MEETING ONCE MORE

Meeting Once More

The Korean Side of Transnational Adoption

Elise Prébin

NEW YORK UNIVERSITY PRESS
New York and London

NEW YORK UNIVERSITY PRESS
New York and London
www.nyupress.org

© 2013 by New York University
All rights reserved

References to Internet websites (URLs) were accurate at the time of writing. Neither the author nor New York University Press is responsible for URLs that may have expired or changed since the manuscript was prepared.

LIBRARY OF CONGRESS CATALOGING-IN-PUBLICATION DATA
Prébin, Elise.
Meeting once more : the Korean side of transnational adoption / Elise Prébin.
pages cm
Includes bibliographical references and index.
ISBN 978-0-8147-6026-0 (cl : alk. paper)
1. Intercountry adoption—Korea (South) 2. Interracial adoption—Korea (South)
3. Adoptees—Korea (South)—Identification. I. Title.
HV875.58.K6P74 2012
362.734095195—dc23
                        2012048181

New York University Press books are printed on acid-free paper, and their binding materials are chosen for strength and durability. We strive to use environmentally responsible suppliers and materials to the greatest extent possible in publishing our books.

Manufactured in the United States of America
c 10 9 8 7 6 5 4 3 2 1

Contents

Acknowledgments	vii
Introduction	1

PART I: MEETING THE BIRTH COUNTRY

1. Shift in South Korean Policies toward Korean Adoptees, 1954–Today	21
2. Everyday Encounters	35
3. Holt International Summer School or Three-Week Re-Koreanization, 1999–2004	52
4. Stratification and Homogeneity at the Korean Broadcasting System, 2003	68
5. National Reunification and Family Meetings	87

PART II: MEETING THE BIRTH FAMILY

6. Stories behind History	103
7. Meetings' Aftermaths	118
8. Evolving Relationship with My Birth Family	133
9. Management of Feelings	151
10. Meeting the Lost and the Dead	163
Conclusion	177
Notes	183
Bibliography	207
Index	219
About the Author	223

Acknowledgments

This book is the happy outcome of twelve years I have spent equally in France, South Korea, and the United States. For that reason, the list of people I should thank is very long, and I can name only a few whose encouragement, help, advice, presence, friendship, and love were instrumental in the process of writing this book.

I thank my French family for being supportive during my studies and rediscovery of Korea. My dissertation owes much to the expertise and affection of my professors Laurence Caillet, Raymond Jamous, and Alain Delissen, to the fun years I spent at the University of Paris Ouest-Nanterre-MAE and the EHESS, and to funding from the French Ministry of Education.

I thank my birth family, and in particular my paternal aunt, for giving me so much time during my stays in South Korea. My research would not have been possible without the goodwill of my many informants at Holt, KBS, and elsewhere, and the advice from Professors Kim Eun-shil, Kim Song-nae, and Song Doyoung. Fieldwork would have been more of a trying experience without the warm presence of dear old friends who made me like South Korea: Lee Soo-jeong, Chung Koomi, Yoon Heuiseung, Chung Minsun, and Lee Sijin.

I thank my husband, Mayu, for convincing me to publish my book in English and for editing patiently the very rough first version. During the year I spent at the Korea Institute, Harvard University, as a postdoctoral fellow funded by the Korea Foundation and the year I served as a lecturer at Harvard's Department of Anthropology, I had wonderful students and met with many distinguished anthropologists and scholars of East Asia. Among them, I thank Carter Eckert, David McCann, Michael Herzfeld, Ted Bestor, Nancy Abelmann, Laurel Kendall, Ellen Schattschneider, Nan Kim-Paik, Samuel Perry, Isabelle Sancho, Seunghun Lee, Jun Uchida, Kyoung-Mi Kwon, Se-Mi Oh, Katherine Lee, Sarah Kashani, Paula Lee, Chan Park, David Chung, and Ed Chang for reading parts of my manuscript, sharing teaching tips, inviting me for guest lectures, and providing pleasant company in Cambridge or in Seoul. Special thanks go to Susan Laurence and Myong Chandra who made the Korea Institute feel like a second home.

I thank Tobias Hübinette, Eleana Kim, Elizabeth Raleigh, Hosu Kim, Kim Park Nelson, Marianne Novy, Joyce Maguire Pavao, and Chris Winston for their interest in my research and for including me in different events and conferences relating to adoption.

I extend my gratitude to Alex Eichler and Nita Sembrowich for editing an early version of this manuscript, to Jennifer Hammer and Alexia Traganas at the NYU Press for their patient support and help, and to several anonymous reviewers for their insightful comments.

I dedicate this book to my daughter, Anouk.

Introduction

In 1999, I returned to South Korea, my birth country, for the first time since my adoption by a French family at age four. I was then twenty-one and a participant in the Holt International Summer School, a three-week program for international adoptees held every summer since 1991 by the adoption agency Holt Children's Services.¹ That summer, I discovered a television show called *Ach'im madang: kŭ sarami pogosip'ta* (Morning talk show: I want to see this person again). At the beginning of my visit, Korean social workers played a recorded tape of *Ach'im madang* in the living room of the Holt guesthouse, where the group stayed. One scene in particular struck me: rebroadcast in slow motion, a Korean mother was shown bursting into tears and rushing toward her twenty-year-old son, who had been adopted in the United States. The palpable tension of the moment was heightened by a tragic melody played in the background, a song redolent of South Korean televised melodrama. That day, in the guesthouse, several adoptees in the audience started weeping at this scene, having succumbed to unknown or unspeakable emotions. After a few days, the social workers, having carried out searches based on each adoptee's adoption file, announced that some of us would be able to meet our birth families: mothers, fathers, brothers and sisters, aunts, grandparents. Thanks to the videotape, participants knew how the first encounter would unfold. Social workers had clearly used the television program as a pedagogical tool to prepare us for our potential meetings with our birth families.

In the history of transnational adoption, the case of South Korea is remarkable for many reasons. The Korean War (1950–1953) marked a change in the care of children from temporary fostering of young war orphans and refugees to definite adoptions into new, foreign families (Marre and Briggs 2009, 8). Since then South Korea has sent abroad approximately 200,000 children who now live mainly in the United States and Europe. It was the number one sending country from 1980 to 1989, number two in 1995, and still number four from 1998 to 2004 (Gutton 1993; Dorow 2006; Selman 2009). But rather than the number of children

>> 1

sent abroad, the most intriguing aspect of the phenomenon is perhaps the sheer scale of the mobilization that has taken place within Korea around the return of adult adoptees to their birth country since the 1990s, and by extension the national significance that has been accorded to meetings between transnational adoptees and their Korean birth parents.[2] As we will see, research shows that the severance of adoptees' ties with their birth country is symbolically repaired in South Korea when birth parents reappear in public with the children they gave up for adoption. But these meetings create a type of relatedness that does not necessarily lead to sustained relationships. If the initial meetings do result in relationships, they do so due to favorable sociological conditions but also to personal choices. And both these sociological conditions and personal choices are subject to changes during the parties' lifetimes. The public meetings between adult adoptees and their birth parents in South Korea thus constitute a fascinating case for those interested in new kinship and contemporary families whose shape depends less on natural reproduction, old customs, and individuals' reliance on an unquestioned life cycle than on politics, technologies, and individuals' strategies. This book explores the representations of transnational adoptees in South Korea by examining official discourses and media as well as everyday interactions between adoptees and South Korean citizens, birth parents and otherwise. Informed by my own experience as an adult adoptee and by two years of ethnographic research in Seoul, this book analyzes the social facts of adoptee reintegration through the lenses of South Korean individuals, families, society, and nation. I contend that South Korean society actually organizes returns and meetings to make departures and ruptures acceptable, as negotiable and conscious choices and no longer as forced or ineluctable events. As we will see, my research suggests that family meetings are a social service organized by the state on behalf of both parents and children.

* * *

The following are two additional vignettes that, in conjunction with the earlier anecdote, relate in chronological order my encounters with the adoptee–birth parent meetings phenomenon in South Korea. These vignettes work together to set the stage for this book's successive chapters that depict the political conditions, social parameters, pragmatic limitations, and multilayered meaning of adoptee reintegration to their birth country and birth families.

Meeting with My Birth Family (July 17, 1999)

We adoptees watched the video of *Ach'im madang* on a Tuesday. By Saturday, we were halfway through the Holt International Summer School program. Most participants were by now displaying unusual signs of anxiety. One of them reminded me that it was "D-day," indicated on the schedule by the innocuous phrase "opening files." All of us were about to find out if the social workers had tracked down our biological parents, or had at least located some of our Korean relatives who were still alive. Since the beginning of our stay they had been involved in conducting searches for our family members while others were guiding us through different activities and observing us to anticipate any negative reactions in the case of disappointment or surprise.

When my turn came, I went up to the room of Mrs. Na,³ the oldest social worker. When I entered the room, she smiled and addressed me in English:

"You're a very lucky girl!"

"Really, why is that?"

"Please sit down. There was a phone number in your files, and we were able to reach your paternal grandmother. Your father passed away in 1993, as did one of your paternal uncles in 1998. But you have another paternal uncle who has been calling every day to see when the family can meet with you. . . . We also contacted your mother, who wants to see you and take you home after your stay with us. She lives alone. You are staying in Korea for a while longer after the program . . . two months, right? We thought that you might want to meet them right after your stay here."

"Well, I am sorry but I have plans . . . I have to go to Japan to meet some friends."

Her face crumpled in indignation. "How can you react this way? Your mother hasn't seen you in seventeen years and you don't want to see her?"

"That's not what I meant at all," I replied. "If they really want to see me, of course I'll meet with them, but I also have some plans to travel."

After scolding me, the social worker asked if I had a Korean friend who could serve as an interpreter during my family reunion. Another week went by, and shortly after the closing ceremony held at Holt Children's Services, I was called to Mrs. Na's office once again. A Korean friend who spoke French accompanied me.

In the office, we waited together for my mother and my paternal aunt, who, as Mrs. Na explained, used to be friends at school. Suddenly, she received a phone call and left the room. A few minutes later, the door opened, and two Korean women in their fifties appeared with Mrs. Na. One woman's eyes were red from crying; the other woman smiled shyly, supporting her companion. They looked inquiringly at my friend, then at me. Mrs. Na laughed, identifying me as their daughter and niece. They hugged me awkwardly for a moment, and then everybody sat down on the couches to have a discussion. The woman who was crying was my mother. Mrs. Na related her impressions of me, based on the three weeks we had spent together. Although I was perplexed, I tried to encourage the two women with a smile.

My Korean friend started translating into French for me as we began our conversation. I was asked about my sister, with whom I had been adopted by the French family. They reproached me for not having brought any pictures, but I restrained myself from saying that I had not really planned on meeting with them. They asked me how long I would stay in Korea. My hands were held and massaged; my features were studied, and I was compared to my father. My paternal aunt had brought photographs: one of them featured me as a baby next to an older baby who was my cousin—my paternal aunt's son. I would meet him as soon as he got permission to leave the army. He was in the middle of his military tour of duty in the region of Kangwon. There was also a picture of my father in his twenties, at my paternal aunt's wedding, in front of a statue of the Virgin Mary. I was surprised to learn that they were all Catholic, like my adoptive family. My mother had left my father and never remarried. She was living with her mother, her younger sister, her sister's husband, and their three children. She worked at an insurance company. At that time, I had difficulty remembering how many aunts and uncles I had just acquired and who was living or deceased.

After these preliminaries, we all went to a neighborhood restaurant. At that moment, I received a phone call from an elderly nun from an Inchon orphanage I had contacted at the beginning of my stay. I had called on behalf of my French family, who had been in touch with her since my adoption, but also in the hope that I could visit the orphanage where I had once stayed. The nun arrived soon afterward, speaking perfect French and English. After we all introduced each other, she started asking my mother questions and translating for me. Thus I came to learn more about the circumstances of our separation. My mother had met my father through my paternal aunt. They had married against the advice of their parents when he was twenty-four and she twenty-seven. Shortly after I was born, they started talking about divorce, but my paternal grandfather was firmly opposed to it. My sister was born two years later. Shortly upon discovering that my father had a mistress, my mother fled to her maternal home. It was not until my paternal grandfather passed away that the divorce was officially pronounced. My mother answered the nun's questions as she ate her meal and kept repeating that she felt guilty for leaving us. We then changed topics: my mother asked what I was doing now. I explained that I had studied philosophy and had recently switched to anthropology. My mother grumbled, "What is she gonna do with that?" Everybody laughed but me.

After this first meeting, we decided on a time when my mother would come to pick me up for a home visit. My newfound relatives decided whom I would visit and in which order. I was ignorant of how many relatives I had begotten, what they were doing, and how to address them. I was vaguely worried by this turn of events and started having the unpleasant feeling of losing all control of the situation. I begged my Korean friend to come see us often to help translate our conversations. She told me not to worry; she and a friend of hers would take turns translating every other day so that I would be able to communicate with my Korean relatives at dinners. She took down all the necessary phone numbers.

A few days later, when the summer school program was over, my mother and my paternal aunt came together to pick me up at the Holt Center in Ilsan. I said good-bye to the few remaining participants, then got into my mother's car, taking a seat in the back. My paternal aunt, in the front seat, looked back at me every now and then with a smile. Sometimes my mother peered nervously into the rearview mirror from behind her big sunglasses, but she did not smile. They were mumbling something to each other. The trip from Ilsan to Inchon seemed endless, and I fell asleep several times.

I ended up spending the rest of the summer with my relatives, though I did manage to visit my friend in Japan as well. Back in France, it took me months to decide that I would switch the focus of my graduate studies from Russia to South Korea. My paternal aunt and her son kept sending me short letters in Korean that I read with my beginner's dictionary and with the help of my interpreter friend, who had come back to Paris. Eventually, I returned to South Korea to learn Korean and get to know them better.

Observing Family Meetings at the Korean
Broadcasting System Studio (June 4, 2003)

What takes place on the television show *Ach'im madang* are first meetings between South Koreans and their long-lost relatives, but in contrast to my own meeting with my birth family, these reunions are well orchestrated and well performed.

On June 4, 2003, at 8:36 in the morning, a flashback reminded *Ach'im madang* viewers of the last broadcast. After her initial presentation on that show, while she sat listening to the next guest, one female participant had received a phone call. Now, the participant was standing at the lectern, wearing a formal outfit. To her right were the show's host and hostess, Lee Sang-byŏk and Lee Kŭm-hŭi, who were retelling her story for a few minutes during which the participant showed signs of impatience.

"Well, now, please step forward. Are you going to call 'mom' [ŏmma] or 'mother' [ŏmŏni] or 'older sister' [ŏnni]? Say what is easier for you."

The participant stepped to the middle of the stage and turned toward the corridor from which the relatives were about to appear. The hostess indicated the entrance with a theatrical gesture. After rocking back and forth nervously, the participant dried her tears and called in a strangled voice, "Mom!"

Applause from the audience and melodramatic music greeted the relatives as they entered onto the stage at 8:38. Round green tags fixed at their collars indicated each person's relation to the participant: "mother," "older sister," "paternal grandaunt," "little brother." While they hugged each other, information was displayed on the screen for the viewers: "Meeting after twenty-nine years of separation." The camera zoomed in on the mother's and daughter's faces. Both of them were murmuring, forehead against forehead. The clip-on microphones they were wearing allowed the audience and the viewers to hear the exchange, but the participant could only sob, "Mom, mom, I missed you so much!" In the background, one of the brothers, obviously embarrassed by this awkward situation, kept his head down, compulsively wiping his eyes that seemed to remain dry.

The melodramatic music lasted only one minute; when it was over, the hosts left the lectern and went to meet the reunited family in the middle of the stage. They tried to separate the family members in order to ask questions and reintroduce them to the audience. In the softest tone of voice, the host said, "The little brothers and the older sister of the participant could call their mother whenever they wanted because she was always by their side, but this was not the case for her." As sobbing sounds continued, he went on: "Ah! You brought some pictures. How old are they in this picture?" The sobs continued, but there was no answer. The hostess seized an old black-and-white picture of the two sisters holding hands. She presented it to the camera. The two girls had the same bobbed hair and the same bangs, which inspired the hostess to comment in a tender voice, "*Ayuuu! Ayuuu!*[4] Their bangs are exactly the same!"

The participant was still crying. The hosts turned toward the mother: "She who was so little when you saw her last, here she is again before your eyes!" The mother grumbled without expression, "As I did not know where she was, I could not find her.... Thanks to her paternal aunt who watched *Ach'im madang*, we were able to find her again." The microphone was then offered to the paternal grandaunt who was the cause of the reunion. "I watched *Ach'im madang* every day! Every day!"

The participant kept talking to one of her brothers, the one rubbing his eyes. She held his head against her head. The camera followed their interaction: "I was the one who used to carry you on my back . . . " "I did not know," he answered, visibly embarrassed. He kept his head down, avoiding her looks by holding his hand above his eyes the whole time.

The camera still followed their interaction and rambling conversation, but it was already time to introduce the participant's husband and two sons. The hostess announced: "Your daughter married early, and she already has a son who is twelve years old. Grandsons, son-in-law, please come forward."

The three people approached from offstage. When they reached the middle of the stage, close to the flowers on the pedestal table, they performed a deep bow to their newly found relatives.[5] The hostess told the children, "Here is your grandmother, here are your maternal uncles." The participant's husband shook hands with his wife's brothers and gave them each a friendly pat on the back. The camera focused on one of the two boys as the host tried to ask him about his feelings, but because they were intimidated, the two boys did not speak much. It was time to conclude the episode.

The hostess repeated her final instruction to the audience several times, "Please congratulate them! Please congratulate them! Please applaud them!" The audience carried out the order. Suddenly the host asked the reunited family to stand in a line. He gave the signal as if they were pupils: "*Ayuuu . . .* ! This turned out so well! Attention! Ready! Bow!" All the people present onstage, including the hosts, bowed together while holding hands, like actors finishing a performance on the stage. The newly reunited family finally exited. The paternal grandaunt tried to greet the hosts again, but they were already looking at their notes to handle the family to be featured next.[6]

Position and Method

The preceding vignettes describe three kinds of family meetings I witnessed in very different modes: as a viewer, as an actor, and as a scholarly observer. They recount, in chronological order, three moments that correspond to three different stages of my status and my position within the family meeting phenomenon. I watched the first meeting on a television screen in a room full of other adoptees from the United States and Europe, but also with the South Korean organizers of the summer school. At the time, I was not aware of the reasons we had to watch that video and what was about to happen, partly because of my poor command of English but also because of my carefree attitude. I then experienced something similar as one of the main actors of a three-party event involving my birth relatives and the South Korean social worker in whose office our meeting took place. Finally, I observed other meetings of adult adoptees and their Korean families as an anthropologist, sitting in a studio audience with the participants of the television program, but also with an eye on the actions going on backstage during the production, on the various preparations that took place before the taping, and on the larger sociohistorical context of these meetings and their aftermaths. These three different moments owe to my position within the phenomenon of adoptee reintegration in South Korea.

When I first returned to South Korea, I was immediately defined by South Koreans as part of a group called the "transnational adoptees." As such, I had to learn about Korean society and about the possibility of meeting with my birth parents, and I had to prepare myself for such an event. As soon as I met with my birth family, I became a "living oxymoron" (Kondo 1990), a relative and at the same time a stranger, and I realized that my birth family and I had experienced our first encounter in very different ways: my Korean relatives had presented a united attitude of knowing sadness as they spoke to and about me, whereas I was far more perplexed by our interaction and was simply smiling at them. They were meeting somebody they thought they knew, someone to whom their relationship was already defined, whereas I was meeting strangers for the first time. At least, such was my reasoning as a French adoptee who was raised in an environment where blood and race supposedly did not matter. They were a South Korean mother and aunt, each in her fifties and somewhat familiar with the televised meeting programs and the general context of family separation, whereas I was a twenty-one-year-old French student who had simply come to South Korea to travel around Asia and have a bit of fun. That I did not cry at the first meeting with my mother and aunt left my family rather stunned. That I suddenly wept alone in the middle of a meal at a maternal uncle's house a few days later surprised them as well—I had just started to grasp what was happening to me. From these initial moments of discordant expectations arose in my own mind several questions about the nature of such reunions: What were the political, institutional, and historical conditions that even made such meetings possible? From then on I also found myself more interested in *Ach'im madang*, the most popular South Korean "meeting program," for I had the intuition that my emotional ineptitude would find an explanation in its study. As I witnessed other, more orchestrated meetings in the KBS studio, inevitably comparing them with my own, I came to see that the form of the meeting was perhaps more important than its content. Moreover, the study of the program's history would tell me about the evolution of adoptees' representations while providing information concerning a larger picture, perhaps explaining why, for example, transnational adoptees, domestic adoptees, and Korean orphans could appear side by side on the same television show.

In addition, I thought I would find clues as to where I stood within, what to do with, and what to expect from my own birth family after the first meeting. If I knew what they wanted and what they thought, I would know how to adjust to the new situation and act properly. My main questions were: What do these meetings *do*? Do they change the nature of transnational adoption? What kind of ties do they create? Does the future of these ties depend on each family's idiosyncrasies and each individual's psychological state? I already had the feeling it was not so: what my relatives wanted and what they thought were not mere matters of psychology or temperament. Rather, these matters had to do with kinship and culture. Therefore, as a social anthropologist, I would approach my relatives as part of Korean society, as the "others." This somewhat deterministic view of culture and kinship was encouraged by my readings on Korea but, later on, was challenged by direct experience and time. In fact, far from sticking to kinship patterns I once read about, my relatives' attitudes and my own still oscillate between pragmatic adaptations that depend on variable personal and familial circumstances, and assigned roles or duties valued as ideals within Korean families.

I had chosen to concentrate in social anthropology prior to my return to Korea, after which my personal story had indeed oriented my interests. This double position required a specific approach that, until recently, filled me with ambiguous if not contradictory feelings that complicated the exchanges I had with Koreans and adoptees alike. In this book transnational adoptees who return to South Korea are only the protagonists of actions generated and organized by Koreans, not informants whose opinion is solicited. That said, I do not mean that adoptees lack agency in these encounters.[7] While my focus is on Koreans, I do report some adoptees' reactions and words on certain occasions, illustrating that they do react and speak out. Because of my double position, I made the conscious decision to rely more on observation than on interviews. Given my phenotype, observation allowed me to witness fleeting interactions, dialogues, and attitudes without Korean people's knowledge that I was an adoptee. Short conversations also let me pass for a Korean resident abroad, which always lightened my interlocutors' mood. To the contrary, in interviews my identity as an adoptee always occupied the foreground, most often leading either to dead ends with persons directly concerned with adoption, such as birth parents (except for today's young single mothers, as we will see), or to repetitive and sometimes off-topic debates on the ever-controversial and ever-sensitive topic of adoption and transnational adoption. I primarily restricted my interviews to people engaged in the adoption process or working as professionals in the production of the televised meeting program. I have included some descriptions of the biographical elements from my own life that chronicle my long-term relationship with my biological family to provide a qualitative understanding of rather private life experiences. Again, that type of material relied more on participant observation of everyday life and spontaneous interaction than on organized and systematic interviews with my relatives.

I stage myself in a larger narrative as being *acted upon* by South Korean society and as being a valuable witness and informant to my own anthropological analysis. The reader will find every now and then auto-ethnographic elements that contribute to the understanding of ethnographic situations I experienced and of the intersubjective evolution of my relationship with my birth family. Yet, this book aims to be neither an adoptee memoir focusing on my interiority or my innermost feelings about being an adoptee, nor a pure reflection on anthropological fieldwork featuring myself as the main character, nor a pamphlet against transnational adoption, nor a manifesto claiming the emergence of a Korean adoptee community. I present case studies in a historical and anthropological frame.[8] My core goal is to offer an alternative to what has already been written on transnational adoption from Korea, and to contribute to new kinship studies and to growing research that examines the impact of transnational adoption on the evolution and representations of family, as well as the human implications of modernity and globalization in Korea and more broadly in Northeast Asia.

To a great extent, it is hard to separate the issues related to transnational adoption in South Korea from its treatment by the media since the late 1980s.[9] Therefore, on top of participant observation and interviews, this work examines the television programs, films, newspapers, and websites that broadcast factual information and "expressive representations" (Appadurai 1996) about transnational adoption. Because of their omnipresence in contemporary South Korea, these sources of media constitute "a significant domain of social life" (Janelli and Yim 2005). Given the diversity of media productions, there are a variety of analytical approaches one may take toward them. On the one hand, my method partly consisted of selecting different types of fictions with related topics such as domestic or transnational adoption and the lives and destinies of orphans, and analyzing them in order to extract structural regularities. I approached these narratives more or less as texts that reflect, through invented lives and events involving fictional characters, some norms and questions relevant to South

Korean society at the time the works were produced (Chalvon-Demersay 2005, 82; Abelmann 2003). On the other hand, I researched and analyzed the reality show *Ach'im madang*. But the textual approach for a reality show had obvious limitations. Previous studies in the anthropology of media have revealed, beyond the meanings within the narratives themselves (fictional or not), the context and the reasons of their creation, focusing on the influence of politics on the production of national cinema and television (Abu-Lughod 1993, 1995, 2000). Studies of television not only can identify political stakes and describe the diversity of national productions but also can focus on their reception by the public and on their material consequences in everyday life (Mankekar 1999). Combining these different approaches, this book describes the production of the South Korean weekly meeting program *Ach'im madang*, exposes its relation to the state, and explores its reception by the public. Because we are dealing here with real people, I am especially interested in the way this meeting program not only speaks of but also may reconfigure family, kinship, and adoption. Therefore, this book is meant to contribute to the anthropology of kinship with a focus on adoption while exploring and articulating several subfields such as the anthropology of media and emotion.

Television and Kinship

Although considered a reality show that uses real participants and true stories, *Ach'im madang* can be considered a certain kind of fiction, one not too far from literary fiction.[10] It produces a more or less formatted narrative that encompasses all kinds of family separation by framing them in a larger national history of war and division. By doing so, it conflates state and family—and serves both. *Ach'im madang* may transmit familial and national values and tradition to viewers, but individuals also use the program for their own purposes, however complex those may be. Therefore, the show cannot be reduced merely to a narrative one should interpret, any more than it can be reduced solely to its political aspect (Ricoeur 1986, 1992). It is ironic that the program's strong emphasis on "real kinship" based on blood necessitates the elaborate construction of a near-fictional narrative that leaves little space for spontaneous attitudes or discourses, and proves to be weak in the face of everyday life's obligations and societal pressures in the meetings' aftermaths. In the second part of this book, a glimpse of these aftermaths will confirm the hypothesis that, in this context, blood is no thicker than water. Here, biological kinship can be experienced either at a symbolic level or, in the long run, through sustained and concerted effort.

Kinship and Emotions

The general narrative produced and reproduced at *Ach'im madang* also enables catharsis for traumatic separations as well as certain patterns of familial construction through the production of proper emotions. The social workers' use of the program video indicated the need to inculcate the right emotions in order to facilitate interactions—not only between foreigners and Koreans but also between children and parents. The ritualized actions undertaken during the spectacle that constitutes the meeting program call for a performative approach (Hughes-Freeland and Markwell Crain 1998; Schechner 1977, 1993; Schechner and Appel 1990). I focus on the making of the show and on the spreading of that particular narrative. Transnational adoptees, as members of a liminal social category, are assigned all kinds of ritualized actions, among which is meeting with their birth families when searches are successful. Even if considered as a political narrative on family separation in the context of national partition, the program *Ach'im madang* seems to soothe familial issues, to work on feelings of loss and resentment, and, in some cases, to build a type of relatedness that has been only recently touched upon and needs further exploration.

The ethnography of televised first meetings between adoptees and birth families provides an entry into the exploration of new types of families that combine biological kinship and chosen relatedness. Far from merely reconstituting the broken ties between individuals related by blood, these collective, carefully orchestrated meetings remind us that blood, while always remaining a liability in the mind of most people (in Korea and in the Western adoptive countries), does not suffice to (re-)create families. The discrepancy mentioned earlier between ideal kinship and pragmatic kinship is mirrored by the meeting's two sequences: the onstage, ritualized, public sequence versus the offstage, freer, private sequence. It would be erroneous, however, to see these two sequences as completely opposed—the "fake" or fictional sequence as opposed to the "real" and true sequence. Together, both sequences form a social reality that individuals who are caught in familial situations deemed unusual need to negotiate at an emotional and symbolic level.

Adoption, Meetings and Postmeetings

Adoption, the creation of filiation among individuals who do not share a blood connection, is quasi-universal but varies from place to place. Adoption always involves three parties: the adoptee, the adoptive parent(s), and the biological parent(s). The three parties' relations are stipulated by tradition or a judicial system. Adoption inside a group or inside one's culture has been the topic of numerous works in anthropology, which usually take into account the three components of the adoption triad (Le Gall and Bettahar 2001; Camdessus 1995).

According to Western norms, adoption establishes definite and official filiation, as opposed to other forms of temporary or informal caring. In this context, adoption is considered a fiction that copies "real" filiation that comes from sexual procreation and is based on blood (Carsten 2004; Schneider 1984). This arrangement frequently results in uneasy feelings for those who experience this type of unusual kinship (Modell 1994, 3–4). Thus, adoption studies in Western countries often focus on the psychology of people involved in adoption, and especially on the adoptee's mental issues (Lévine 1996). They also compare and discuss the advantages and drawbacks of the different systems of adoption—open, plenary or closed, simple, "*sous X*" (born to unknown mother), and so forth—and describe the evolution of adoption laws and practices (Fine and Neirinck 2000; Ouellette 2009). In so-called traditional societies, anthropologists study adoption as only one modality of child circulation among a multitude of other practices (Lallemand 1993; Bowie 2004). In adoption, the child can often be seen as a gift that groups exchange the way they exchange women. In this case, adoption builds an alliance between adoptive and birth parents (Lévi-Strauss 1985; Jack Goody, 1969). This is not the case in Korea, where, until recently, adoption was almost exclusively a means to find an heir and prolong the Confucian patriline (Peterson 1996). But there are many other forms of adoption worldwide that sometimes give the choice to the adoptee, sometimes disturb generational order when a grandmother becomes a mother (Bowie 2004), and sometimes entail more or less contact—and no alliance per se—between the donor and receiver, as in Western open adoption cases nowadays.

Transnational adoption is yet another kind of adoption that has as many facets as there are countries involved. It obviously places limits upon the possible alliance between donors and receivers or the openness of adoption. This book, however, shows how Korean society, beginning in the 1990s, has developed a focus on reunions that supposedly "reopen" adoptions after several decades. Is the strong Korean emphasis on blood enough to reconstitute wholesome families? Do the outcomes of these televised meetings between adoptees raised in Western countries and their Korean birth parents substantially differ from the meetings described in the context of domestic adoption in Western countries?

Transnational adoption started on a significant scale in the second half of the twentieth century and developed considerably during the 1980s and 1990s

(Selman 2009). Early on, in Western countries, studies on transnational and transracial adoptions were contained primarily within the fields of psychology and social work (Frances Koh 1981).[11] Later, they also motivated research on adoption laws in the countries that provide children, and research on international laws (Marre and Briggs 2009). After 2000, adoption studies became a subfield of research across various disciplines. Research on transnational adoption often focused on how adoptive parents negotiate race and culture regarding the incorporation of adopted children in their family. It also looked at the construction of the adoptees as objects of desire, exchange, and consumption through the erasure of their past and previous relationships (Eleana Kim 2010, 10–11). But for a long time physical and cultural distance were indeed obstacles to examining the entire triad of transnational adoption. In the academic world, voices of birth parents and of adoptees themselves were missing, and their representations of transnational adoption unknown.[12] Recently, the field has seen the emergence of important research on the birth parents' societies (Johnson, Huang, and Wang 1998; Johnson, 2004; Jung-woo Kim and Henderson 2008; Joo-lee Lee, 2007) and adoptees' communities (Eleana Kim 2007),[13] with more and more adoptees entering the various academic fields to write about adoption. Even more recently, studies on adoption have started looking at the different ways in which transnational adoptees and their adoptive families engage with birth countries and birth families.[14] These studies revolve around three types of discourses concerning transnational adoptees' returns to the land of their birth, family searches, and meetings with their birth families. Widely accepted by adoptive families and other types of nontraditional families in the United States and parts of Europe, the first discourse claims that returning to one's birthplace to look for one's origins, roots, or genetic heritage is good and healthy (Dorow 2006). This position has the backup of media and DNA technologies and feeds on a global consciousness (Volkman 2009). The second discourse, expressed by unconditional partisans of nurture against culture, sees the adoptees' search for birth parents as a threat for adoptive families who are supposed to embody the principle that blood does not matter. Searches and returns are depicted as confusing experiences (Howell 2009). In between these two positions, the third one is yet uncertain as to the benefits of finding one's birth parents and points at the difficulties that may arise in the wake of this discovery while, at the same time, stating that the will to know is legitimate. Anthropologist Barbara Yngvesson (2002), for example, has collected the testimonies of many young adult adoptees from Sweden who have returned to their various birth countries and who keep in touch with their birth parents. Through these stories, the reader gets only indirect glimpses at these ties and at the birth parents' lives and experiences because the focus is on the adoptees' subjectivities. These adoptees voice doubts regarding the future of their relationships to their birth parents, but most care about them very much and are ready to invest time and resources in these ties. My work on the meetings and postmeeting relationships between adoptees and their Korean birth parents is an attempt to explore further this new type of kinship located in between spaces and in between biological and social kinships. A common problem is that in most cases, transnational adoption is constructed by the law as a replacement of blood ties, so when the figure of the birth parent reappears, it disrupts the myth of adoption and seems to threaten identities. Now, social anthropologists have recognized new types of relatedness that challenge that dichotomy: the potential ties between sperm or egg donors, or surrogate mothers with the families they helped create; or between adoptees and their birth parents. By calling these ties biogenetic, one implies a pseudoscientific distance, a relatedness based on some kind of knowledge on paper that responds to curiosity or pragmatism. This seriously limits the understanding of the emotional and social repercussions of these types of relatedness in people's lives (Strathern 1992; Carsten 2004). Meetings between adoptees and their birth parents within domestic adoption have been the most thoroughly described as being beneficial (Carsten 2004, 104) and as leading to new paths within contemporary kinship where people have to venture "without maps" (Modell 1994). But it is clear that returns that lead to meetings between birth parents and children after transnational adoptions present a case substantially different from the preceding examples because many birth parents actually spent time with their children before their separation, and because their views on parent-child relationship may differ from those of their children: an ideal kinship "map" in their minds may inform their attitudes and decisions regarding these ties. Adoptees may have their own "maps" as well. Yet once the meeting has occurred, the relatedness it creates may change quality through time according to multiple parameters, despite the fact that it is based on blood.

In line with the third position regarding family search, meetings, and postmeetings, I argue that no matter their outcome, the meetings are beneficial for both adoptees and birth parents despite their different cultures and experiences, so long as one does not mistake the meetings for a reconstitution of biological families and what they usually imply in economic, legal, and emotional terms. Instead, I show that the meetings in South Korea are a process of recognition of blood ties that, at the same time, reestablishes symbolic continuity and aims at the acceptance of difference and loss in order for individuals to "live better"—that is, without overwhelming feelings of resentment or sadness. This new type of kinship and relationships between adoptees and birth parents that may ensue involves conscious "effort" and "work" as much as in the "self-conscious" relationship between adoptees and adoptive parents (Modell 1994, 13). By focusing on transnational adoptees' meetings with their Korean birth parents, I define the different types of relatedness that can emerge from these meetings by looking in particular at the birth parents' circumstances, values, and representations. My own case study provides insight into the everyday, ongoing building of those relationships in the long run. Somewhere in between my idiosyncratic experience and the structural traits of Korean kinship and social organization that pertain to what scholars call Korean culture lies the reality of postreunion relationships that other adoptees may build with their own biological relatives.

Outline

This book is divided into two parts: the first is concerned with the national, public, and collective aspect of the return of Korean adoptees to their birth country; the second turns toward the more private and interpersonal aspect of adoptees' reintegration within their birth families.

Chapter 1, after a brief summary of the history of transnational adoption from Korea, describes how the South Korean representations of adoptees changed from negative to positive over time in official discourses owing to the globalization of Korea and the construction of the Korean diaspora.

Chapter 2 contrasts these official discourses of reintegration to the everyday encounters adoptees are susceptible to experience. A series of impressionistic vignettes stresses that the pace of change in people's everyday reactions, opinions, and prejudices may be slower than in political discourses in the national and international spheres.

Because of these discrepancies between official discourses and the real interactions between adoptees and South Koreans, chapter 3 shows how South Korean society undertakes symbolic actions to integrate international adoptees as an ambiguous group that stands in between cultures despite the enterprise of recuperation described in the first chapter. We will see, however, that if the symbolic actions obviously stand for rites of passage—of incorporation—their goals are unclear.

Next, chapter 4 revisits the televised meetings mentioned in introduction and sheds light on a different moment, venue, and means of integrating international adoptees to the motherland. Even if some participants cannot find their relatives after their appearance on the show, they are nonetheless, despite their nationality, somewhat reintegrated within the Korean people via the television program hosts' discourses on physical resemblances, and production of collective emotions related to family separation and of the collective memory of an antediluvian universe where family relations were unproblematic.

The last chapter within part I, chapter 5, shows how this television program is a ramification of meetings of the divided families separated by the war and by the partition between North and South Korea. In other words, through television, transnational adoptees are integrated in the greater history of the nation and into a narrative of loss and sadness that covers up individual circumstances and responsibilities.

Confining the role of television to state propaganda—in the ideological assertion that the war is the ultimate cause of the migration of 200,000 Korean children—is to limit the comprehension of its use by South Korean society and especially the birth families themselves. This book sheds light on a still understudied facet of the media's place in societies in the anthropology of media. In fact, the first part lays out the social, political, and historical context and the collective and external conditions of possibility for transnational adoptees and their birth families to meet. The televised meetings are the moment and space where the state and the families intersect.

Part II of this book analyzes the narratives of family separation created by the televised program participants even in a context of strict limitation of time and the larger enterprise of standardization of the collective memory as seen in chapter 4. Adding to the literature on child circulation and its conflict with internationalized norms of plenary adoptions, chapter 6 describes similar practices of rural, poor Koreans and how one exclusive option became the rule after the Korean War: transnational adoption. The stories this chapter relates challenge the war narrative and put a name on the persons who decided to divide their own and others' families.

Chapter 7 consists of ethnographies of first meetings between transnational adoptees and their birth families. These examples are representatives of the different outcomes of the family meetings. It analyzes the socioeconomic situation of the birth families and infers the future of the relationships not so much in terms of failure or success but rather as more or less sustained modes of relatedness. Meetings that lead to the severance of ties seem like failures insofar as one sees the family relationship monolithically: either as presumably complete relationships based on biological kinship or simply as nonrelationships.

To better illustrate the point that between these two poles there exist other possibilities of relatedness for transnational adoptees and their birth families, chapter 8 provides the readers with my own experience of "relating" to my birth family over the course of a decade. Anecdotes will convey a sense of how flexible and fluctuating my relationship with my birth family feels, but how real and no less important than my relationship with my adoptive family for the ongoing construction of who I am.

Going back to the televised meetings, chapter 9 focuses on this specific feeling of relatedness as orchestrated, performed, and expressed through tears by the media and the people. It tries to answer these questions: Why are these meetings necessary? Why are they considered the "best" meetings? By channeling and taming ambiguous emotions of anger, guilt, and resentment ritually, the program is a mediating agent that produces that specific feeling for the best interest of the various parties involved. In that sense, we can see the media as an instrument of social welfare for the people involved in adoption, both domestic and transnational.

Finally, chapter 10 draws a parallel between feelings for the lost and feelings for the dead. Within this frame of interpretation, the televised meeting appears as a cathartic moment of potential closure for all parties, one that produces a certain order within families. The meetings create relatedness, leaving open options of relationships—including the cessation of contact—but they never reconstitute families according to the ideal model of biological kinship.

The conclusion ties together the themes laid out throughout the book and enlarges the scope of this study, which has targeted mostly the South Korean side of transnational adoption with its specific theoretical interest in kinship and media. I engage in a dialogue with other scholarly works that focus on other countries and common themes such as the globalization of kinship, the politics of reproduction, and the idea of return—in the hope that others might generate further research on transnational adoption in birth countries.

PART I

Meeting the Birth Country

1

Shift in South Korean Policies toward Korean Adoptees (1954–Today)

> Korean adoptees bring in needed hard currency for Korea—roughly $15 to $20 million a year. They relieve the government of the costs of caring for the children, which could be a drain on the budget. And they help with population control, an obsession of the Korean government.
> —Matthew Rothschild (1988)

> Children who were adopted to developed countries in the 1960s–1970s received a good education and became competent adults. That is why it is in our interest to ensure the creation of a network.
> —*Dong-A Ilbo* (08/02/2004)

Today, returning adult adoptees are considered a resource by the South Korean government in the context of globalization. Since the 1990s, the positive image of successful adult adoptees' return to South Korea has tended to supplant the negative image of unfortunate babies being sent abroad for transnational adoption. This chapter is about the changing public opinion about transnational adoption in South Korea, a lens through which we can uncover the changing place of South Korea in the world. The phenomenon of return may have several conflicting interpretations, but adoptees' personal quests primarily depend on their birth country's will to establish an institutional structure that welcomes them.

Overseas Korean Adoptees: A Visible Population

Since 2005, May 11 is the national "Day of Adoption" in South Korea.[1] Unlike in the past, journalists, politicians, and adoptees today speak openly of international adoption. Between 1953 and 1988, adoption of Korean children was hidden from the Korean public despite ever-increasing rates. Official figures reflect a clear boost in the 1980s, which was obviously related to the South Korean government assuming control of the four main adoption agencies (Eastern Social Welfare Society, Social Welfare Society, Holt Children's Services, Korea Social Services), and to the easing of the adoption process that followed.[2] But for a long time, responsibility for the increase in adoptions was attributed to foreign countries and the adoption agencies they established in South Korea after the war.

The 1988 Olympic Games hosted by Seoul were an economic and diplomatic success that awakened national pride (McDonald 1996, 252). The efforts made for the Games' organization were fueled by a "popular desire for a successful summer Olympics in Seoul" (Eckert and Lee 1996, 347). But the economic miracle was not the only topic on which journalists focused. Matthew Rothschild, an American journalist writing for the *Progressive*, launched a wave of criticism at the young republic with an article entitled "Babies for Sale, Koreans Make Them, Americans Buy Them."[3] The magazine cover exhibited a cartoon of a stork whose bundle contained a baby with slanted eyes sitting on batches of green bills. A few months later, a headline in the *New York Times* read, "Babies for Export," beginning a domestic and international scandal.[4] These few articles had an enormous impact in South Korea, where they were publicly debated.

After the 1988 crisis, transnational adoption became a regular topic for the media. Many television programs and newspapers articles[5] were and still are cast in the same mold, as evidenced by such titles as "From Outside: International Adoption; From Inside: Child Traffic"[6] and "Children Still for Sale."[7] But in the 1990s, the South Korean media, while deploring the "still ongoing adoption industry,"[8] tended to stress the causes of child abandonment. Most of the 1990s documentaries targeted especially teenage mothers, who were directly linked to the transnational adoption issue: since the mid-1990s, more than 80 percent of babies given up for transnational adoption—still between 2,300 and 2,400 each year since 2000—have been born to young single mothers.[9] The inhumane ways the mothers supposedly abandon their babies—often right after birth in places such as trash cans or toilets—are emphasized by the media.[10] It seems obvious that national shame led to the accusation of single mothers, who are made guilty of a morally disruptive act, a crime, or a sin against the nation as much as against their child or life in general.

On the other hand, statistics, debates, and exhortations to adopt domestically have become inescapable in the public discourse.[11] One program broadcast in 1993 announced the national ambition as follows: "Abandoned children: Let's stop international adoption in 1996. Report on domestic adoption."[12] Domestic adoption had become the controversial subject par excellence. As a means of follow-up, social workers, especially from Holt, started contributing regularly to this type of program on adoption. In another broadcast of 1999 they were invited not to be blamed in public but to contribute their expertise as the most convincing advocates for domestic adoption.[13] Seen at first as the main child-trafficking institution, a supply for foreign countries, Holt Children's Services transformed over a decade into a pioneer for children's rights and the foremost potential child supply for South Korean families in the context of a decreasing birthrate. A glimpse into the history of Holt Children's Services will provide us with an appreciation of South Korea's peculiar adoption history and culture.[14]

Holt Children's Services: From Blame to Sanctification

The target of much outrage and criticism in 1988, Holt is today regarded with respect. Its advertising posters are openly displayed in public places, even in subway cars: the posters invite South Koreans to "experience the joy of adoption" (Bourbon-Parme and Tourret 2004, 76). Holt's changed status in South Korean society parallels the change of attitude and policies of the government vis-à-vis transnational adoptees.[15]

From 1950 to 1953, the Korean War featured South Koreans allied with Americans in opposition to assailing North Koreans allied with the USSR and China. Each side invaded the other's territory, one after the other. A stalemate resulted in the separation of the two parties by an artificial frontier fixed on the thirty-eighth parallel by the United States and the USSR on July 27, 1953. South Korea had undergone the most destruction and was the poorer of the two states in 1953. Damages were both material and human. Historical sources converge to assess an exceptional number of family separations in Korea due to the lasting division of the peninsula.[16] Yet it remains to be seen if this separation phenomenon is really unique in history,[17] or if its perception as unique depends on values and social structures specific to Korea.

In postwar South Korea, there were indeed multitudes of orphans, mostly taken care of by foreign institutions. In the 1960s, an American military official wrote: "It is certainly unrealistic at this point for Koreans to think in terms of a welfare state" (Wade 1966, 90). As a matter of fact, Americans blamed the successive military regimes for the precarious nature of the South Korean social welfare system (Eckert and Lee 1996, 347–387). They also deplored a common trait of all postwar societies (Sorlin 1999): the lack of interest and involvement of Koreans in the plight of orphans (Wolfe 1966,

120–121), which they often opposed to the generosity of the foreign militaries and missionaries who opened the first dispensaries, hospitals, schools, and orphanages (Beach 1966).

Many war orphans were spontaneously adopted by American military personnel, as we will see further on. But these informal adoptions were often canceled, either in Korea or in the United States.[18] Welfare institutions anchored their influence in South Korea through Protestantism and American capital.[19] Among all the foreigners who had a strong impact on Korean society, Harry Holt, founder of the adoption agency that bears his name, stands out as the most famous. Transnational adoption as an American practice came into existence in 1954, under the quasi-mystic momentum of this fervent, middle-aged Protestant from Oregon. His Korean right-hand man and friend, David Kim, relates Holt's life and accomplishments in a biography that is close to a hagiography. A heart attack in 1950 provided a turning point to the rich entrepreneur's life as he realized he had never done anything to earn his salvation (David Kim 2001, 69). He survived and began searching for his life's mission. In 1954, in Eugene, Oregon, Harry Holt watched with his family the documentary *Lost Sheep* that featured a South Korea ravaged by war and reduced to a desolate land where millions of orphans wandered (Marre and Briggs 2009, 6–7). Holt recognized in them the mission given to him by God (David Kim 2001, 67). He would meet many administrative obstacles, but American legal officials finally granted Holt the authorization to adopt eight orphans, mostly mixed-blood children he went to fetch by himself. His return to Portland's airport in 1955, with eight babies in his arms, made the headlines of American newspapers, and many couples decided to follow his example.

After 1961, Holt devoted his life to Korean orphans and moved permanently to South Korea. With his personal fortune, he built the first orphanage in Ilsan, a northern suburb of Seoul, which was to soon welcome 700 children. In 1964, a group made up of 133 couples from all over the United States left Los Angeles on the same plane for Korea. The children they had seen in pictures for several years were waiting for them. Harry Holt died that same year, at fifty-nine, and was buried in Ilsan. His wife, Bertha, who had remained in the United States, came to settle in Korea and take over her husband's mission with one of their biological daughters, Molly.

Until 1988, Harry Holt's life and work were little known to South Koreans. The first children to be sent abroad were children who were considered "mixed-blood" (*honhyŏla*). Their mothers were Korean, and their fathers were foreign military, mostly Americans. When they left the military bases where they had been assigned, many of these men abandoned their Korean girlfriends, who stayed behind, often treated as prostitutes by their neighbors. Their children suffered the effects of strong prejudices. Mothers and children were the first and main targets of Holt's proselytism (David Kim 2001, 88). While sharing the disapprobation directed at these women in their own society, Holt believed they were not definitively condemned. Biracial children—especially of African American fathers—were the fruit of sin, but remission through conversion was still an option. The drop of American blood invalidated the Korean blood and constituted a sufficient reason for exclusion from Korean society. Holt clearly believed that these children ought to be repatriated to the land of their fathers. As years went by, however, biracial children became rare and were replaced by wholly Korean children who left their birth country in ever-growing numbers. Changing American immigration laws also played a significant role in this migration.[20]

At least twice, Korean interests conflicted with American interests within Holt (David Kim 2001, 340–341). Kim, who worked at Holt-Oregon, the American branch in charge of recruiting prospective parents, mentions the tension in his book and attributes it to the unequal collaboration of the countries. Americans were advantaged and started using the money from the Korean office to extend their activities in other countries.[21] On the other side, money from the Korean branch was soon the target of embezzlement by an employee involved in a political campaign. The crisis was inescapable. The financial conflict became a dispute over authority between Koreans and Americans (David Kim 2001, 340–341). Finally, in 1978, the South Korean government seized control of the parent company. The appointment of a Korean general director did not yet unseat Bertha and Molly Holt, Harry's wife and daughter, who became the board's copresidents. Their role became largely one of representation. After Bertha's death in 2000, Molly kept working in collaboration with the successive Korean presidents of Holt, ensuring that they respect her father's wishes and the Protestant spirit of the company. In 2003, I heard her say about the possible candidate for the Holt presidency: "Well, as far as he's a Protestant, it's fine!"

After 1978, the number of adoptions at Holt increased considerably, reaching a peak of 8,837 children sent abroad in 1985.[22] The election of a Korean general director resulted in the easing of adoption procedures, a reason that Holt and the other three national adoption agencies became the first targets of South Koreans' anger in 1988. A documentary shows protesters invading the headquarters of the Korean Welfare Society and the president's office on January 25, 1989. Led by a female university student, the protesters accused the agency of causing national shame by favoring international adoption rather than domestic adoption, the former being much more profitable than the latter.[23] Attacking adoption agencies was also a way to reject foreigners, especially Americans, with whom the roots of the institution lay; it was a keen expression of South Korea's refusal to depend on the United States. At that time, South Koreans had started to take pride in their economic achievements. From then on, Holt was constantly pointed to for its expertise in all matters related to Korean children, even in affairs not related to adoption.[24] For example, in a rather suspicious television program from 1992 entitled "Mysterious Document: I Want to Know: Handicapped Children,"[25] the public incidentally learned of an inquiry concerning stolen children: a mysterious woman would approach a young mother carrying a baby in a market, start talking to her, and follow her home. She would bring alcohol and flowers with her and stay a long time, until the young mother needed to go outside again and would ask her to look after the baby for a few minutes. The unknown woman would then take advantage of the mother's short absence to leave with the baby. The police had interviewed the victims, and all their descriptions of the criminal matched. Because she had to dash out as quickly as possible, the strange woman sometimes left her shoes behind. One victim also found a wallet with Japanese currency inside. The first suspicions naturally led the journalists to adoption agencies. Holt employees had to deny these implicit accusations of stealing babies for dominating powers by explaining adoption procedures. After the broadcast of this documentary on the program, a female representative of Holt came to the studio to share a disturbing experience. A poor woman had come to the agency: she ardently wished for a child, but because she was short on money, she was not able to sign the contract and left in distress. A few days later, the Holt counselor called the woman to ask if her desire to adopt had been fulfilled. The woman told her she had found a child. It was probably an illegal adoption, the social worker speculated with a gloomy face.

The program moved on to a different story: an investigation begins in a provincial police station, where a woman has been arrested after getting caught stealing a child. She confesses with downcast face: "I could not have children. I wanted a child. . . . I wanted to raise a child." Another day, policemen found a woman with a newborn child. However, she had no birth certificate for the baby, which would have proved that she had given birth to him in a certain hospital. As a conclusion, the host states that the issue of stolen children is all the more alarming given that there is a real "lack of children" in South Korea.[26] These statements implied, wrongly, that a correlation exists between stolen children (by foreigners) and decreasing fertility rates. After the 1988 crisis, the main adoption agencies had to send their spokespersons to the different television channels' studios to respond to the most extravagant accusations.

* * *

Since the 1990s, the state has endeavored to promote domestic adoption, asserting that it "brings happiness to families and welfare for children" within South Korea. The promotion of domestic adoption has become a leitmotif in the media: South Korean families are followed by cameras during the procedure and are praised as examples of tolerance and patriotic spirit. Childhood and adoption specialists who come to the studio are invited to share their expertise.[27] Praised as models of civic virtue, the same adoptive families reappear in subsequent programs.[28]

According to the Korean media, American adoptive families are models for South Korean society, which is still evolving and improving. Discourses emphasize the need to take into account the individual versus the collective and the respect for human rights.[29] The tone aims for edifying, but it veers closer to didactic: "When our country will be more open-minded, we will pay more attention to individuals." The program aims to "see how in this age, societies change, evolve. Let's be more open!"[30] The purpose is to usher South Korean society into modernity by "writing a new history of family" thanks to the practice of domestic adoption.[31] Following America's example of domestic adoption is all the more justified when it becomes evident that international adoption is not always beneficial to Korean children.[32] The values of Christianity are also palpable in Koreans' regard for human life. In 1994, a South Korean pastor adopted a baby that a garbage man had found in the trash.[33] Several couples, members of the same parish, followed his example and adopted a number of children from an orphanage in Kyŏngju.[34]

Adoptions within South Korea have increased, while international adoption has slightly diminished. In 1999, a television report announced that 1,770 domestic adoptions had taken place that year compared with 2,436 international adoptions.[35] In 2001, there were 1,700 domestic adoptions and 2,400 international adoptions.[36] In 2002, there were 1,694 domestic adoptions and 2,370 international adoptions.[37] In October 2008, the South Korean government announced that domestic adoptions had outnumbered transnational adoptions (1,250 that year) for the first time.[38] Domestic adoption today involves more girls than boys. Social workers explain that it is most often the desire for a child that motivates the adoptive families. So, South Koreans still adopt boys out of duty toward the patriline, but they adopt girls for pleasure: the first argument is that girls are supposedly easier to raise and emotionally more supportive, which makes them better caretakers in general than sons.[39] The second argument is that sons still carry on filial duties and the patriline while girls "leave their parents' house anyway [when they get married]." So, there is so much at stake in the adoption of a boy that it makes that choice very difficult.

The Holt family is now sanctified as a model of generosity and piety. In later years, Bertha and Molly Holt came to seem fully integrated, always appearing at galas and banquets in their traditional Korean dresses (*hanbok*) and giving speeches to South Koreans in perfect Korean. Photographs show them surrounded by South Korean celebrities and politicians. Bertha's funeral in 2000 led to a national day of mourning, conducted by President Kim Dae-jung. The media covered the event thoroughly.[40] Molly Holt, the last representative of the illustrious family and heir of her father's mission, has become a frequent guest on television shows, where she is asked to talk about her father and her peculiar family with great respect and apparent sympathy.[41]

This change in the image of the Holt family and institution is due to the promotion of domestic adoption over transnational adoption by the same institution that was the target of so much criticism at the end of the 1980s. To honor the Holt family in public is to approve of their work and mission and to depict adoption in general as a positive practice. This change coincided with the rise in the 1990s of a new world order.

Korean Adoptees in Korean Globalization

Since 1993, the Ministry of Health and Welfare has taken inventory of the number of adult adoptees coming back to South Korea each year. Increasing steadily, that number has passed from 1,276 in 1993, to 2,760 in 2001, and probably to over 3,000 today.[42] In parallel, adoptee associations have been flourishing for those who want to create judicial, financial, and educative means to stay in South Korea.[43] These associations for transnational adoptees in Korea receive funding from the government and from private anonymous donors. Several big firms sponsor many events for transnational adoptees living in Seoul, and each year, several universities offer adoptee association members scholarships to attend Korean language classes (GOA'L 2003, 43). Politics, economics, and academics play equally prominent roles in the return of international adoptees.

Abroad, communities of Korean adoptees are more and more active and more visible as well.[44] In 2004, at the occasion of the fiftieth anniversary of international adoption, a large group of adoptees gathered at the Sofitel Ambassador Hotel in Seoul, with the South Korean press covering the event over four consecutive days. According to one article:

> The big gathering of international adoptees is an international event. Its goal is to allow adoptees born in South Korea, who were scattered in the

entire world, to make friends and exchange their opinions on South Korea. In 1999, this gathering took place in Washington, D.C., in 2001, in Oslo, Norway, and this year, in our country.... There are twice as many participants this year as last time [in Oslo]. The 430 participants came from the United States, from Sweden, from Germany, etc., from fifteen different countries.[45]

Titles show that journalists prized testimonies from the most successful adoptees: "University Professors, Aerospace Engineer: Two Examples of Success."[46] The same few exemplary individuals are interviewed several times, and their optimistic discourses serve as titles: "We, Korean Adoptees Are Strong";[47] "I Overcame the Wound of Being Adopted to Become a Missionary of Adoption";[48] "Korean Adoptees Were Born from the Heart of Their Adoptive Parents";[49] "To Be Adopted Is to Be Born from the Heart."[50] According to adoptees themselves, international adoption is a benefit. In the midst of this very optimistic atmosphere, only one article (out of twenty-one) displayed a critical title that recalled the debates of 1988: "Please Stop the Export of Babies!"[51]

To South Koreans, this collective return marks adoptees' attachment to their homeland while making palpable the existence of a community of people of Korean descent abroad. Articles reporting on the end of the gathering are revealing: "200,000 Adoptees Live Homesick for Their Birth Country Which Did Not Take Care of Them";[52] "I Didn't Know I Would Walk Again on This Land: 430 Adoptees Rediscover Their Motherland, with Beating Hearts";[53] "Inside, My Heart Cries: 'I Am Korean!'";[54] "We Leave Again Bringing in Our Heart the Love of Our Motherland."[55] According to the journalists, the four-day gathering generated a patriotic feeling for the motherland in the participants. The press attributes to adoptees a strong love for their birth country, an inborn national sentiment common to all people of Korean descent. This interpretation is put forth in the hope of fostering a positive image of their birth country in transnational adoptees but also of changing the representation of transnational adoptees in South Korea. This change in official attitudes occurred in the 1990s and coincided with the rise of mainstream globalization theory.

* * *

Globalization is a fact, in the sense that nations and cultures are becoming increasingly interconnected through travel, media, and economic exchanges. The effects of globalization add up to something like a new consciousness of belonging to one global community (McLuhan and Powers 1989). These effects manifest in complex ways that have very little to do with economic or environmental concerns; they belong instead to the realm of culture and identity. On the one hand, there exists a positive vision of an economic globalization, under capitalist and liberal tenets, in which nations wish to take part. On the other hand, there exists a negative vision of a modern, homogeneous world that societies resist (Appadurai 1996, 11). At present, it is admitted that the negative representation of globalization has generated, on the contrary, not only resilience but also a reassessment of reified cultural and national identities (Wolff 1991). By challenging the concept of nation-state, globalization motivated a state-controlled redefinition and regrouping of the Korean diaspora.

Originally, the term "diaspora" referred to specific historical phenomena like the dispersal and delocalization of the Jews, the Armenians, and the Greeks (Bordes-Benayoun and Schnapper 2006, 19), but over time it acquired a larger and more complex definition, which today implies several of the following elements: a collective trauma, the memory of forced dispersal and exile, the myths of a motherland, alienation in the country of residence, conflicts with the majority or mainstream culture, nostalgia or the desire for return, continuous support from the birth country, the promotion of movements for return, and a powerful collective identity expressed through various media (Clifford 1991; Anthias 1998). Yet some diasporas are experienced and perceived as "reproduction of cultural phenomena through creolization and hybridization" (Agnew 2005, 5). In other words, diasporic phenomena, viewed from certain angles, can be valorized as positive, creative, and profitable (Bordes-Benayoun and Schnapper 2006, 14). In the new world order, migrations are often a choice (Ong 1999), and if they are not, they can be turned to one's advantage.

In the 1990s, the South Korean government recognized an indisputable fact: the presence of millions of people of Korean descent outside of the national territory. At the end of the nineteenth century, Koreans began to migrate to the United States. After the Japanese colonization of Korea from 1910 to 1930, it was widely held among Korean intellectuals that a nation could exist while being dispersed. Rather than disappearing after leaving the colonized motherland, identity survived in faraway places, where Koreans often expressed a stronger patriotism than did those who were subject to Japanese rule (Schmid 2002, 20–22, 22–38). After the Korean War, emigration increased, and the U.S. Immigration and Nationality Act of 1965 encouraged Koreans to go to the United States (Kitano and Daniels 1988, 105; Abelmann and Lie 1997, 49–84). Today, Koreans are spread throughout 160 countries of the world, representing more than 10 percent of the global Korean population (Abelmann and Lie 1997, 50): 2 million are in China, 1 million in the United States, 700,000 in Japan, and 500,000 in Central Asia (or the former Soviet Union), with others in Canada, Latin America, and Europe (Hübinette 2005).

* * *

Like other nations, South Korea sees globalization as a state of the world that is advantageous for the national economy but nonetheless a problem, a threat to Korean culture and identity (Alford 1999, 143). President Kim Young-sam (1993–1998) expressed this thought clearly:

> Globalization must be underpinned by Koreanization. We cannot be global citizens without a good understanding of our own culture and tradition. Globalization in the proper sense of the word means that we should march out into the world on the strength of our unique culture and traditional values. Only when we maintain our national identity and uphold our intrinsic national spirit will we be able to successfully globalize. (Young-Sam Kim 1995, 268–273)

Based on Kim's vision, the Korean definition of the diaspora is to this day a construction engaged by the state to encompass any person of Korean descent who lives abroad, engendering within him or her a sense of community and a strong attachment to the birth country. For this purpose, the South Korean government created in 1997 the Overseas Koreans Foundation (OKF), "a non-profit organization affiliated with the Ministry of Foreign Affairs and Trade. Its establishment was agreed upon at the '1st Overseas Koreans Policy Committee' in 1996, and followed by the announcement of the 'Overseas Koreans Foundation Legislation' (Law N° 5313), which was passed in 1997" (Overseas Koreans Foundation 2004, 5). The first objective of the foundation was the economic prosperity of South Korea:

> The Overseas Koreans Foundation will be the solid basis for constructing the "Leading Economy in Northeast Asia." In this sense, the overseas network will be specialized in various social, economic, . . . educational, cultural, and professional fields. Using this network system, the Foundation will promote an extensive ethnic community consisting in the 1st, 2nd, and 3rd immigrant generations and consequently enable them to contribute to the homeland. (OKF 2004, 5)

By way of metaphor, OKF is described as the "home for the 7 million Koreans living overseas [who] had no choice but leave their homeland [and] are struggling single-handed in the world." OKF promises: "We will embrace you with motherhood.... We will proudly remember [our history].... We will protect your ethnic identity" (OKF 2004, 15–20). The contact with Korea is established and maintained thanks to an educational system that covers all fields of knowledge. It is also upheld through the organization's "heritage camps" and language classes. Teaching Korean culture is indeed necessary for the management of economic potentialities but is also an end in itself, as the condition for ideological control of the Korean globalization. Teaching aims at stirring consciousness and sentiments of belonging, patriotic emotions, or "ethnic structures of feeling" in the absence of a state clearly defined by its territory (Appadurai 1996, 144–149; Lutz and Abu-Lughod 1990). In 1998, the Ministry of Health and Welfare inaugurated the OKF Cultural Awareness Training Program for Overseas Adopted Koreans (Eleana Kim 2010, 180).

Like Korean emigrants, Korean adoptees are de facto integrated into the Korean diaspora. According to the U.S. Immigration and Naturalization Service (INS), Korean children adopted in the United States since 1954 represent up to 13 percent of all emigration to the United States from Korea.[56] After leaving Korea as orphans, adoptees can be regarded as Korean Americans. Therefore, the loss implied by transnational adoption is transformed into a gain. During the 2004 gathering, the media participated actively in the elaboration of a strategy of South Korea's globalization, as passages from these two articles reveal:

> No complete research on the Korean adoptees has been realized so far in South Korea for the following reasons: they are dispersed in the world; their lives differ from one place to another.... But on the basis of the existing studies it is possible to note down several common particularities. According to one study conducted during the first international gathering of Korean adoptees, 70% of the adoptees interviewed were university graduates, 25% of them had a master's (which is superior to the general mainstream American society's rates of college graduates: 45%).[57]

> It will not be only a reciprocal exchange between adoptees but the occasion to create a network of international relations.... Especially, Korean specialists aim to prepare during the gathering a program for a better knowledge of international adoptees and a better worldwide management.... The professor Lee Nam-sŭn from Hallym University thinks that

adoptees can create connections between their birth country and their adoptive country. They can constitute a central human force in this enterprise. That is why it is in our country's interest to manage the situation well.[58]

The image of social and economic success of this Korean community in the world is brought out not only to justify transnational adoption *a posteriori* but also to underline the economic asset it represents for the nation's future. Since 1999, transnational adoptees who want to return to Korea are given special status as overseas Koreans with a two-year F4 visa by the Ministry of Justice. Based on ethnicity, the F4 visa makes up for the lack of South Korean citizenship of individuals who can prove their Korean origins: emigrants ("Korean-born alien"), their immediate family, and transnational adoptees who may not be related to anyone.[59] South Korean citizenship is significantly extended by the issue of the F4 visa (Hübinette 2002, 7). Obtaining the F4 visa is a privilege; the recipients must find "white collar jobs." This mandate evidences the construction of a hierarchy within which the most educated and wealthiest groups are better considered and offered more advantages by the motherland. Transnational adoptees are clearly seen as part of a qualitative immigration, objects of a brain drain. OKF also keeps in touch with transnational adoptees who have already returned to their birth country. In 2005, the day before my birthday, I received from OKF by express mail an English DVD with Korean subtitles entitled *Mochŏn* translated as "Coming Home" ("to come back to one's mother" in Chinese characters). The gift reminded recipients of their time in South Korea by showing a group sharing the same cultural experiences. In 2006, OKF contacted me via e-mail to ask for the references of my PhD dissertation in order to update its database of studies on Korean transnational adoption.

The South Korean government targets immigrants depending on their diplomas and tries to expedite foreign investments while staying ethnically homogeneous. For economic reasons, the politics of belonging and the legal status of foreign people of Korean descent have considerably changed. Korean babies and children were sent to transnational adoption on the basis of their invalid family ties that denied them the status of person. But as globalization emerged as a new world order, they have been called back to their birth country. In this instance, the ethnic blood supersedes the patriline's blood. The return of these scattered Koreans, and their possible stay in South Korea, turns globalization's threat to identity into a promise of spiritual and material improvement based on the contribution of the diaspora (Ong 1999, Watson 2004).

The two acts of the transnational adoption drama—the departure of poor children from a birth country torn by a recent war and the return of successful young adults to a developed nation proud of its achievements on the global scene—must be understood in a larger political and economic context that fluctuated over fifty years. The happy return organized by the South Korean government seems to undo the sad departure induced by foreigners, somewhat erasing adoptees' difficult experiences and promising an easy integration and bright common future. A lower-scale analysis deconstructs that narrative, however, and reveals that this official discourse is flawed at several levels. We will next examine how the construction of Korean adoptees as members of the all-encompassing diaspora does not always translate well in everyday life when adoptees encounter South Koreans in the streets. The status of returnees physically "contaminated," or at least psychologically and culturally influenced by their life abroad, remains problematic to South Koreans despite the varying political readings and uses of their experiences in the course of history.[60]

2

Everyday Encounters

One day of the spring of 2001, I went to a local flower shop to buy a bouquet for my paternal aunt's birthday. My poor command of the language drew the attention of the female shopkeeper. The woman frowned, and her face darkened when I disclosed that I was adopted. Even though I told her with pride that the flowers were for my aunt who lived close by, she asked no further questions. Instead, she lowered her price, gave me the bouquet, and refused any extra money I tried to give her. Her husband came over and asked what the matter was. She grumbled an explanation and gestured at me with a sharp nod of her chin. She looked annoyed while he said nothing, and I left their shop confused. She knew I had found my Korean relatives, but that did not change the reality of my adoption abroad, which she deemed sad or shameful. This was the first of several similar encounters I would experience over and over again during my stays in Korea.

Spending time in South Korea, I came to realize that the image of transnational adoptees was always put in relief by way of comparison with the image of the orphan, of emigrants' children, and other figures of marginality. Either in fictional accounts or in firsthand and secondhand life stories, all categories of ethnic Koreans kept crossing paths, forming a hierarchy based on their degree of Koreanness. Put together, these discourses on each group described the dynamics of marginality as a system. They helped situate transnational adoptees in the stratified social landscape of modern South Korea.

Defining Koreanness

Because I had to learn Korean in order to conduct fieldwork, I spent months at different language institutes in Seoul in 2000, 2003, and 2004, which introduced me to very tangible representations of transnational adoptees. Language institutes are places where Korean teachers and young international students—the majority of whom are emigrants' children and transnational adoptees—experience difference and debate about who and what they are.

All language institutes are similar microcosms that produce culturalism, that is, an essentialized definition of culture.

At the Korean Language Institute (Yonsei University), the mostly female teachers were fond of discussions about Korean society. Because they enjoyed hearing their students' opinions, they often turned debates or presentations into occasions for the confrontation of representations. Defining one's own culture and other cultures was a constant exercise in the classrooms. Although classes generally proceeded smoothly, questions about Korean society would occasionally produce ambivalent reactions. Teachers usually tried to answer students' questions about Korea in a straightforward manner, but they often put an end to heated discussions with a simple assertion: "That's the way it is in Korea." They often perceived questions as criticism, complaint, or mockery and would try to rectify hasty judgments and clichés. When I was attending an advanced-level course, all classes of the same level had to prepare a show for the end of the semester. One Japanese male student suggested parodying Korean people, but the teacher told him sternly that it was a poor idea: other classes in the past had taken this slippery path, and "nobody [had] laughed because it was not funny." In my classes, students asked questions such as: "Why is Korean society so conservative?" "Why can't girls smoke in the streets?" "Why are long sleeves, stockings, and covering tops standard in the middle of the summer?"[1] Students mentioned their own and other foreigners' misadventures. Students in one class, made up mostly of Americans and Europeans, decided one day to discuss a delicate subject: cohabitation before marriage. The young Korean teacher's embarrassment did not deter them from this topic but instead had the opposite effect: they took a malicious pleasure in lingering on the topic. Looking for reasons to explain hostile attitudes in another class, one teacher complained that she was regularly facing students—especially from Western countries—irritated by the situational difficulties caused by their status as foreigners in Seoul. She considered the summer session the most trying of all. "Heat and humidity wear down even the most patient and open-minded students," she asserted.

But criticism and mockery sometimes went both ways. Korean teachers also formulated judgments about students of different nationalities. A few of them cited trips or studies in foreign countries as a basis for judgment. Defining the culture of others was sometimes based on positive criteria: what Russians eat, how the French dress, how Turks look. In one class composed only of Asian students, one professor laughed as she recalled an elderly Caucasian male student who scared her "because he was so hairy." Defining the other could also be based on negative criteria, especially when it came to foreigners of Korean descent: what made them different from true Koreans was what they lacked and what they did not know. This was the case with emigrants' children (*kyop'o*) and foreign adoptees (*haeoe ibyangin*). Either directly or indirectly through short sentences improvised for vocabulary practice, teachers gradually subjected foreigners of ethnic Korean descent to open mockery and half-spoken criticism. One day, a *kyop'o* girl was called "tomboy" (*namja katta*) because of her unkempt appearance; another was given a cold smile and asked to conjugate "to be vulgar" (*yahada*) because her tank top was too revealing. Meanwhile, her friend, a foreign adoptee, received exaggerated compliments on her "traditional beauty" (*chŏnt'ong mi-in*). "She has a large and round face, an exposed forehead and neat makeup," said the senior teacher. The recipient of the compliment smiled but was not pleased, as we had learned earlier that traditional beauty also implied a small chest and a wide waist "which looks like the larger part of a fish." Because the definitions of beauty, modesty, and femininity obviously stemmed from ancient Korean standards, foreigners did not match these references. Instructors proffered harsher remarks on both the appearance and the behavior of foreigners who happened to display Korean features, and girls were always more targeted than boys. These remarks were based more on stereotypes than on facts; at that time, even South Korean youth did not match the ancient standards.

* * *

Theoretically, Koreans' social life is based on the combination of three fundamental social ties. What differentiates overseas Koreans from South Koreans is their lacking one or several of the three ties. Once, the Chinese characters lesson drifted into a discussion of these three social ties.[2] The teacher explained:

> First of all, there is the blood tie or *hyŏl-yŏn* (character *hyŏl*: blood). Then comes the soil tie or *chi-yŏn* (character *chi*: land, soil). In Korea, for the presidential elections, regions vote overwhelmingly for candidates born in those regions. Our president Kim Dae-jung comes from Chollanamdo, well, all the people of that region voted for him, or at least almost all of them.... Last comes the school tie or *hak-yŏn* (character *hak*: school, university). Students usually meet their future spouses at the university. That's why girls start using makeup, growing their hair long and untied as soon as they enter the university. The school tie is crucial when it comes to finding a job. If an older student (*sŏnbae*)[3] with whom you built strong

ties finds a job in a company, he will help you get there as well. If you lack one of these ties, it is difficult to live in Korean society. Even *kyopo* students (emigrants' children) who have relatives in Korea and want to come back to Korea to live and work have a hard time finding their feet. They don't belong to any network and often ignore their necessity, rules, and existence. They say they try to "make friends" with Korean students but after several months, *kyopo* state difficulties in sustaining friendships with native students.⁴

The articulation by the teacher of these three principal social ties implies that several categories of individuals lack them partially or completely and find themselves diminished, incomplete, and inferior to mainstream Koreans. This articulation also contains the principles of a classification. Although she mentioned it first, the teacher did not provide any detail about the blood tie. Neither did she develop the concept of the soil tie. The blood tie seems so universal that it does not need an explanation or commentary. Yet the blood tie's preeminence was implied when she gave an example relevant to emigrants: "Even *kyopo* students who have relatives in Korea" have a hard time fitting in. According to this discourse, emigrants are more integrated than orphans or foreign adoptees in Korea, but all experience discrimination.

These three principles are well ingrained in South Koreans' minds and appear in a range of cultural representations from fictional depictions in the media to anecdotes reported by social anthropologists. Stereotypical representations of orphans are relevant to the understanding of how transnational adoptees are still perceived in South Korean society.

Transnational Adoptees Compared with Orphans

The blood tie is indeed the connective basis whose absence is most likely to provoke Koreans' prejudice. Various sources concur to show how adoptees who have not found their birth parents are comparable to orphans who, in general, are considered uneducated, poor, and ineligible for marriage.

In 1993, the television show *Jeremy* earned an award for best drama in South Korea.⁵ While I was surveying the collection of videos on adoption and child care at Holt Children's Services, an employee especially recommended that video as "of interest" (*chaemi itta*). As a matter of fact, the plot constructed an enlightening comparison between a Korean orphan who remained in Korea and his brother who was adopted abroad.

The first scene takes place in a Seoul train station. On the platform, a poor, desperate woman sits on a bench with her two young sons. She tells them to stay where they are and wait for her on the pretext that she has to run some errands. She hastily descends the stairs and gets on the first train leaving the station. As the train passes the two patiently waiting boys, the mother, crying, sees them for the last time. The older son notices her and understands that she is abandoning them. The two brothers start crying loudly, and soon passersby gather around them. The next scene is set in an orphanage. The two brothers are forcibly separated by a female nurse and the male director of the institution. The younger brother is adopted by an American family, while the older brother, too old for adoption,[6] stays in Korea and grows up in institutions.

With the shot fading, the viewer realizes the two first scenes, in black and white, are childhood memories that the older brother retains as an adult and shares with a female friend. He tells her about his desire to find his little brother. She decides to help him, and both of them go to Holt Children's Services, where the social workers give them access to the adoption file. They learn that his brother's new name is Jeremy and that he now lives in America. They also learn that it is possible to contact him. The bilingual female friend contacts Jeremy, who appears to be eager to meet his older brother. Jeremy decides to fly to Korea as soon as he can.

In the next scene, the characters are in Kimp'o Airport, where Jeremy arrives from the United States. The meeting is happy but reserved. Jeremy is visibly rich, dressed in preppy clothes. His conservative haircut and silken scarf indicate his social class. The Korean actor who plays Jeremy overenunciates each English word. The three characters go to the older brother's comfortable apartment. The friend serves as an interpreter to enable conversation between the siblings, but after a while she has to leave. The two brothers stay together, eat, communicate in rudimentary English or through signs, and get to know each other better. Always at home, the older brother has only brief conversations on the phone every now and then. After several days spent together, Jeremy asks his brother what he does for a living. He does not receive an answer.

One evening, the two brothers and their female friend go out to a restaurant. On their way home, several mafia members (*kkangp'e*), who had been hiding in their cars close to the apartment, encircle them and threaten them with guns. Everybody ends up in a police station, where Jeremy, in a state of shock, asks for an explanation. How can his brother be involved with these criminals and live in such a violent environment? The older brother does not answer and keeps his head down in silence. An orphan, he could not earn an education and advance in society through legal means. The mafia was his sole resource and provider. Revolted by this revelation, Jeremy decides to shorten his stay and return to the United States. The atmosphere is sad and tense.

The last scene shows Jeremy alone at the airport. Suddenly he sees his brother exiting a taxi. Before the final separation, Jeremy bursts into tears and cries: "Who did this? Is it Holt? Is it our parents? Who did this?" The older brother turns his head away and leaves the airport without a word, brokenhearted.

This fictional narrative about orphans' fate in South Korea was confirmed by a French priest, whom I interviewed in 2001. Living in Suwon, he was the tutor of several young male orphans, taking care of their educational and professional development with the help of two Catholic Korean women who volunteered several days a week. The orphans and the priest lived in the same house, governed by order and discipline after Don Bosco's example.[7] One of the Korean women prepared a meal in the kitchen as the priest and I spoke. A teenager came in, fastidiously put his shoes in a low entrance closet, politely greeted us, and went up to the second floor. Outside the house, many dogs barked at passersby. The priest explained that each boy had his own dog and was responsible for its care. That way, he said, the boys would learn the notion of responsibility. The orphans had different schedules: the two or three youngest left for middle school and came back home together. Others attended high school, and the oldest were apprentices in shops. The priest said that by learning a profession, they would avoid the only other alternative available to them: delinquency and, eventually, criminality. Society rejected and despised them, impeding their chance of success. "Delinquency is seen as the attribute of the orphan," he told me resignedly, "but in fact it is a consequence of social prejudice and poverty."

Ethnological texts and interviews concur in classifying the blood tie as the basic tie on which the other bonds depend. Being an orphan in South Korea not only puts one in a disadvantageous economic situation but also makes one a lesser candidate for marriage. Anthropologist Laurel Kendall (1988, 88–91) narrates the life story of her main informant, a female shaman. She notes the extreme reaction of the young woman, who rejects her lover and their infant after discovering that the man has no family. This example equates the orphan with a beggar. The lack of a family to raise and support a child leads not only to poverty but also to the impossibility of alliance (marriage relationship) and legitimate lineage. Kendall shows how her informant's lover has hidden from her his background as an orphan; how she had to search on her own for his true identity, which meant searching for his family; how she rejected him and refused to raise their daughter after she had learned the truth; how she considered him and their baby both bastards.

According to this logic, social abnormality is irremediably transmitted to the descendant. It is also notable that the crucial ties are patrilineal as opposed to german (sibling relationship): the informant's lover has an older sister and an older brother, but she focuses only on the absence of his parents. Like his siblings before him, he will probably never marry. Kendall expresses her surprise at the extreme reactions of her informant, but despite an excessive dramatization, the story reveals a reasoning that explains and justifies her behavior. Though it is not clear, the parents must have died when their children were young; their death has the same effect as if they had never existed. Kendall questions her informant's choice to later marry a poor widower. That widower once had parents, once was married and had children. Contrary to the death of a child's parents, the death of the parents of an adult is seen as natural and without social implications. His status as a widower does not endanger his inclusion in the patriline.

"In our country, not having parents is like not being human," confirmed one of my Korean female friends. When I met her, in 2001, she had recently fled her home after her wealthy father disowned her for living with a self-educated, poor orphan. She had persisted in dating and living with him, and she was working hard to study and make her choice successful. "If I gave up with him, I know my father would welcome me home again," she said with a sigh. "I still visit my mother and my sister when my father is out." Marriage as a social recognition of the union seemed simply impossible in this situation. The relationship with an orphan eclipses any existing filiation. Breaking up with him would lead to reconciliation with her father and reintegration into the family. When I saw this friend in 2007, she had just attended her younger sister's wedding at the Ritz-Carlton and told me her father's rejection of her seemed to have weakened with time. But as of 2011, both father and daughter still held their antagonistic positions.

Molly Holt, daughter of Harry Holt, has devoted her life to Korean orphans. Her more than fifty years of experience leads her to claim that orphans still do not have opportunities to climb the social ladder, get married under normal conditions, or reintegrate with mainstream society. During an interview, she provided me with a striking example of a Korean orphan with whom she had maintained contact:

> Now, he's thirty-five or something, often comes to my home and has a beautiful wife. She can't talk and has one disabled hand. Orphans marry orphans or disabled people. When the child is adopted in a Korean family and is old enough to know it, he gets terrible discrimination. He said: "Why did I have to go to a Korean family? When they had guests, I had to

hide in the kitchen and eat the leftovers. . . . I was never treated like a son."
It's true, they should have protected him, but he was treated like a hired
man; that was the truth.[8]

This example illustrates the supposed fate of orphans adopted domestically, as opposed to the fate of orphans adopted abroad. This orphan compares his situation with the one he imagines for a foreign adoptee. Even his marriage does not satisfy him:

> He said: "I had to marry a disabled person," but I told him: "You know you were a lucky boy, maybe your wife is disabled but she's a wonderful person"; also they have two beautiful children, they are really smart. And of course, because he married her, her family just did everything for him. They bought him a house, got him a job and everything, . . . but he was still unhappy, he said: "Send me to America." I said: "It seems that you're doing ok . . . " "Yes, but I always get treated like an orphan.[9]

The grateful attitude of the parents-in-law indicates that the handicapped are usually unable to marry. Consequently, the proposal from an orphan is, in this case, providential. Molly Holt's discourse, very much focused on the man's material comfort, indirectly mentions his probable strong dependence on his in-laws. His situation is close to the *terilsawi*, or a son-in-law living at his wife's parents' place and commonly referred to as an adopted son-in-law, and often associated with a poor foster son (Roesch-Rohmberg 2004, 83). His marriage thus did not enhance his social status but rather stressed his inferiority. Molly Holt's story might have been biased due to her total involvement in transnational adoption. The example she chose, like the drama *Jeremy*, is an implicit justification of the ongoing dispersion of orphans abroad, since those staying in Korea are condemned to marginality. The adoptive filiation and the lesser alliance with a disabled woman prevent this man from completing the integration into society that filiation and alliance usually imply.

Many other figures of extreme marginality based on the lack of ties haunt the image of the orphan and, by extension, the image of the transnational adoptee. People often link the origins of orphans with the possible prostitution of the unknown mother. This linkage places the moral heritage of orphans in the shadow of illegitimacy. At my request, a Korean friend tried to remember the first time she heard of international adoption. After a moment, she recalled seeing a documentary at a movie theater in 1991: *The Unsolved Arirang*[10] *of Susanne Brink*.[11] Due to her natural beauty and her sad story, Susanne Brink had become the emblem of unhappy transnational adoptions. I found a short documentary entitled *Susanne Brink: 10 Years Later* among the Holt videos. The Munhwa (culture) Broadcasting Corporation (MBC) team had traveled to Sweden to produce a summary composed of vignettes of Susanne's mistreatment by her Swedish adoptive mother, abandonment by her Swedish boyfriend after giving birth to their daughter, betrayal by some Koreans who claimed to be her relatives in order to get money from her, and, finally, her finding her real biological Korean family. Despite the shocking elements of the dramatized story, my friend retained only vague memories of the documentary. She made a comment revealing her subconscious thoughts, surmising that, at some point, the heroine might have been a prostitute to make a living. Even if this was an error in memory or a misunderstanding, it illuminates the persistence of a well-known cliché: the unwed single mother as an immoral woman.

Another case illustrates the problem generated by the unknown identity of the biological parents of orphans and adoptees. A female American adoptee of Korean descent has been dating a Korean American man for many years. They are both in their late twenties. She would like to be introduced to his parents, but they are reluctant to meet her. She knows they would rather introduce their son to the daughter of a Korean family they know well and with whom they share common values and cultural mores. The adoptee has failed to find her biological parents after several visits to Korea. "Her mother may have been a prostitute," insists the man's mother. The social abnormality of prostitution is thought of as biological, genetic anomaly that can be transmitted to the offspring.

As we have seen, being an orphan makes marriage difficult; being single is itself a form of marginality. Single Korean women over the age of thirty usually feel socially ill at ease due to the pressure exerted on them by their environment. A thirty-five-year-old, single Korean woman I met in Seoul several years ago told me that her grandfather still gave her New Year's pocket money along with her young nephews and nieces because she was still single and considered a child. One evening, we had dinner with several friends, among whom a twenty-six-year-old single man was conspicuous. The hosts, a married couple, kept referring to my friend and the single man by means of compliments and innuendo. In her desire to find a serious partner, my friend seemed to appreciate the hosts' help. But after the attempt failed, she revealed to me that she was planning on leaving soon for Europe to flee familial pressure, begin a new life, and maybe find love.

A conversation with a married Korean woman uncovered an interesting association of ideas: Koreans familiarly call single women in exile *kuisin* (ghosts), a term that originates from the Chinese characters *kui* "demon" and *sin* "god" and refers to the ghosts, bad spirits, or souls of the dead who return from the otherworld to haunt the living. These single women are considered outsiders, strangers to the society of normal, married couples. The lack of the marital tie afflicts other existing ties. It can undo family and blood ties, leading to exile and death "far from home" (*kaeksa*). My informant was worried that one of her university friends had become a *kuisin* to her family and friends. The term *kuisin* reveals that the representation of social abnormality implies the idea of death and, therefore, generates fear. Celibacy may also lead to illicit sexual encounters that result in illegitimate children. Therefore, the representations of orphans and adoptees are closely related to the representations of single mothers who are regarded as potential prostitutes. It is interesting that single men, who also, in some ways, do not comply with society's rules, are not called *kuisin*. As a matter of fact, Korean men have the power to ignore their illegitimate children without having to deal with the consequences.

In Korean representations, the marginality that might have characterized someone's life tends to be accentuated after death: the deceased then becomes dangerous and inauspicious. Again, although unmarried men can also experience discrimination in society, they do not generate the same scary representations as women. Resentment is attributed to women, which explains their tendency to become haunting ghosts and restless spirits. This is a leitmotif in Japanese and Korean horror movies. Koreans and Japanese explain that in their patriarchal societies, women are more likely than men to die unsatisfied.

The dead separate into two categories: those who died naturally and are given rituals by their descendants; and those who died accidentally, too young to be married, without descendants, or in a state of extreme frustration (Baptandier 2001, 92–93). It is widely believed that individuals who die without having married or without legitimate children are the most inclined to become restless spirits and haunt their relatives and, sometimes, all of society. Nobody will perform the rituals needed to appease, liberate, and untie the nostalgic or resentful dead from the living world. They will not turn into auspicious dead or benevolent ancestors—who are said, in Buddhism, to escape the cycles of reincarnation. The difference between not having descendants and having illegitimate children is that, in the first case, rituals can be performed and adoption can solve the problem. In the second case, illegitimate children simply reproduce the marginality of their unfortunate parents.

Discrimination against orphans and single mothers and their offspring is exacerbated in the case of biracial individuals and their Korean mothers, two other figures of marginality who have suffered from great prejudice in postwar Korean society. The rejection of biracial people is not unique to Korea (Watt 2009), but it explains, as mentioned earlier, the origins of transnational adoption in Korea. As we have seen, the first children to be adopted in the United States were from Korean mothers and foreign fathers. Their physical characteristics were irrefutable proof and a sign of their essential otherness, especially half-black children.

Address Unknown,[12] a film by Korean director Ki-duk Kim, uses a biracial character as an emblem of the hardship of the postwar era. Throughout the story, all the central figures are afflicted by misery and hatred: the dog butcher,[13] the sight-impaired girl, the American soldier, the biracial boy, and his Korean mother. The latter two live together in an old, abandoned bus where a picture of the father, an African American soldier, is seen on a table like a relic of a happy past. The young man experiences isolation, the malevolence of neighbors, and discrimination in finding a job. He cares for his mother, whom the villagers call a prostitute.

In an outburst, he kills his employer, the dog butcher. He then returns to the bus, destroys the portrait of his absent father, and leaves on his motorcycle. Going at full speed on a narrow path, he falls from his motorcycle headfirst into the frozen mud of a rice field. His stiff body remains planted like a stick until his only friend finds him the next day. His friend is a member of a respectable family whose father was awarded war decorations that he constantly wears. Yet this respectable young man also eventually falls from grace. After shooting an arrow at the American soldier who abused the sight-impaired girl with whom he is in love, he is arrested by the police. His father wants to take the blame for the crime, but his son refuses this sacrifice. The car transporting the convict to jail passes by the old bus, in flames. From a distance, the young man witnesses the suicide of the abandoned mother. She immolates herself while holding the body of her son.

Delinquents, prostitutes, singles, handicapped, and biracial individuals are all marginal figures, the objects of strong stereotypes in Korean society. They share the common trait of absent or severed ties to social life. Like restless spirits or *kuisin*, they already belong to a parallel world that has negative effects on the normal world. They cast shadows upon those who approach them. An orphan's state is permanent, and nothing can change it, whereas a "normal" person's state fluctuates during life and can quickly fall into marginality. Abnormality, as we have seen, is essentially thought of as a lack of social ties. The missing tie could be the blood tie, soil tie, or school tie. The absence of the blood tie at birth or its loss at some point has implications for the remaining ties and eventually results in one or another form of marginality.

The example given by Molly Holt shows the following causal chain: orphans cannot go to school and pursue a career, which leads to a marginal marriage or celibacy. The example given by Kendall can be schematized this way: discovering the absence of potential parents-in-law causes the woman to reject her lover and their child, and eventually leads her to marry another man. That cause-and-effect series of events constitutes a vicious circle.

As subjective as they are, these stories illustrate a system of representations, a logic implied in the combination of ties the informants cite when explaining a problematic social situation. These stories that relate to orphans in South Korea illuminate the far-reaching effects of the missing blood tie. It is fair to say that these aspects of marginality are thought of as dangers latent in orphans and foreign adoptees (Douglas 2001), liabilities transmitted through blood, legacies from marginal parents that will be passed on to illegitimate children. Despite the new policies of belonging initiated by the government, as seen in the previous chapter, the nature of the blood of adoptees is still dubitable unless they discover the identity of their parents.

The comparison of foreign adoptees and domestic orphans is often implicit in the attitudes and silences of Korean people, although the term "orphan" (*ko-a*) is never used. When interactions are short, as with shopkeepers or cab drivers, attitudes express compassion and pity rather than hostility. Irremediably negative, adoption, whether domestic or transnational, generates culpability and requires some kind of compensation. Here, my experience as an adult adoptee provides ample material for anthropological analysis.

The first time I lived in Korea for a long period, I registered at the National Institute for International Education Development (NIIED), which was the cheapest public language institute in Seoul. This was my first formal course, but because I had independently learned the alphabet and basic grammar, I chose to attend the second level. Most of the other students in my class were the sons and daughters of Korean emigrants (*kyop'o*) from North America, South America, Europe, Central Asia, China, Japan, and Australia.[14] The majority of them could speak adequately, having grown up with parents speaking Korean at home. After a few weeks of struggling to keep up with my peers, I learned of a scholarship that the main teacher would award to the best students. In the middle of the semester, I was surprised to receive one of these scholarships. A Chinese *kyop'o* also received the scholarship, but our situations were very different. In discussing the fact with some classmates, we concluded that the Chinese boy received the award because he probably was poor. My peers presumed that in my case, receiving the scholarship was an encouragement, a sign of sympathy, or a compensation for my adoptee status.

Additionally, at the end of the semester, I received a distinction from the teacher—a form identifying me as an "exemplary student" (*mobŏm haksaeng*).

During that same semester at NIIED, a female teacher expressed special concern about me and one day revealed the reason: she was a single older woman who had grown up as an orphan. Through her intelligence, strength, and endurance, she had succeeded in her studies and obtained a diploma that enabled her to teach at that school. She encouraged me to persevere in my studies as she had done. She thought we shared the same status, the same inferior position relative to others.

The reduction of transnational adoptees to the same status as orphans used to be the most prevalent response among South Koreans, but it is now often mixed with a more valorizing assimilation with emigrants who reside abroad. We will now see the important implications of this assimilation and show that the positive official discourse about the Korean diaspora is reflected in people's attitude toward either transnational adoptees or emigrants' children, but always with ambivalence.

Transnational Adoptees and Emigrants

Many South Koreans consider foreign adoptees to be ambiguous beings and treat them either with scorn and pity or with envy. They presume that a foreign adoptee today was a domestic orphan yesterday. In *Jeremy*, the poor orphan with no prospects left Korea to be adopted and later returned rich, educated, and speaking English. Like the emigrant of Korean descent, Jeremy has an open door to the world, a status some might envy, especially given contemporary South Korean striving for higher education and a cosmopolitan lifestyle (Seth 2002, 100–131, Prébin 2011).

On my first stay in Seoul, I observed that my foreign accent generated questions from vendors and cab drivers always eager to start a conversation: "*Kyop'o aniseyo*? [Aren't you the child of emigrants?]" or "*Ibyangin iseyo*? [Are you adopted?]" This preliminary question quickly revealed that *kyop'o* and foreign adoptees returning to Korea are a well-known phenomenon. I answered once that I was *kyop'o* in order to gauge my questioner's reaction. The cab driver responded by simply asking which country I was from, when I had left Korea with my parents, and whether I had relatives living in Korea today. I said that I lived in Paris, that my parents and I had left Korea when I was four, and that I had uncles and aunts on both sides who currently lived in Inchon. He believed me without any problem. This information led to other questions: "Do you like Alain Delon and Brigitte Bardot?" "What do your parents do for a living?" "Is Paris as beautiful as people say?"

I usually answered such questions about my origins by identifying myself as a foreign adoptee. In these situations, the person's reaction was more hesitant. My interlocutor often became silent for a moment before curiosity overcame embarrassment: "When were you adopted?" "Were your adoptive parents nice to you?" The questions focused not only on my adoptive family but also on my Korean birth family: "Did you find your birth mother?" "Did she remarry?" "What about the rest of the family?" "What do they do?" After revealing that I had found my Korean mother, along with two grandmothers and a bunch of uncles, aunts, and cousins, I seemed to detect in my questioner a kind of satisfaction, a genuine sense of relief. I was always then warmly congratulated: "*Ch'ukhahamnida!* [Congratulations!]" I was sometimes told to quickly learn Korean, which implied that I had to spend time with my birth family.

Above all, many Koreans assume that all foreign adoptees have rich adoptive parents. I received many self-serving invitations from Korean women of all ages who dreamed of seeing Paris and wanted me to reciprocate. I had to explain over and over that my parents were not rich, did not live in Paris, and had a somewhat small house. In addition, many Korean students said that they also envied my fluency in "foreign languages," not taking into account that French is my native language.

The comparison of foreign adoptees with emigrants is natural to Koreans, and also to the persons who are compared. Adoptees and emigrants easily get acquainted either in their home countries or in Korea, especially while attending the language institutes of Seoul. In 2003, during a class at the Korean Language Institute, a teacher asked me about my nationality and my studies. She was delighted to hear that I was studying anthropology, a discipline she deeply appreciated, and tried to speak a few words of French she had learned in the past. One day, a Japanese student dared to ask me directly what I was, "really." Most Japanese and Korean Japanese know of overseas Japanese but only discover the phenomenon of transnational adoption when they spend time in Korea. They wonder about the identity of the foreign adoptees they meet at the language institutes of Seoul. In contrast, the *kyop'o* who come from Europe and the United States are already aware of transnational adoption. I told the Japanese student that I was French, born in Korea, and that I had been adopted. The student started asking more questions: "Which mother do you consider your real mother . . . ?" But at that moment, the teacher tried to help me, she thought, by declaring that I was *kyop'o* like most of my classmates. I contradicted her, arguing that *kyop'o* (emigrant's child) and *ibyang* (adopted person) were very different. The teacher looked troubled and turned toward the other students: "Is it not the same thing? [*ttok-kach'i anayo?*]" An awkward silence fell over the class. The teacher imagined that her intervention would ease my integration as a foreign adoptee. Indirectly, she also expressed her inner feeling that being an emigrant was better than being an adoptee.

Because their parents have left Korea, emigrants' children seem to retain the blood tie and the soil tie (through the relatives who have remained in South Korea) but to lack the school tie. According to the teacher's discourse, the blood tie is more important than the soil and school ties. Thus, emigration is, in theory, a lesser form of marginality. South Koreans, however, may consider emigration a willful betrayal of the motherland. This opinion can lead to a negative attitude toward emigrants and their children.

A senior female teacher at the Korean Language Institute expressed her scorn toward emigrants by calling emigration an irreversible loss without much reward: "When you emigrate, you lose your roots [*ppurirŭl ilko*], you are like a tree without soil [*ttang*] to plant its roots in the long term; Koreans must live in Korea [*hanguk saramdŭri hanguke saraya toemnida*]."[15] This determinist and organicist view of Korean identity as linked to the land affirms that emigration is always a deceitful illusion, a soon-to-fail venture. The teacher invoked the well-known 1992 riots in Los Angeles, when small Korean businesses became the main targets of a black community angered at the beating of an African American by the police. Many Korean emigrants were ruined and had to start over from scratch or return to South Korea (Abelmann and Lie 1997).

Emigrants usually have relatives—uncles, aunts, cousins, and sometimes grandparents—who still live in Korea and welcome them when they return. Nobody questions these emigrants' origins and blood ties. However, emigrants can face problems in integration involving their own kindred, through whom they have soil and blood ties that should ensure their social identity even if they do not reside in Korea (Shima 1998). A young emigrant citizen of Germany spent *Ch'usŏk* (a harvest festival often referred to as the Korean Thanksgiving) visiting ancestors' tomb with his relatives. Soon after the visit, friends found the German *kyop'o* crying in his room. He told his friends how the head of his patrilineage (his oldest paternal uncle) mistreated him during the festivities in spite of objections by his paternal aunts. This rejection indicated that he was not considered a full member of the clan on the basis that his parents had migrated to Germany and were absent on that crucial day. This contradicts the accepted reality that today most Koreans do not live exactly where their family originated (Shima 1998). The blood and soil ties that exist in theory through relatives who stayed in Korea do not ensure the inclusion of the emigrant in reality.

Emigrants' children returning to Korea lack one tie without fail: the school tie. By contrast, their parents often belong to high school alumni associations whose influence is reportedly very strong, especially at the government level. The Chinese characters teacher described school, and especially the university, as the most crucial network on which a person's future depends. Because it determines economic achievement, the school tie has come to supersede other ties in the contemporary era (Hwang 2004, 351). But South Koreans usually surmise that emigrants' children and transnational adoptees had good educational opportunities and were able to attend one of the prestigious Ivy League schools.[16] In the globalized world, the education in a Western country has challenged the ties contracted in Korean schools and universities.[17] In general, this shift benefits emigrants and adoptees who attended good schools in the United States. Back in South Korea, they are often offered jobs that require English speaking and sometimes welcomed by potential parents-in-law. This new ranking of school ties adds nuance to the simple system of social strata Koreans evoke spontaneously.[18]

Despite continuous efforts to clarify their identity, foreign adoptees remain an ambiguous category, sometimes compared to Korean orphans and sometimes to emigrants' children. Discourses reveal a tendency to associate the transnational adoptees and emigrants' children with one another, as they resemble each other in attitudes, mannerism, gestures, and languages. This resemblance allows one to ignore the negative aspects of transnational adoption but does not entail unquestioned inclusion: emigrants' children also encounter prejudice. On the basis of the education criterion relevant to the context of globalization, the taxonomy of adoptees and emigrants (that have one term each, *ibyangin* and *kyop'o*) significantly changed in the 1990s and confirms the elevation of transnational adoptees in South Korea. Whereas in the past they were called "adopted child" (*ibyang-a*), which placed them on a par with "orphan child" (*ko-a*), they became "adopted persons" (*ibyang-in*) and more often now "compatriot adoptees residing abroad" (*ibyang tong p'o*), which assimilates them with emigrant Koreans residing abroad (*kyop'o*) as *kyop'o* and *tongp'o* are used indifferently to talk about overseas Koreans. The Chinese characters *tong* and *kyo*, respectively, mean "same" and "life abroad," and *p'o* refers to one mother's womb. With this semantic evolution and the blurring of category lines, one dominant idea emerges: the strict definition of social identity based on the three ties has become a rather loose one revolving around blood or ethnicity. It is at least a politically correct way of including adoptees within Korean society.

It is clear that despite the inclusion of foreigners in a broader definition of Korean identity, old representations of otherness remain and resurface in ordinary encounters, interactions, and conversations with South Koreans, against official discourses crafted by the government. Caught between nations and cultures, transnational adoptees impersonate the marginal figures described by anthropologists Arnold Van Gennep and Mary Douglas: they harbor potential powers but also present danger forever, making their integration as desirable as it is arduous (Van Gennep 1981; Douglas 2001).

We now turn to an illustration of how institutions such as Holt and OKF cooperate to maximize adoptees' potential positive attributes while reducing their negative attributes through special education programs and ritualized performances.

3

Holt International Summer School or Three-Week Re-Koreanization (1999–2004)

> Koreans pretend to organize all this for us [adoptees], but I think they do it for themselves.
> —Participant, HISS, 2000 (interview, 2002)

Holt Children's Services officially initiated the Holt International Summer School (HISS) in 1991, but it was launched informally in 1983 by David Kim for the first returnees (2001, 320–321). Today this three-week program includes different types of activities: a "heritage tour"; classes related to Korean culture; a social welfare tour that requires participants to visit orphanages and single mothers' houses; and a family search, which is undertaken by social workers from the information they find in participants' adoption files.[1] As a participant in 1999, I paid only $1,000 for a three-week course including airfare, stays in luxury hotels, and meals in the best restaurants. In fact, although transnational adoptees may represent a targeted clientele of regular consumers,[2] the nominal cost of these programs leads one to wonder if the economic aspect of the enterprise is not somewhat secondary. And even if a large part of these programs is devoted to travel, Korean adoptees are not perceived as mere tourists. As seen earlier, strategies of globalization are openly advocated by South Korean officials, but apologies are also systematically made in public by OKF representatives and politicians.[3] This suggests that the programs represent a compensation or a gift to returnees (Mauss 1990; Sahlins 1988). I took part in HISS in 2004, this time as an assistant, in order to look more closely at the dynamics of the program.

I argue here that the sequencing of the programs indicates that they stand for rites of passage for adoptees who return to South Korea. They, however, integrate adoptees less to their motherland than to the remote diaspora. In other words, they may further reinforce adoptees' separations from Korean society.

Apprenticeship of Childhood

Every year, the program offers the same range of activities in its cultural classes, with minor variations. Therefore, despite their brevity, these activities appear to provide a mandatory corpus of knowledge. During their stay at the Ilsan Holt Center, where all the classes took place, HISS participants made only brief excursions to Seoul with the assistants—an American adoptee in 1999 during my own participation in the program and myself in 2004—to go shopping, see the Korean performance of an American musical (*Fame*), observe a traditional performance, and attend a dinner theater. Study time and leisure time were clearly delineated, and some participants complained about the lack of freedom and autonomy. Although brief and superficial, this accelerated apprenticeship was part of a child's education. Korean adoptees were all adults in age, yet they had to be reeducated from the beginning, that is, disciplined.[4]

Prior to their flying to Korea, HISS participants had to complete a form and read the rules. In 1999, they had to promise to respect South Koreans by avoiding any provocative outfits (no tank tops, no miniskirts). Although no uniform was required, participants received a T-shirt bearing the Holt logo and seemed to be regarded as school students. During the program, participants could not smoke cigarettes in public or drink alcohol, especially at Ilsan Holt Center, "so that mentally challenged residents would not try to imitate them," social workers explained. Going outside the center after nine o'clock at night without an escort—a social worker or a volunteer—was forbidden so that nobody would get lost. Participants were also compelled to attend all the classes indicated on the program. The whole program was described on a poster in both Korean and English. Completion of this learning program, combined with a good attitude, would be validated at the end by a diploma.

When they first arrived at the center, participants received instructions from the volunteers. Adoptees themselves, these volunteers stayed with the participants the whole time they were at the center and helped social workers, who usually returned home at night. Volunteers led a tour of the big house built by the founder himself. Bedrooms with *ondol*, the traditional Korean floor heating system, and mattresses on the floor hosted three or four participants—genders separated but nationalities mixed. Everyone was instructed to wear plastic slippers inside the building and to take them off at the entrance to bedrooms, and to fold his or her personal mattress every morning and put it in the lower compartment of the closet along the wall. Accommodations were simple, and disabled residents of the center did most of the cleaning and maintenance. Two friendly Korean women came every day to prepare meals, except when the group ate out on special occasions. Participants took their meals in the living room. Led by American participants, the group said grace in English before sitting down. Food was generally good, varied, and not too spicy, since the previous years some adoptees had had stomachaches and had to be taken to the hospital, recalled a social worker. Participants rotated dishwashing after each meal.

Participants, who in 1999 and 2004 came from the United States, France, Norway, Denmark, and Germany, got to know each other despite the language barrier. On July 26, 2004, after everybody had arrived, a minibus bearing the Holt logo drove participants, volunteers, and social workers to Holt headquarters, an office building located in Map'o district, in western Seoul, close to the north bank of the Han River, for the opening ceremony. The Korean president of Holt, the council board president and daughter of founder Harry Holt, Molly Holt, the president of the sponsorship department, and all the employees of Post-Adoption Services attended the event. Plastic folders containing booklets published at Holt, a notebook, pencils, and a badge with the name of each participant were set on tables forming a U in the center of the room in front of a little stage. A piano stood next to a cross at the back of the room under a South Korean flag. From a wooden lectern engraved with a Protestant cross,[5] the program administrators delivered brief welcoming speeches in front of a banner reading: "Welcome Overseas Korean Adoptees to Holt International Summer School 2004." The banner featured a scene by the famous painter Hong-do Kim (1745–1815?) entitled *The Village School*.

Holt staff sat on the right of the platform in three rows of chairs, those with higher rankings in front. Sponsors were represented by severe-looking elderly women. They observed the adoptees with rapt attention, taking their charity responsibilities very seriously. Social workers assigned seats to participants while a young employee took photographs using a professional-grade camera. Once everybody was seated, the ceremony began. The strict spirit of the event was at once imbued with Protestant values by means of the opening prayer, improvised by Molly Holt. She stood and prayed with her eyes shut, followed by all: "Lord, here is the group of young Korean adoptees who are back to their motherland this summer. . . . Please protect them and help them through this experience."

Accompanied by a pianist, the "Holt Choir," made up of male and female staff from Post-Adoption Services, performed "God Will Make a Way," a song composed in English for this occasion.

God will make a way
Where there seems to be no way
He works in ways we cannot see
He will make a way for me
He will be my guide
Hold me closely to His side
With love and strength
For each new day
He will make a way
He will make a way
By a roadway in the wilderness
He will lead me
And rivers in the desert will I see
Heaven and earth will fade
But His word will still remain
And He will do something new today
With love and strength
For each new day
He will make a way
He will make a way

Religious in nature, these lyrics seemed applicable to anyone, like the Gospels or the Psalms, their obvious sources of inspiration. In this context, the lyrics identified adoptees as people in difficulty, a bit lost and in need of a guide to find their way. God was their guide, but as helpless children, they would also receive help and encouragement from Holt staff. After the song, each participant introduced him- or herself in English—first name, last name, and citizenship—and was applauded.

In 1999 and 2004, all participants were over eighteen, as mandated by the program. The oldest participants were in their early thirties, and some were married with children. A majority were graduate students or professionals who had worked for several years and found it frustrating to be treated like children in primary school. As the days went by, more and more complained about the constraints imposed by the program on leisure activities and about the impossibility of sleeping late: volunteers had to wake participants up in the morning, sometimes by banging a spoon on a pan. The participants played their role haphazardly. At first, at registration, they had paid little attention to the program activities and schedule. Everybody grew impatient to start traveling, or anxious to get information about birth parents. Contrary to the participants' desires, organizers took the classes very seriously: professors came from the best institutions in Seoul, and adoptees were told to show the greatest respect and interest in front of them. At the end of each class, each professor was politely thanked by all and received a gift from the volunteer or a social worker: a watch and the Holt T-shirt.

In 1999, the program included several activities that could form part of a Korean child's curriculum. Confirming the stereotypical love of Koreans for music, there were four hours of "Korean songs," ranging from nursery rhymes and love ballads to the national anthem. Introduced as an opera singer, the music teacher broke into the national anthem with a powerful voice. The first piece in the booklet, the anthem, was followed by short nursery songs, a popular modern love song, and two versions of the classic national folk song "Arirang"—a love ballad about abandonment and female resentment. Four hours were not enough to complete the ambitious repertoire. Participants were also taught for four hours traditional drumming using four percussion instruments (*samulnori*). Students learned by repeating and imitating their professors' techniques of using onomatopoeic sequences (*k'ong, ttak*).

In 2004, the fiftieth anniversary of transnational adoption, the OKF's program was included in the HISS program. These extra classes, which took place in the ballroom of a hotel in Suwon, where participants and organizers alike stayed for two days, included three-hour craft class where they decorated a box made of Korean traditional paper (*hanji*, made after a late Chosŏn technique from the bark of the mulberry tree).

The 1999 and the 2004 HISS schedules included eight hours of *t'aekwondo*, the national martial art, which is as commonly practiced by Korean children as the piano. In the studio, participants not only had to participate in the physical exercises—stretching, positions, and kicks—but also had to memorize synchronized sequences under the supervision of the master. While participants mocked each other's clumsiness or complained that their bodies hurt, the instructor and his assistant remained extremely serious and hounded anyone who showed signs of laziness or stiffness. Discipline was strongly emphasized. Participants had to quickly learn how to salute, bow, and count in Korean so that the class could proceed smoothly. In 2004 at times very young pupils came to the studio to train and serve as examples to the adult beginners. They avoided laughing at the foreigners, whom they instead ignored, simply following their master's commands with rigor and steadiness. To broaden their physical training, participants spent four hours learning the rudiments of the traditional "mask dance" (*ttalch'um*) in the gym of the Ilsan complex. In 2004, in addition, the group was initiated into *t'aekkyŏn*, an ancient fighting technique that preceded *t'aekwondo*, supposedly dating back to the Three Kingdoms period (57 BC–AD 668), for which participants put on a special white outfit. They came out of the room exhausted.

The 1999 program included four hours of elementary Korean cuisine classes at the Ilsan Holt Center. What was at stake in food was no less than cultural identity. With soft voices, the four instructors, all Korean women in their fifties, explained their gestures in Korean: "Now I mix with my fingers . . . much better with fingers!" They made their students taste the food, putting it directly into their mouths either with the cooking chopsticks or by hand; they fed them in a motherly way, as if they were their own children, and did not forget to compliment girls on their beauty or to laugh with tenderness at boys' lack of skill. Toward the end of class, when the *kimch'i* (pickled, fermented cabbage) the students and instructors had produced together was still marinating in plastic pans, the social worker took a picture of everyone exhibiting their rubber gloves stained with red pepper powder. Participants were given a booklet in which all the recipes made that afternoon were printed in English. That evening, the whole group enjoyed this homemade feast.

Additionally, the HISS program incorporated ten hours of Korean language lessons. The plastic folders distributed at the opening ceremony contained the first volume of a Korean language handbook and accompanying tapes. As an introduction, the professor from Seoul spoke in praise of the native language, which he called the "most difficult in the world but also the most scientific" thanks to the creation of the Korean alphabet (*hangŭl*) by the enlightened King Sejong (1397–1450), who reigned from 1418 to 1450. He added that giving up the old Chinese character–based system for the new Korean alphabet had enabled the country to achieve record rates of literacy and, much later, the easy application of Korean for computers.

Finally, the program included six hours of Korean history. The professor from Seoul talked first of the different kingdoms that eventually united, covering the territory now occupied by the two Koreas. At the end he spoke of today's Korean nation, which, he added, includes the Korean diaspora. The professor's solemn voice crescendoed as he concluded with these exalted words: "You, adoptees, belong to the Korean diaspora, the fourth diaspora in the world; you are smart, educated, and Koreans are proud of you. You are the ambassadors of Korea!" At this, American, French, German, Norwegian, and Danish participants applauded. The message was clear: any person of Korean blood is welcome in Korea and, despite nationality received through adoption, has to represent Korea abroad without bringing too much foreignness to Korea. This will to win over adoptees was made all the more explicit in the way the professor praised participants' education and professions. He proceeded by asking each participant to write a note indicating his or her status, studies, or profession. Those who were graduate students were publicly distinguished from the others. In 1999, one American who studied at the University of California in Berkeley was especially congratulated. In 2004, one American who was a university professor received marked admiration.

Most participants had been adopted as babies or very young children. Thus, the school program and the infantilizing treatment described earlier make some sense when one considers how, at some level, the adult adoptees are still thought of as infants when they first return to their native country. Yet learning is not enough; knowledge has to be validated by diplomas and certificates. Remarkably, the imposed activities culminate in a graduation ceremony and an honorary citizenship ceremony that stand for adoptees' replacement school and soil ties. With this symbolic acquisition of ties, adoptees reach a new status, at least in the eyes of the organizers and within Holt. Going back to one's childhood is only the preliminary step in one's entrance to adulthood.

HISS participants were rewarded with a numbered certificate bearing their name in English and in Korean, and a picture of the founder kissed on the cheek by a Korean child. Underneath the picture was written: "Founder Mr. Harry Holt (1905–64). He founded Holt for Homeless Children and he was taking care of the children in the love of Christ at Ilsan Centre until his death." In fact, the certificate was given during the closing ceremony.

On July 28, 1999, Reverend Song, Korean president of Holt Children's Services, extended his congratulations to the group and was answered and thanked in Korean by the two spokespeople ("Address in Reply"). I was one of two students who gave this short Korean speech written and rehearsed with a program volunteer. In the 1999 closing ceremony, "Singing in Unison" consisted of singing the South Korean national anthem, learned during singing class. On August 16, 2004, the "Address in Reply" was given in English by the American university professor. A small group performed with drums for two minutes ("Students' Performance"), a routine for which they had a few hours' rehearsal. The ceremony also included the national anthem, indicated as the "National Ceremony." While visiting, learning, playing, and eating, adoptees had contracted duties and obligations vis-à-vis their motherland. Although the opening ceremony welcomed them as ignorant foreign youth, the closing ceremony celebrated their newfound status as knowledgeable adults conscious of their roots. Despite some hesitation and mispronunciation, staff and sponsors enthusiastically applauded the success of the Holt International Summer School.

> July 28, 1999
> N° 99-18
>
> CERTIFICATION OF STUDY FOR HOLT
> INTERNATIONAL SUMMER SCHOOL
>
> This is to certify Ms Elise Prebin (Cho Woo Jung) completed the whole course of 8th Holt International Summer School.
>
> Rev. Song, Jae Chun, President
> Holt Children's Services, Inc.,
> Seoul Korea

Similarly, for the last night of the trip, the 2004 OKF tour participants returned to the Ritz Carlton in Seoul, where the program's opening ceremony had taken place a few days earlier. The closing ceremony, a gala, was held in the ballroom in the presence of people, like Molly Holt, who were important in adoption circles. An ice sculpture at the entrance signified the grandeur and solemnity of the event. Each participant was called to the stage to receive his or her personal certificate, stamped with the seal of the OKF and signed by the then president Lee Kwang-kyu.[6] The ceremony concluded with a group picture taken on the stage. Then all were free to tuck into the abundant buffet.

The certificate distributed to HISS participants at the Map'o mayoral house perhaps best expressed the political aspects of adoptees' reintegration in 2004. The Honorary Citizenship Certificate reveals the ambiguity of adoptees' citizenship. That morning, social workers had asked participants to dress up. At the mayoral house, the group entered a room in which four members of the mayor's administration, including the mayor's representative, invited everybody to sit down in a certain order: seats were numbered, and each adoptee received a card imprinted with a number and his or her name. A photographer attended the event but took pictures only when each adoptee received a certificate and shook hands with the mayor's representative.

These multiple certificates demonstrate the South Korean government's intention to attract, welcome, and integrate adoptees. Accepting the certificate is not a choice but an obligation and an honor. In addition, these are not sham certificates: they bear serial numbers. The recipients' names are evidently registered, and the same person cannot receive this distinction twice. At the mayoral house, one participant stayed apart and observed the others. I asked her why. "I have already received one of these, last year," she told me, "because I volunteered for an association of disabled children in Seoul."

This particular event took place in Map'o district, but similar events can take place in other districts, depending on specific programs (Eleana Kim 2005). They all show that the concept of soil tie has evolved at the same time as the concept of citizenship (Hwang 2004). They confirm that the old concept of "homeland" or "original village" (*kohyang*), on which the soil tie (*chiyŏn*) is based, remains with few adjustments a criterion for integration and the definition of social status. Certificates validate this reeducation and give a territorial identity to international adoptees, replacing the school tie (*hakyŏn*) and the soil tie (*chiyŏn*) in the absence of the blood tie (*hyŏlyŏn*) if one's birth parents cannot be found. Thus, the entire program allows tie-deprived adoptees to reach the status of persons, which is ultimately very reassuring to Korean society.[7] Highlights of the program often appear on South Korean television (either in the news or in special shows about adoption) and mostly focus on adoptees' ability to mimic Koreans by speaking a few words in Korean, eating Korean food, or performing rituals.

Rites of Passage to Adulthood

In 1999 and 2004, the initiatory nature of the program was reflected in other kinds of apprenticeship, some more complex than others, that reached beyond the childhood sphere: the practice of etiquette, the practice of the tea ceremony (which was explicitly linked to a rite of passage to adulthood, or capping ceremony),[8] and training in the traditional wedding ceremony. This was the most constraining part of the program.

In 1999, the class took place in a classroom inside the Ilsan complex, presided over by elderly women, regular volunteers or sponsors at Holt. The class included a tea ceremony and male and female bowing. Before beginning training, participants put on their custom-made traditional costumes. Dressing was very complex and required help from two volunteers. Wanting a photo, some participants posed by putting an arm around a friend's shoulders, a move that uncovered their underarms under the short bolero. At this sight, the older Korean women grumbled with disapproval and pointed out the guilty to those who had not seen what happened. The unruly females were immediately taught to avoid this improper gesture. Those who behaved properly received compliments and smiles. All participants quickly became hot in the big room, where the air-conditioning was inefficient. But it was only the beginning of a long training in measured greetings, deep bowing, and careful handling of the wooden tools for the tea ceremony. For one entire afternoon, "etiquette classes" taught participants table manners and how to bow before parents or grandparents. Young Korean children learn these postures early and execute them easily when circumstances require. But adult participants had a hard time: knees cracked, and arms remained bent. The end finally came, and all dutifully thanked the patient instructors by bowing in the way they had barely mastered. A group picture was taken to conclude the afternoon.

In 2004, participants were also initiated into traditional culture for one entire day at Myung Won Traditional Tea Academy, located in Pukch'on, one of the richest neighborhoods of Seoul, behind the presidential Blue House. Participants were given English brochures that explained the rules of how to sit depending on the shape of the table and the number of guests, the way to drink alcohol before elders, and the symbolism and virtues of tea. Repeating the different sequences of the tea ceremony in traditional costume was tiring and monotonous. The instructors were older Korean women with severe expressions. Once again, the air-conditioning did not work. Irritated by the constant compulsory group activities and disenchanted by the recent news that she would never find her birth parents due to lack of information, one of the oldest participants started expressing resistance. She showed uncommon clumsiness when it came to pouring the tea, distraction when she ought to bow, and a general bad attitude. The Korean woman who taught her ignored this behavior and did not lose her cold smile and her strictness, repeating the same gesture again and again until the recalcitrant student got it right. In general, when bows were too stiff, or not low enough, Korean instructors did not hesitate to press reluctant backs and necks with vigor.

The several hours of training ended with the distribution of yet another certificate stamped with the foundation seal and personalized with the Western and Korean names of each adoptee. The first page bore a poem in Chinese, the language of the ancient literate elite, that here served to emphasize the traditional and refined character of the ceremony. At the end, participants, two by two, applied their new knowledge to this event, which was described as a capping ceremony. They walked slowly toward a little stage where the instructors stood: the elegant president of the foundation and one male employee who was forced into this role at the last minute for his imposing size and looks. The traditional master of rites is indeed always a man (Kendall 1996). Although reluctant, he quickly put on the black hat made of horse hair called *kat*, cleared his throat, and started reading the protocol in Korean, which was directly translated into English by one of the Holt social workers. Each participant held a little piece of paper on which the response to the speech was written in English on one side, Korean on the other.

> **STUDENT RESPONSE REMARK ON ACCEPTING THE ADULTHOOD**
>
> As we have much to learn we are especially thankful for your presence and teachings today. As we accept our coming of age we will follow the teachings of pursuing happiness, balanced discipline, and our duties and responsibilities to the society.

This collective answer, written by Koreans, puts adoptees in an inferior position: they "have much to learn," and they are "thankful" to their Korean instructors for giving them a Korean education. Only this ritual performance explicitly ensured them a symbolic adult status. "The society" referred, of course, to South Korea. Instructors created this special rite of passage for transnational adoptees, a group of young people without ties whom they must define socially and help think differently of their relation to their birth country.

Symbolic entrance to adulthood is really complete after the performance of a wedding ceremony, which 2004 OKF tour participants practiced for hours. This training involved not only two volunteer couples but also a number of extras who acted the roles of parents, master of ceremonies, or commoners. Measured bows, steps, and greetings were repeated dozens of times until the ceremony could take place properly. Everybody took pictures or filmed the scene. The typical screeching music was played on tape when the prospective couples entered the room with majesty. The audience of extras was again in traditional costume. The couples walked up to the stage and performed the different sequences, grooms facing brides, while some participants acted out disputes between in-laws.

Along with previous studies, my research suggests that infantilized adoptees are forced to act in certain ways and to accept certain discourses during the cultural programs. These programs grant them Koreanness while turning them into objects of consumption for the Korean public (Eleana Kim 2005, 49, 67–68). But foreign tourists, Korean emigrants' children (*kyopo*), and even biracial children with one Korean parent have all been observed performing wedding and tea ceremonies as recreational activities when visiting South Korea. These ceremonies look like mock rituals or games entertaining foreigners and Koreans alike—as opposed to authentic marriage rituals for Koreans. So where do the ceremonies performed by transnational adoptees stand? Do adoptees receive a special treatment compared with these different groups? At the NIIED, where I studied during my first stay in Seoul, the cultural program attended by a majority of emigrants' children and a minority of biracial children and adoptees was composed in the same way as for the HISS or OKF tours, although it was specifically a Korean language program.

But both tea and wedding ceremonies were reduced to the minimum. The ceremonies involving exclusively transnational adoptees do not appear to stand on the same level of symbolism as the other groups' performances. They are taught more thoroughly and forcefully—for several hours. Like other cultures, Japanese, for example (Nakane 1970), Korean culture can be called a "culture of diploma," very much codified. Transnational adoptees are indeed a problematic category—more so than foreigners without Korean ancestry and individuals with one or two Korean parents—in a society where individuals' status should be defined as much as possible; in this respect, rituals and certificates are culturally appropriate, even expected. According to Mary Douglas's analysis, transnational adoptees who first return to their birth country are considered "matter out of place," that is, a source of disorder and danger. Ceremonies and rituals turn their formlessness into a creative source of enrichment and transformation for their birth society (Douglas 2001, 162–163).

In contrast to the other groups enumerated earlier, adoptees do not perform the wedding ceremony independently from other ceremonies. It is only a stage in a larger process of making them adults; it goes beyond the sphere of game, play, or consumption and implicitly expresses a wish for preferential marriage between Koreans or persons of Korean descent. It could very well make adoptees pass from a dispersed community into a restricted endogamic group (where one marries exclusively someone who belongs to the same group).[9] Potentially, the symbolic couple is a unit for production of Korean children. The alliance is implicitly proposed to adoptees as an alternative to adoptive—and foreign—filiation. A ubiquitous element of any such program for transnational adoptees, the wedding ceremony emphasizes the importance of blood. It is the Korean blood in adoptees' veins that should be preserved to ensure the perpetuity of Korean culture and identity.

If the analysis stopped here, the programs could stand as a means of symbolic reintegration and compensation for the rupture that occurred in the past with the sending away of the adoptees as infants for international adoption. However, a third aspect ought to be explored: the tour of welfare facilities, a logical process that seems to lead to the reproduction or continuation of transnational adoption.

Reproducing Transnational Adoption and the Diaspora

The adoptees' three-week stay included a "social tour" of adoption facilities. Like the classes, this social program took participants back to childhood, but this time it was their own specific childhood. This aspect of the program reimmersed them in the experience—even the trauma—of adoption, seemingly in contradiction with the various elements of reintegration described earlier. It suggested that adoptees not only become members of the diaspora through initiation and reeducation but that they also reproduce the diaspora by tacitly approving and taking part in the international adoption system, as we will see. Thus, their action confirms their separation from the motherland.

After a visit to the tomb of the founder Harry Holt and to the Ilsan museum that commemorates his life and work, the group went to Seoul for a guided tour of the offices of parental counseling, Post-Adoption Services, and the nursery where babies are readied for adoption. At the nursery, a few hundred meters from the main office, participants were invited to play with and hug the babies. An employee took pictures. Some adoptees burst into tears and left the room.

The next visit took the group to an orphanage in the countryside. The whole afternoon was spent with the orphans. Some participants were surprised to see that several orphans were already teenagers. Most orphans stayed in Seoul orphanages but got transferred to the countryside if they were not adopted. The woman who directed the orphanage explained that all children were going to school and that social workers were helping them find jobs. At age eighteen, they had to leave the institution and live independently. The group split up and joined children in different age groups for various activities. Some made necklaces out of beads; some took a dance class; others participated in sports. A volunteer, either a Korean student or a Korean mother, guided each activity. Before leaving, a group picture was taken with the children.

Additionally, adoptees who wanted to have a look at their files had the option of returning to the orphanage that had hosted them in the past. That day, I escorted two Norwegian participants to an orphanage in Inchon, Star of the Sea (*haesŏng*), which happened to be where I had stayed with my younger sister in 1982. One participant and I were given copies of our files, and I saw a picture of my sister that I had never seen before. Then we toured the establishment, guided by a nun who related the history of the place, which had been founded before the Korean War.

The social program ended with a visit to Aeranwon, a single mothers' house. Several expectant mothers had volunteered to meet with adult adoptees for a discussion. The two groups could ask questions of each other, supported by one Holt social worker and the director of Aeranwon. The expectant mothers introduced themselves: name, age, stage of pregnancy, and choice for their child: domestic or international adoption. Several started weeping, and somebody held out the box of tissue that had been provided in the middle of the table. Adoptees, through a series of careful questions, were led to say their life was successful and happy where they were, but that they nonetheless searched for their biological family. The young women explained the circumstances of their pregnancies, which were often hidden from their own families. For most of the women, their young age and financial situation, as well as general social pressure, did not entice them to keep the child. This last visit of the social circuit left the group with a painful feeling. So, in parallel to the accelerated apprenticeships of Korean childhood, adoptees were made to understand their own Korean pasts. This way, adult adoptees observed every step of international adoption within South Korea and were likely to better grasp the process through which they themselves had gone. Within the span of a few days, they occupied all the positions that composed their story, from being a single mother's baby to being an orphan dandled by foreigners. But this was not all.

Following the same logic as the apprenticeship, the HISS "social tour" was crowned by an ultimate stage in the participants' transformation. At the end of the program, if a baby was available for adoption at an adult adoptee's destination (and healthy enough to travel), that adoptee had to escort the baby on the plane trip, regardless of the adoptee's age or previous experience with children. In 1999, a twenty-year-old French adoptee had to travel from Seoul to Paris with two babies. Participants must give the baby to the adoptive parents upon arrival, along with some small gifts and Korean baby clothes. Participants agreed to serve the adoption agency when they registered for the program, and it was stipulated that the agency would reimburse the cost of the program if escort occurred. In 1999, I brought a few-months-old baby to Paris, and the agency reimbursed me for the cost of my stay in Korea. During the plane trip, a steward presented himself as a young father and took the baby in his arms each time he cried. Taking care of a Korean baby shows the adoptees' tacit acceptance of the system they came from, but it is also the last rite of passage in a full circle: adoptees who were sent out of Korea in childhood come back and leave again as adults who will give Korean children away for adoption, like Koreans before them.[10] By escorting a baby for adoption, adoptees also pass from the status of objects to the status of main actors, or rite masters of ritualized representations: they ensure the baby's passing from one world to another. One is initiated only upon becoming the initiator. Therefore, the program ensures adoptees' integration less into their original society than into the Korean diaspora as defined by the motherland.[11]

Focusing on the emergence of a transnational adoptee community, previous research (Hübinette 2005; Eleana Kim 2005; Jo 2006) has analyzed transnational adoption from South Korea within the scope of "cultural activism."[12] This approach supposes that a minority or diasporic group reacts collectively and consciously to prove that it differs from a definition originating from a hegemonic national discourse.[13] This approach highlights conflicts between adoptees and organizers that are expressions of adoptees' agency, constituting a refusal to be won over by official discourse serving an economic agenda (Van Gennep 1981; Grimes 1985, 1990; Segalen 1998). But it is important to note that South Koreans deemed the ceremonies successful and repeated the program year after year.[14] Journalists attested to the good atmosphere of the gathering of 2004 and organizers to the success of each HISS. The latter ignored adoptees' complaints and mockeries and almost always managed to make them act in the right ways. In fact, no adoptee avoided any activities; all adoptees thanked the organizers and applauded at the end of every program. Rituals are less a question of belief than a question of action and performance (Bourdieu 1972; Schechner 1977, 1990; Boëtsch and Wulf 2005; Hughes-Freeland 1988). The American adoptee who demonstrated reluctance at the tea ceremony ended up reading a thank-you note at the HISS closing ceremony of 2004. The organizers said they had chosen her because she was an English professor who would speak well in public, but they also tamed her somewhat by making her read the note.

Even if the rituals that adoptees go through seem to aim at their reintegration into Korean society, the programs validate separation rather than integration. The departure for adoption is not the separation phase of the process, and the motherland is not the starting point of the rite of passage. For the program's organizers, the starting point is abroad. Thus, leaving the adoptive country constitutes the separation phase; the stay in South Korea is the transition phase for the adoptees' initiation, which includes isolation, rules, compulsory learning, and performing rituals. The return to the adoptive country is the real integration phase. The wedding ceremony and the baby escort produce fully initiated adult adoptees who can perpetuate transnational adoption in place of Koreans. Therefore, their status as adoptees has been reinforced. The diaspora as a frame of interpretation for transnational adoption entails only a voluntarily limited integration, insufficient within South Korea but operational abroad.

In the context of globalization, transnational adoptees occupy a middle-ground sociological status in Korea, a status that still retains an ancient ambiguity while edging closer to full Koreanness. That new status stresses inalienable, deep blood of ethnicity, as opposed to the superficial layer of foreign culture deposited by a contingent history of nurture abroad. This status will be corroborated by the analysis of the very popular "meeting program" *Ach'im madang: kŭ sarami pogosip'ta* that depicts not only the further building of a community of blood, tastes, and emotion but also the construction of a dominant narrative of dispersal that takes transnational adoptees back to the stagnant postwar history of Korea. Sociological status is therefore complemented by a historicized status.

4

Stratification and Homogeneity at the
Korean Broadcasting System (2003)

Wednesday, June 4, 2003, 8:30 a.m.: a happy bird's singing signaled the opening sequence of *Ach'im madang* on KBS. Shortly after, a trumpet played an optimistic major chord in arpeggios, and an energetic, happy melody began. The thirty-second animated film featured the host and the hostess as main characters: their caricatural big heads wore a frozen smile and hinged on top of small bodies. They arrived on a tandem bicycle from a green countryside planted with apple trees. Once they reached the foreground, the two characters bowed toward the viewers. They went by the window of a house. On the edge of the window a cup of hot coffee was still steaming, and a television was turned on KBS: on the screen, a middle-aged woman with short black hair was crying in the arms of an old woman with white hair arranged in a bun. After this scene, the two hosts were suddenly riding a car in the midst of an urban landscape. They took a ramp and drove by an apartment where the television also was on; on the screen appeared the regular studio audience of *Ach'im madang*: an old man with his white hair and his paternal look sat among an audience composed of middle-aged women. Smiling, they all applauded with enthusiasm. Suddenly, the couple rose toward the setting sun in a small red plane. Then the melody decrescendoed.

Ach'im madang still plays today every morning of the week for an hour, with a different theme for each day. "Family matters" is a fair way to sum up the general subject of the program; topics range from couples' issues to children's education. As the opening sequence indicates, the Wednesday broadcasts focus on family searches and meetings, by far the most popular theme among my informants and the most popular "meeting program" (*mannam-ŭi pansong*) in South Korea. Gathering seven to eight participants who are all looking for parents and siblings they lost several decades earlier, the Wednesday morning talk show usually allows some of them to be recognized by relatives who, either during or after the show, can call the number that appears on the screen during the broadcast. Every broadcast ends with the hosts telling the viewers that the participants receive presents and gift certificates from the companies that sponsor the show. Then the scenario writer tells the lucky participants to come again the following Wednesday to meet their relatives. If for some reason the participants cannot meet their relatives during the show, their meeting is organized by the scenario writer another day, somewhere near the studio, and is filmed by a cameraman. The following Wednesday, these meetings are broadcast as flashbacks. After the meeting has been broadcast live or by flashback, KBS offers the members of the reunited family a DNA test at Seoul National University Hospital, but the results of the tests are never mentioned in subsequent broadcasts. The host Sang-byŏk Lee and the hostess Kŭm-hŭi Lee are celebrities in South Korea, whereas the old man featured in the animated film, Dong-kyu Park, is known as the son of a famous poet, Mokwol Park.[1]

Ach'im madang met with success as soon as it first aired in 1997. This owed partly to the popularity of the two hosts at the time.[2] The same year, the host of a KBS news program announced that viewers had selected *Ach'im madang* as the best program on KBS.[3] According to the scenario writer, since 1997, no year had gone by without the four-person team in charge of the talk show winning an award. Despite an early time slot that restricts the audience to housewives and older people (Tsuya and Bumpass 2004), *Ach'im madang* was one of the top twenty most popular television shows in South Korea for more than a decade.[4] The outreach of the Wednesday broadcast is enlarged by the KBS website, on which people can watch the show for weeks after the television broadcast.[5]

In this program, transnational adoptees effectively enter a system of representations that clearly classifies people in terms of degrees of marginality (as opposed to full Koreanness), while stressing resemblances among all people of Korean descent. The program aims at creating a community whose disparities and diverse fates should be redeemed by the collective memory produced on the spot. The objectives of the Korean program and the reactions of participants are obviously not always in tune, but there is little room during the broadcast for spontaneous and personal voicing of opinions, and, if anything, the show's longevity attests to its appeal to the Korean viewers. Therefore, the program's narrative on family separation—and by extension on transnational adoption—is indicative of representations that are widely accepted by the South Korean population.

Marking Differences

All of *Ach'im madang*'s participants share the trait of searching for biological families from whom they were separated for several decades. But they are also subjected to systematic "social distinction" over the course of the program (Bourdieu 1987). Since the program's debut, transnational adoptees have appeared on *Ach'im madang* next to orphans and domestic adoptees, but according to the program's scenario writer, they benefit from a structure originally conceived for Koreans only:

> Even if international adoptees as well as Korean participants have the opportunity to apply for the program, all of you can't take part in it [for lack of substantial information]. To tell you the truth, . . . our team thinks we should accept more international adoptees [in opposition to domestic adoptees or orphans]; consequently, we're making some efforts for this purpose. . . . Members of our team wish many adoptees to find their families; we do research and as far as it is possible, we decide to help you and will endeavor in the future.[6]

In this speech to a large group of adoptees, the scenario writer insisted that their participation in the Korean program depended solely on a deliberate choice by the team. Far from being necessary, the decision to group foreign adoptees with orphans and domestic adoptees was a mark of generosity but it was also an "effort," a task of social work. With these words, the scenario writer anticipated criticism from foreign adoptees whose candidacies were rejected for lack of clues or information. At the time of my fieldwork, foreign adoptee cases were only considered during a short period of the year. Recorded in the summer of 2003, the seven broadcasts of *Ach'im madang* I examined and sometimes attended featured one-third foreign adoptees and two-thirds domestic orphans and adoptees.[7] The hosts often reminded the Korean public that foreign adoptees were special visitors to Korea, as they mainly traveled in the summer to take advantage of long vacations. Their intrusion obviously needed an explanation.[8]

The participants also differed in the way they were treated by the scenario writer before the broadcast and by the hosts during the broadcast. Usually, several months went by between registration and participation, during which time the scenario writer and a younger assistant worked together, tracking inconsistencies, contradictory elements in participants' biographies, and above all "negative feelings" expressed by the participants. In 2003, the transnational adoptees that I accompanied went through an accelerated process, due to their limited stay in South Korea. They were treated first, always cordially, avoiding long waiting hours, whereas the older Korean candidates were treated last, often with anger or contempt, as they were seldom articulate and behaved submissively. Several Korean candidates who did have information were eliminated on the grounds that they could not speak clearly in front of the camera, while some transnational adoptees were accepted despite scarce information. During this preliminary session with the prospective participants, I was struck by the differences in attitude on the part of the scenario writer and her young assistant toward foreigners versus Koreans.

During the broadcast, the discrimination continued. Several Korean viewers I questioned about the program in the course of my fieldwork pointed out that foreign and domestic adoptees clearly appeared wealthier than orphans, but domestic adoptees were never valorized in the hosts' discourse, whereas foreign adoptees were. The status of Korean participants can be determined through indirect indicators that fall into three categories: dress, attitude, and speech. First, observations of dress indicate varied status as some participants were dressed neatly and simply, and others dressed up to perform on television. By dressing up, several participants seemed to compensate for their lower-to-moderate economic standing. The few participants who had a neglected appearance also qualified as belonging to the lower economic class.[9] Second, attitudes often indicated the lower economic class of the orphans in contrast to the foreign and domestic adoptees. Many orphans responded to questions by mumbling, stuttering, or keeping their eyes downcast.[10] They answered the hosts' questions in a childlike, demure manner, even though they were often older than the hosts. Adding to the effect, the hosts employed a soft tone to reassure them. Third, language was sometimes an indicator of the level of education. In front of the camera, a female participant revealed her lack of manners by using vernacular to explain why she had a scar: "I got a stone at my mug [*pagi tŏjyŏtta*]." The hostess suavely corrected: "Yes, you were hurt by a stone thrown at your forehead." The audience and the participant herself laughed,[11] but her words and attitude were obviously not appropriate for a person appearing on a televised program watched by millions of viewers.

Additional information on social status came out indirectly. The hosts seldom asked questions about material or marital conditions of participants who were appearing for the first time. In specific cases, however, certain questions arose. For example, a female participant, a blind older woman, declared that even with her handicap, she had been able to study in a school for the sight impaired, marry, and gain wealth.[12] She insisted that she did not look for her lost family members hoping that they would take care of her, but rather because of her tender feelings for them. Her elegant clothes and expensive jewelry confirmed her words. The hostess asked another older female participant if she was married.[13] The hostess merely wanted confirmation for the viewers of what she already knew and had written on the paper she held during the show at the lectern. Later, the scenario writer explained to me:

> Maybe parents looking for their kids were poor and couldn't take care of them. Usually they send another kid but don't go by themselves and don't show up. They think maybe the kid is going to be offended or upset once she or he knows the truth. Also, because they are old they're afraid the kid thinks they want to depend on her or him financially. But no! They don't really think that way, they just want to find their kid. Before they die, they want to find them. They want to see their face. More than a long-term relationship, they want to know what happened to them and just to see them. No biological parent is allowed to appear in the show. Only adoptees are allowed and parents can contact them if they want to.[14]

Marital and economic situations play a key role in the decision of the biological family to contact the participants and, consequently, in the scenario writer's choice of participants. This is information that viewers and concerned family members care about. For the meetings, most participants arrived with their spouse, children, and occasionally mother or mother-in-law. After the reunion, the hosts called them to join the participant and his or her newfound relatives. They asked the children their age and grade in school, but never asked any questions of the spouses. In this instance, the biological family was more important than the allied family. Nonetheless, the latter had to be present to enable the meeting and to guarantee the independence of the two parties.

Most Korean participants, whether orphans or adoptees, were married unless they were young,[15] as in the case of a twenty-six-year-old female participant,[16] and in the case of a twenty-year-old male participant and his seventeen-year-old sister.[17] These young orphans were not married, and the hosts stipulated that, in both cases, the older sibling worked. Young and old participants chosen for the show demonstrate self-sufficiency and proper activities, as opposed to the aforementioned poor orphan stereotype usually held by South Korean society. Like middle-aged, married participants, the young and old domestic participants demonstrated that they provided for their own needs, so that their lost relatives would feel at ease contacting them.

Transnational adoptees seemed generally more relaxed than the Korean participants. They smiled confidently and amicably. Whereas Korean participants had to stand and approach the lectern next to the hosts to speak, foreign adoptees, the majority of whom did not speak Korean, remained seated and conversed through a Korean interpreter who stayed with them for the duration of the show. Some of them arrived at the studio with their adoptive parents, who took seats in the audience. The hosts addressed them with compliments and friendly questions. The hosts asked foreign adoptees what they did for a living, a question they seldom asked the domestic participants. For example, the public got to know that one male adoptee worked in construction, one was a cartoonist, one was in the military, one was an engineer, and another was a business consultant; that a female adoptee worked in the hotel business, and another was a nurse. The scenario writer released these details to the hosts prior to the show. By stressing this information during the broadcast, the hosts demonstrated the success of transnational adoption. This success was thrown into greater relief because transnational adoptees' former status had been the same as that of the domestic participants. Now, the foreign adoptees were often presented as more socially advanced than the latter. In fact, more than emphasizing social advancement, the show most often defined social normalcy. Foreign adoptees all had a professional occupation or were receiving a higher education and were introduced as respected citizens abroad. The questions about occupations posed to the foreign adoptees—who tend to be younger than the domestic participants, and primarily looking for their parents—had the same function as those posed to young orphans: proof for biological parents that their children were independent and would not ask for money or support. But in the case of foreign adoptees, the questions about their profession also had the effect of valorizing them. In contrast, just knowing that an orphan "has a job" sufficed, and older domestic participants were not even asked about their jobs. The avoidance of an otherwise quite common question in everyday interaction, even between people meeting for the first time, suggests that the hosts wanted to conceal the supposed disadvantages encountered by older orphans.

Ach'im madang hosts liked to evoke the foreign countries that participants came from. Transnational adoptees also wore badges with the colors of their national flags. Being a foreigner earned valorization. A female participant who had emigrated to the United States, after spending her childhood and adolescence as an orphan in Korea, registered for the program to look for her father, whom she was able to meet the week before her departure for Florida.[18] The camera zoomed in on her American passport and, although she did not have to wear a badge, the host commented on her new place of residence in a short, improvised epilogue: "Now in Florida, it is 3:00 a.m. because of the time difference with South Korea." Then, he moved on to the introduction of the next participants: "X, thirty-four, was adopted at age eleven through Holt adoption agency.... He came from France. Ah! There, Florida, here, France; we really live in the age of globalization [kŭrobarŭ sidae]."[19] The host used the English word "global" instead of the Korean word segyehwa (globalization), which made his comment even trendier. The host saw foreigners' participation in his Korean program as a sign of globalization, and watching Ach'im madang from the United States proved at least the globalization of the South Korean media. The adoptee from France was accompanied by a Korean female who bore a tag that read "interpreter" (pŏnyŏk). The hosts thanked her for volunteering and making the procedure easy. They also asked her if the program was broadcast in France. She answered in the negative. "Not yet in France," concluded the hosts,[20] obviously excited by the idea that their program could conquer a public thought to be international but still of Korean descent.[21] The host also insisted on the simultaneity of lives in this "imagined community" scattered throughout the entire world at that very moment. As Benedict Anderson has pointed out, the media create the consciousness of simultaneity despite distances, a necessary condition to the national sentiment of community, which used to be a characteristic of the nation-states (Gellner 1983) but now extends beyond state boundaries (Anderson 1983, 23–36).[22]

Ach'im madang's organization clearly included transnational adoptees in a hierarchy South Koreans could relate to. And although it stated that they belonged to the category of incomplete people, it also conferred on them a social status superior to that of Korean orphans or domestic adoptees. Beyond this classification that combines both negative and positive representations of transnational adoptees, the success of the program is due to the atmosphere of the show that makes it "drama-like."

A Dramatic Spectacle

Transnational adoptees have access to many different means of search, including ads in newspapers and journals; ads on the Internet (several websites are devoted to all kinds of family searches,[23] others more specifically to international adoptees' searches for their birth parents);[24] ads in magazines and newsletters produced by adoptee communities and associations; or even services provided by local police stations. Since the 1990s, the four main adoption agencies have also offered postadoption services to adoptees who return to South Korea (Bai 2007), and this is indicated on the American embassy website.²⁵ But according to all the people I encountered in 2003–2004, the KBS program was the most efficient way to find one's relatives. In 2003, I asked scenario writer Yŏng-sŏn Ho, a thirty-five-year-old woman, about the future of the show. She pouted and said she was unable to predict anything. She just had to "make the program last" by screening the participants who had the most clues regarding their past. She stressed that the still high rate of success—up to 30 percent in 2003—had in fact been decreasing since 1997, the year of *Ach'im madang*'s debut. That year up to 70 percent of the participants were able to find their lost relatives. In more recent years participants—including transnational adoptees—had had variable results: "According to the last reports, in 2001, two transnational adoptees out of eleven found their families; in 2002, eleven out of twenty-five; in 2003, five out of twenty."²⁶ The success of the search at *Ach'im madang* depends on the quality of information about one's birth family but also on the popularity of the show and vice versa. The popularity of the show itself depends on the program's level of suspense and drama. That dramatic quality is the result of the collaboration of the different agents of the program to create emotion.

The way the scenario writer referred to participants and the way the hosts addressed them confirm that above all else they were part of a spectacle. And despite the sincere claims that the program provides social welfare services, people's acceptance to the program depended on the rules of the entertainment industry (Hübinette 2005). The hosts' popularity²⁷ and the quality of the spectacle offered by the program were often such that viewers, transported by their enthusiasm and empathy for the participants, made inopportune phone calls that interrupted broadcasts.²⁸ Emphasizing the importance of good performance, the scenario writer referred to participants as "those who perform" (*ch'uryŏnja*).²⁹ She was the one who selected those elements of their narratives that she deemed relevant and the one who made participants rehearse their texts. Participants' status as performers was confirmed by the coupons they received as a kind of remuneration for their performance at the end of each broadcast. A few minutes before the end of the broadcast, the phone number and the website of *Ach'im madang* were displayed one last time for the benefit of viewers. Then the hosts announced that participants would receive a 100,000 won coupon to be used for the purchase of any department store products, courtesy of a cosmetic company.³⁰

In the midst of their chatter, the hosts occasionally defined what constituted a "successful" broadcast. The case presented in the introduction struck me because the host orchestrated the theatrical bow that concluded the action. Emphasizing the skill of the actors who had just performed a dramatic scene of tears—"Ah, it went very well [*Ayuuu! Chal toessŏ*]."³¹ —the host expressed genuine professional satisfaction at a well-done performance. To make the audience hold its breath, the hosts had to manage suspense, continuously encouraging the hope for a meeting, provoking and channeling emotions. During one broadcast, the production team received phone calls for two different participants. But the first phone call disclosed that the relative sought by the blind, elderly female participant had died. At this news, the participant could not hold back her tears.[32] During the second phone call, another participant wiped her eyes and in a shaking voice asked her older sister, who was on the phone, "Has our father died?" The communication was suddenly interrupted. The two hosts exclaimed: "*Aigu!*" and quickly congratulated the participant. The host said with satisfaction: "Two phone calls, it went really well today!"[33] By controlling information and emotions, the production team stirred up the audience's curiosity. The two participants' distress did not prevent the host from openly expressing happiness at the fruit of his work.

For dramatic purposes, the hosts sometimes dragged out the question-and-answer period before the relatives' appearance longer than was necessary. During the sixty minutes of the program, moments of tension or high emotion such as the meeting scene or the phone calls were followed by light moments when the hosts made jokes and told unrelated anecdotes. This irreverent attitude set the professionals apart from the guests. Far from being out of place, their ability to make jokes provided balance and regularity in a context prone to excess. In this regard, the alternation of dramatic music with calm and soothing music, the presence of the professional public, played a crucial role. A professional public composed of middle-aged women[34] was a collective actor that laughed, cried, and exclaimed at specific moments, all of which, together with the different melodies, permitted a better orchestration of the program. Present onstage, surrounding the participants, the public shared similarities with the chorus of a Greek tragedy. The professional public fueled and guided participants' feelings as well as those of the viewers. It punctuated the spectacle so as to avoid outbursts and incidents. One day, a female participant burst into tears when her relatives appeared. Unable to control her emotions at the end of the dramatic melody, she fainted in front of the camera. Her relatives had a hard time lifting her up from the floor. Despite the close-up perspective, one could notice the nervous movements of the host hovering behind the appalled relatives, trying to get the woman to stand again. He shouted in a rude manner: "Don't do that! Don't do that! [*antoae! antoae!*]."[35] His tone and his partner's panicked look at the camera gave away what they believed was their failure.

During broadcast, the hosts' sympathy and compassion were expressed by their interjections: "*Aigu!*" They offered words such as "tears come to my eyes"[36] or described for viewers the tears of others: "If you could help them . . . the mother and the sister are crying while looking for their son and brother."[37] The relatives who arrived from backstage also expressed emotions that were at once very strong and very codified, like the little brother of the female participant described in the introduction, who kept his head down, rubbing his eyes though they seemed to remain dry.[38] All states of mind of the people involved in the family meetings are blended: the consciousness of being onstage and of having to properly play a role, the shock of finding a lost relative. What people remember from the KBS program is the image, which turns up again and again, of relatives weeping as they embrace. The production team calls this climax the "scene of tears." A documentary broadcast in 1997 played some of *Ach'im madang*'s most beautiful scenes of tears in slow motion.[39] Most of these favorite scenes staged a mother and her daughter. We will see that this representation of family meetings reflects a social reality. Sometimes, the mother wore the traditional outfit (*hanbok*), an identity marker for Koreans, who wear it mostly for special occasions. From backstage, she dashed in and accelerated to embrace her daughter. In general, tears (*nunmul*) are a leitmotif of South Korean popular culture, but the analysis of *Ach'im madang* reveals how tears are created in a very concrete manner and taught through the rehearsal preceding the live broadcast. The prepared development of the program's action, the actors' different roles, the speaking time allotted to each, the alternation of tense and relaxed moods, all contribute to the flow of tears. During the program, many participants cried in the middle of their narratives. Like the anxious participants, women who constituted the paid audience prepared their colorful handkerchiefs, holding them folded in small squares in their palms, in anticipation of the contagious emotion.

In 2003, while conducting fieldwork, I rented a room in a boardinghouse in Seoul. One Wednesday morning, the landlady of the boardinghouse dashed out of her bedroom in tears and started preparing my breakfast. I was concerned and asked her what was wrong. She laughed while wiping her eyes with the corner of her apron (I could tell she was being careful not to disturb her makeup): "It is nothing, haha! It is only *Ach'im madang*!" Crying is not the prerogative of women in Korea. In fact, men can express their emotions as openly as women, although they are often described as taciturn, expressionless, abrupt, and laconic.[40] South Korean sociologist Dongwon Lee reports the confession of a journalist at the newspaper *Hankyŏllae* about *Ach'im madang*: "Every Wednesday morning, when I leave for work, I avoid my wife's eyes. She asks me if I cried again. I am ashamed" (2000, 324). This man felt ashamed of crying in front of his wife but at the same time was eager to tell his interlocutor how emotional he could be. In certain instances, emotions are compulsory (Mauss 1968). My analysis aligns with the constructionist argument (Harré 1986; Armon-Jones 1986), which posits that emotions, far from being natural and spontaneous, are inscribed in a series of sequences codified and constructed to allow the proper expression of emotions at the right moment, with the right intensity, in a given culture, as "emotions are statements about, and motivations for the enactment of cultural values" (Lutz 1983, 247). Emotions are instilled through a long preparatory process and through tricks such as pushing emotional participants to tears by questioning them relentlessly. Yet, to analyze the construction of emotions is not to question their strength or their authenticity. In South Korea, to say that one has cried at the sight of the dramatic scene of tears is to prove one's humanity. But tears also signify something particularly important about Koreans.

No matter the outcome of the participants' search, the emotion generated at *Ach'im madang* is a vehicle that is supposed to spread a sense of community among Koreans. In the narrative produced on the show, the social differences between Koreans and foreigners, individuals with or without relatives, between participants, viewers, and hosts, between young and old generations, fade in the eyes of the viewers. That narrative is about a hypothetical common past; it creates a collective memory.

Building of a Community

In the broadcast, homogeneity was first based on the detection of physical resemblances among the different family members. It was always the hostess who asked the participants to turn toward the camera after the confusion of the meeting.[41] She told them to move or stay in a line; sometimes she extended a guest's arm or hand and posed it in a showy flourish. When old photos showing participants with their siblings were displayed, the hostess would laugh and say, "*Ayuu! Ayuu!* They have the same bangs!";[42] "*Ayuu!* They look exactly the same, only their expression is different!";[43] "*Ayuu!* You have the same eyes!"[44] One participant brought an old picture of the mother she was looking for. The hostess exclaimed: "You look like her!" although such similarity was not obvious at all. Sometimes, she jubilantly addressed the public: "They look alike! Turn toward the camera so that we can see you!"; "Except the eyes, he and his older brother are very similar: the lower part of their face."[45] Another day, the hostess asked the participant and her mother, a woman of fifty-seven, to exhibit their hands in front of the camera: "Show if you look alike or not." The mother declared that their hands were the same. The hostess checked while holding up the two women's arms: "Yes, you have the same short fingers." The camera zoomed in on the two chubby hands.⁴⁶ On one occasion, the identity of the person who came from backstage was questioned, but the host's desire to see resemblances was not so easily quelled. The two women did not bear any notable resemblance, yet the hostess tried to find their common points: "Your lips are similar but not your eyes . . . maybe your ears, don't you think?"⁴⁷ The hostess finds, stresses, and sometimes invents resemblances between blood relatives, that is, the evidence of consanguinity.

Through a discourse on physical resemblances, the hosts managed to include transnational adoptees within the realm of ethnicity. One transnational adoptee was asked about his first impressions of Korea. He expressed a feeling of comfort due to his late adoption, which did not erase his memories of a previous life in Korea. The host asked via the interpreter, "Do you like Korea?" "Yes," the adoptee answered, "it is kind of familiar to me. I feel good in Korea." The hostess remarked, "Yes, we all have the same slanted eyes."⁴⁸ A few weeks later, another transnational adoptee was asked similar questions and answered them in a more explicit manner: "What is your impression traveling in Korea?" The adoptee responded, "The first time, I was shocked to see so many Asian people, but little by little, it helped me define my own identity." The two hosts commented: "Yes, he grew up only surrounded by Caucasians [*paegindŭl*]; here, we all have the same features."⁴⁹ This discourse concerning physical resemblances was all the more convincing in the case of international adoptees: although foreign nurtured, they spontaneously expressed their nature. On the show, blood was said to make people look for each other and reunite, as a kind of metaphysical determinative. The term "blood tie" recurred frequently in the discourse of the hosts, especially when they were commenting on a meeting scene. One day, a male participant found his relatives thanks to his older sister, who had been watching the program the previous Wednesday and had recognized him. "Because of blood ties" (*p'itch'ulirasŏ*), explained the hostess.⁵⁰ When an American adoptee arrived onstage accompanied by the U.S. state senator Paull Shin (only his Korean name, Ho-bŏm Shin, was given), the hosts asked how they had met each other. They had met two years earlier at a Protestant church and had become friends. The hostess commented on their friendship: "That is the blood tie" (*kŭge p'itch'uliji-o*).⁵¹ To explain friendship by referring to blood ties is to recall people's common Korean origin. Earlier in the program, siblings' blood and the blood of two nonrelated transnational adoptees were described using the same term: *p'itch'ul*. Here there is assimilation of one family's blood with one nation's blood. The two kinds of blood are conflated by the hostess to reaffirm the way in which a family search belongs to a collective and national register we may designate an "imagined community" (Anderson 1983). The hosts go so far as to include adoptive foreign parents in this powerful ethos. One day, the host told a foreign adoptee that her Caucasian adoptive father "looked a little bit Asian." The interpreter translated the remark to the father, who smiled and said: "Yes, I have been told the same thing several times." The host nodded with respect and added with a smile: "Maybe in a past life, who knows . . . ?" The audience laughed.[52]

The community of tastes, especially of culinary tastes, parallels the sharing of physical features. It is related to corporeity.[53] Korean food constitutes a vector conducive to the expression of identity. On one occasion, the hostess made comments on the strong ties between the participant and her biological relatives whose meeting was featured in a flashback. During the short sequence in which the participant's siblings were gathered around the same table, the hostess said, "Like her mother in the past (who has passed away), she especially loves *chapch'e* (a noodle dish with meat and vegetable)."[54] But because I had been the eyewitness of the whole family reunion as their interpreter, I knew that her mother's favorite dish was *kalbi* (barbecue) and not *chapch'e*. In the same vein, a transnational adoptee was asked about his first impressions of Korean cuisine and whether he liked it. "Yes, I really like Korean food," he said. The host asked, "Do you have memories from your previous life in Korea?" "Yes," he answered, "I ate a rice cake . . . and I got very emotional." The hosts were delighted.[55] The national tie is created through the consumption and sharing of common food (Nelson 2000, 76–78).

The community of taste extends to a community of feelings. When tender emotions are expressed during the broadcast, they are always interpreted by the hostess in terms of *chŏng*, a feeling usually seen as typically Korean. Stemming from Chinese characters, the term *chŏng* means at the same time "feeling," "emotion" (*kamjŏng*), "compassion" (*yŏnmin-ŭi chŏng*), affection, tenderness, and attachment. "To have a lot of *chŏng*" (*chŏngi manta*) means "to have a good heart" or "to be generous and sensitive." If "*chŏng* grows," it means that an attachment born from physical proximity has, over a long period, come to link two people who are not related by blood. Koreans often say, when parting from one another: "I will miss you; I got attached to you [*chŏngi tŭrŏsŏ* . . .]." The hosts render *chŏng* as a feeling that is sometimes intimate and private and at other times collectively felt. Korean blood conveys the feeling of *chŏng* without distinction of gender or age (Hee-kyung Lee 1995). Korean studies scholars consider the concept of *chŏng* one of the ideological foundations of national identity. In the first Korean novels from the beginning of the twentieth century, the value of *chŏng*—its authenticity and spontaneity—was recognized and spelled out (Jager 2003, 20–21). Koreans think of it as a purely Korean emotion, natural evidence of a higher and more universal morality than the one attached to restricted relations dictated by Confucianism (Jager 2003, 24–26). Even the few adoptive parents present during broadcasting could be granted a degree of Korean identity, through their Korean child. An adoptive mother who sat next to her daughter was overwhelmed by the tearful atmosphere. When she started crying, the hostess commented: "The feeling called *chŏng* is something universal [*chŏng iranŭn ke kongt'ong ida*]."[56] By this observation, she included the foreign women within the realm of Korean emotions and ethos: *chŏng* implied the shared suffering of persons who are strongly attached to each other.[57]

The Collective Memory

The construction of a homogeneous community enlarged to the dimensions of the world would have seemed a vain enterprise without the evocation of a common, ancient origin to ease the tension. The building of a community at *Ach'im madang* had its basis in the evocation of moments, places, and idealized relations that fed the emotion triggered by the meetings and turned it into a longing for an indefinite past, or nostalgia. The hosts kept evoking globalization, as we have seen, but they also reconstituted the countryside village as the original frame of Korean identity. *Ach'im madang* confirms that the elaboration of a nostalgic discourse is indeed the corollary of "global consciousness" (Robertson 1992, 156–162; Appadurai 1994, 41).

South Koreans love Korean television dramas (*tŭrama*),[58] which they tend to watch with assiduity and prefer to foreign productions (Dong-hoo Lee 2004, 39). They discuss dramas during family reunions, and with coworkers, neighbors, and roommates. Anthropologist Nancy Abelmann argues that South Korean series reveal much about the state of the society and the debates that are going on concerning different social issues. Most of the dramas depict families; all are fictitious. Although exaggerated, the plots, the emotions, and the characters of South Korean dramas reflect the contradictions and the complexities of the society's "compressed modernity" (Abelmann 2003, 22–32). Abelmann describes the way in which popular series fuel conversations in her informants' families and how that, in itself, contributes to the evolution of representations, which in turn have an impact on reality. South Korean sociologist Dong-won Lee argues that *Ach'im madang's* success derives partly from its closeness to the genre of drama that is also concerned with family matters.[59] He notes how many Koreans appreciate

Ach'im madang as a program "more dramatic than a drama."⁶⁰ Anthropologist Choong Soon Kim evokes the "tragic saga of family separation" (1988, 5–9). Here, the use of the term "saga" imparts a literary, mythical, and almost sacred aspect to these family stories, which are in the end similar to each other. The meetings' happiness is thought of as the achievement of a quest spanning several generations. That is why there is such an emphasis on the time of separation, as systematically indicated by the subtitles: "Meeting after Forty-Two Years" or "Meeting after Twenty-Five Years." It also implies that the saga has a happy ending. Experiences of family separations are turned into a kind of narrative that viewers can recognize and to some extent anticipate, having a beginning, a middle, and an end, and involving certain types of characters, as dramas do.

Ach'im madang's assimilation with dramas indicates that viewers consider the popular program as occupying a place somewhere between a reality show (because actors do not play a role different from their own selves), a dramatic fiction, and also literary fiction. Nostalgia has been accurately described as a longing for a past experience not based in reality. It can immerse people in a past that is not their own or project them into a future in which the present is already in the realm of a fantasized past (Appadurai 1996; Robertson 1992, 159; Tonkin 1992; Lowenthal 1989).⁶¹

Under the guidance of the scenario writer and the hosts, participants staged themselves in narratives of memories. Misfortunes became events, twists and turns, and adventures the audience would listen to with more or less curiosity, depending on the quality of the narrator. Once the hostess called a female participant the "heroine of a success story" (*sŏngkong-ŭi chu'inkong*). Dong-won Lee reports that one of the participants he interviewed described herself "as a drama heroine" (*tŭrama-ŭi chuinkongchŏrŏm*). Through the program, she sublimated her unhappy childhood.⁶² The program's participants had valid reasons to look for their lost relatives, but nostalgia was provoked on *Ach'im madang* by techniques such as the use of flashbacks during broadcast, the "narrativization" of memories according to a certain format, or the playing of a specific melody at a specific moment, as mentioned earlier. Nostalgia itself is a kind of fiction, "as an imaginary which is shared, as socialization and as communication" (Heinich 2005, 68). *Ach'im madang* employed a variety of methods to produce this "collective nostalgia."⁶³

At once unique and common to all Koreans, memories from childhood were often fixed in a graphic way at *Ach'im madang*. Participants were invited to represent in a schematic manner the places they remembered by drawing on a board that the camera would show in a close-up. Most of the drawings were of natural or urban landscapes. Rather than landscape drawings, foreign adoptees presented maps of houses in which they lived long enough to remember the setting and the furniture. Graphic and discursive individual expression sometimes contributed to the success of a search, but primarily staged on television a different time-space, emotional landscape, or "univers de mémoire" (Munn 1995). Drawings of villages and of past everyday life reminded participants not only of their childhood but also of the presence of those who vanished.[64]

The drawing styles were limited in number. The recurrence of certain patterns indicated high codification of details, which in turn contributed to the construction of the archetypical village. One day, the host declared: "All our participants brought maps of their villages: they always represent the countryside of our childhood, with its streams, its trees, and its mountain behind the village [*tuittongsan*]."[65] Through the drawings, the village became a common notion not only for Koreans who lived in the countryside but also among urban dwellers who imagined scenes of the countryside (Nelson 2000, 73). The clumsy drawings constituted a kind of biographical genre, with conventions, for "ordinary people."[66] But the hosts' words soon transformed the participants' maps into the "countryside of *our* childhood." From the individual biographical elements, the hosts draw the material for the recollection of their own childhood to create a collective memory of Korean childhood framed within the countryside village. The participants' life stories and memories were imbued with the fictive and aesthetic quality of literary narratives. At least as much as they served a practical purpose, these poor and monotonous maps played a symbolic role. Together, the generalization and the idealization of places effected a detachment—that is, a collective sublimation of memories that the program reconstructed and reinterpreted. The fates of small numbers of people became representative of the community's destiny. The experience of separation was generalized: separation from one's childhood time and space, from one's family, from the older generations, from the dead and one's ancestors.

One of the functions of the three officiates of the program was to plunge participants and viewers into the past and to reconstitute briefly all these now missing elements. It was a spatiotemporal movement. The animated film of the opening sequence itself constituted a metaphoric rendition of the entire program: the two hosts come from the countryside on a tandem bike, cross the city by car, and finally take off in a plane for an unknown destination. Wherever they go, they occasion family meetings and sow nostalgic memories of the past. But they only pass by and never stop. As quickly as they appear, they disappear again. Consequently, a brief memory is the real end of the program as it satisfies a basic psychological need: to temporarily rebuild what knowledge is unable to grasp, that is, the time of childhood (Ricoeur 1992).

Beyond the functional objective of the meeting program, the hosts undertook an enterprise of transmission of values—conservative ones—to the participants but also to the audience. Anecdotes were always broached first by the host, then remarked on by the professor and sometimes the hostess. One day, the host began with a story about a tree:

> In our village, there was a huge acacia on the riverbank and everybody in the region knew about that tree, beautiful and immense. One day, the schoolteacher came to our home and was drinking with my father in the acacia's shade. He became dead drunk and I had to escort him home. As we were crossing the river on the stone walk, he suddenly declared he had to go somewhere. I was just a child and it was very embarrassing. I felt I was waiting for an hour! (audience's laughter) While he was urinating, I was collecting stones here and there to keep busy. . . . (audience's laughter) Ah, no one can forget memories from childhood.[67]

The real point of the anecdote was the simple comment that concluded it: "No one can forget memories from childhood." The story itself was trivial. Then the host asked: "What about you, professor, do you have any memories from childhood like this one? Do you have any stories about trees?" The professor added his own tree story:

> Yes, in fact, in our village, there was a spring and on its banks there were poplars to which cows were tied during the day. That area was always littered with dung. . . . Because the wind always blew in the same direction, trees developed only on one side. At school, at drawing class, we were always told to copy these trees.[68]

The host's memory and the professor's memory were considered valuable and worth sharing by the hostess. She was unable to provide similar stories from her own childhood: "As I grew up in the city, my memories are poor compared to yours. I have no stories like this." The host concluded: "Until middle school, children should all be educated in the countryside and move to the city starting from high school."[69] From a seemingly neutral opening topic the conversation moves to a crucial discussion about children's education. Most comments made by the hosts and the professor function as endorsements of the return to nature and the old village as opposed to the city, of interpersonal relations as opposed to the anonymous and individualistic urban life, of anchorage to a permanent place as opposed to aimless travel.[70]

To go back to the countryside is to return to the real and metaphoric places of one's childhood but also to reaffirm ties with older generations.[71] During one broadcast, the host asked the son of a participant who had just found her family: "What do you think of your mother's generation? Because of poverty, many people of your mother's generation suffered familial separation."[72] Similarly, under the cover of joking, the host reproached a participant's youngest son for his lack of empathy. The child simply did not look sad enough.[73] The hosts and the professor were conscious of the way the program could transmit values from the "good old days" to the young. This romanticized, virtuous past that one should spend all one's lifetime longing for was also depicted as the bleakest era in the nation's history, so that older people's achievements could appear greater.

During the program, only the hosts addressed Dong-kyu Park directly, with a polite "Professor" (sŏnsaengnim). The professor never had contact with the participants. A character in the opening credit animation, he always sat in the first row among the participants and female studio audience, in the place of honor to the right of the hosts. Outside of the program, he is famous as the eldest son of the writer and poet Mok-wol Park and also as the author of literary and biographical works. Celebrities were welcome on the show, as indicated by the presence of U.S. state senator Paull Shin, who accompanied the American adoptee during one broadcast.[74] Shin, adopted in his late teens by an American military officer, was famous in South Korea for his autobiography, which had become a best seller. After his marriage, he had become a doctor, then a state senator. He had returned to South Korea, found his birth parents, and helped them to emigrate to the United States.[75] Having overcome his low status and become influential and famous, he personified success and filial piety and was a model for orphans and adoptees, whose condition he shared a long time ago. The professor and the senator-writer belonged to the same generation, and both had written biographies that resurrected the same period of South Korean history. A generation shares the common experience of a peculiar historical event or moment.[76] These two men were linked as contemporaries and by virtue of their writing about the lives of ordinary people who shared their own exceptional destiny. They contributed to the placement of the program in a literary narrative. Models and authors of the collective memory, they were given much speaking time (Halbwachs 1994). Collective memory is constituted by the multiplicity of individual memories, but it is shaped by a few prominent individuals, who make it the official memory. The hosts' comments were like interpretations, fixings of the past moments recounted by each participant in the form of moving, amusing, or tragic stories. Their comments depersonalized individual discourses to make of them collective cultural capital. They also provided the participants with a certain view of their own lives. There was of course an obvious contradiction between the evocation of a difficult, dark, and bleak past—the context of familial separation—and the reconstitution of a happy childhood spent in the ideal countryside village. Collective memory is partial by definition (Finley 1981; Todorov 1995). Participants became a contingent presence; they disappeared after having offered material that the hosts and the professor subsequently worked to shape into a consumer good. Their stories also melted into the larger national narratives of war and partition.

The analysis of *Ach'im madang* shows that adoptees are not simply caught in the dichotomies of acceptance and rejection, discrimination, and favoritism. The conscious effort to make them pass from one pole (the marginal, resentful, orphan) to the other (the successful, happy, diasporic Korean) is as obvious as the will to reconcile their ambiguous identities and finally assimilate them with all Koreans through the narrative of a common past. But the performance of rites and the construction of a collective memory both function in a time-space that differs from that of ordinary social interactions. They wishfully color difficult social realities in continuous endeavors because their gains are never assured.

The Korean War, to which we will turn next, plays a crucial role in the overall biography of transnational adoptees. The war is conceived as the ground zero of South Korean modern history, against which the ideal past it erased is put into painful relief, and from which sprang forth all ills, including all family separations.

5

National Reunification and Family Meetings

In 1999, my paternal grandmother expressed great joy at meeting again with me, the older of her favorite son's two daughters who had been left by their father at the orphanage Star of the Sea (*haesŏng*) in Inchon. She cried in silence, compressed my hands for a long time, looked at my palms in the hopes of reading a promising future, asked me for forgiveness, and confided to my interpreter with a sigh: "To find Woo-Jung [my Korean name as it is spelled in my adoption documents] again is like meeting my North Korean relatives again. We watched television often in case she would appear on the screen."

In line with the official discourse, my grandmother referred to the war and to the partition even though, occasionally, she would also mention ordinary familial problems: my birth parents' divorce, difficult material conditions after my grandfather died, my father's inability to take care of us once my mother had returned to her maternal home, and so forth. With the establishment of a Communist regime in 1945, which brought occupying Soviet forces to Pyongyang, and the general worsening of living conditions, 3.3 million North Koreans left for the South until 1949 (Kim 1988, 30; Foley 2003, 66–67). Because he had previously been a functionary in the police force, my grandfather felt he was in a dangerous position and consequently decided to leave for South Korea. My grandmother, who was pregnant with her second child, joined him; she left their four-year-old first son behind with relatives, thinking their separation would be only temporary. But, caught in the conflict, my grandparents were never able to go back to North Korea. They settled as well as they could at the southwest tip of South Korea, first in Mokp'o, then in Inchon. They managed to raise their four children who were born in South Korea during and after the war. My grandmother's words link the relatives left behind in North Korea and the two grandchildren relinquished to an orphanage who were adopted abroad. Her words confirm the historicized interpretation of her family's story. For my grandmother, the separation from her first son and the separation from my sister and me are two comparable losses, two episodes of the same sad story. Indeed, the recurrent meetings of the divided families provided by the media have helped to shape this conflation of transnational adoptees with North Korean relatives in people's minds and hearts. This conflation is significant because it places adoptees within a political framework where they are part of the enterprise of unification launched by South Korea in the late 1990s—they are in fact frequently taken to the border during the motherland tours and asked to wish for the unification. This conflation also helps Koreans to express their complex feelings regarding both issues but does not mean that they cannot differentiate them.

Origins of the Format: 1983 Telethon

In producing *Ach'im madang*, KBS was reusing in 1997 some techniques that had proven efficient during a gigantic telethon organized in the same studio in 1983 for the purpose of reuniting relatives separated during or after the Korean War. Each week, the dramatic scenes of the weekly talk show echo the 1983 telethon in form and content. It was an event that deeply marked the South Korean population and still resonates today, as the suffering of the war and the postwar period has not been forgotten:

> *Ach'im madang* is not the first program devoted to family search. Almost any Korean remembers the program for the families divided by the Korean partition. This program was maintained from June 30 to November 14, 1983, and for 138 days, Koreans felt passion for the divided families' meetings. At that time, more than 53,536 out of 100,000 cases were broadcast during the program; among these persons, 10,189 experienced the joy of meeting again their relatives. Even if 14 or 15 years have passed since then, the viewers of *Ach'im madang kŭ sarami pogosipta* ("I want to see this person again/I miss this person") remember the emotions of 1983. (Dong-won Lee 2000, 326)

To dismantled families who had been separated from loved ones for more than thirty years, and who had come to view their circumstances with resignation, 1983 provided the first opportunity to express their repressed emotions with any degree of openness. The telethon coincided with a dazzling expansion of media technologies (Choon Soon Kim, 1988, 120–121). *Ach'im madang* is in itself a commemoration of the telethon and constitutes at once a more trivialized and a more sophisticated version of the somewhat spontaneous and unpredictable movement of 1983.[1] Launched by the South Korean Red Cross, which supported the inalienable rights of individuals to be reunited with their families, the process of reuniting families kept fluctuating owing to various uncertainties introduced by the Cold War (Foley 2003). After 1970, following a period of hostility and tension, the South's attitude toward the North started to improve (Choon Soon Kim 1988, 102). On August 12, 1972, the president of the South Korean Red Cross proposed negotiations for "the prompt solution of purely humanitarian problems." Several meetings ensued but were stopped suddenly by the North Koreans' withdrawal from the negotiating table. From 1973 to 1983, North Korea made multiple terrorist attempts on South Koreans and Americans stationed in the demilitarized zone (106–107). Finally, because of Pyongyang's hostile attitude, the prospect of reuniting divided families across the thirty-eighth parallel became utopic. South Korea decided to reunite families that remained divided within its own national territory (98–122). Massive direct participation and an unprecedentedly large viewing audience led KBS to change its programming to allow more time for the Telethon (109–112). The success of the telethon was reflected in the unprecedented airing time and the all-time high viewing rate (112). Of course, the viewing audience of 78 percent was not limited to members of divided families (127). Using new media technology, the telethon enabled searches to be conducted with a great deal of success not only nationally but also internationally (111). The year 1983 marked the beginning of this collective passion for meetings of divided families, a passion that would continue to grow in the following decades.

The two studios of KBS are both located in Yŏŭido.[2] The oldest and main one is still the symbol of the family meetings that first took place outside. Once I watched a documentary made in 1985 by KBS to commemorate the forty years of separation that many families had experienced after 1945. The documentary recalls the big moments of the telethon. It shows a monumental stone staircase leading to a vast esplanade with multiple entrances to the massive building. For this event, all the paving stones were carpeted with cardboard signs and papers bearing the names and birth dates of the lost. Signs even covered the cars that were temporarily parked in the vicinity. Some people spent hours, if not days, in that place, reading all the signs, one after another. Others were found sleeping on the steps. To this day, the esplanade is called the "Meeting Plaza." Sculptures of embracing figures or relatives running toward one another are still in place there. Some songs were written for the occasion and sung in the plaza.[3] Today, *Ach'im madang* is produced in this site of memory (Nora 1986). The building itself is imposing.[4] I noticed that when *Ach'im madang*'s participants first arrived at the studio's main entrance, they looked impressed and kept their voices low, as if in a sanctuary.

After a troubled period that saw an increased American presence in South Korea, negotiations between the South and the North Korean Red Cross started again on May 27, 1985. This time, the negotiations resulted in an exchange of visitors to both capital cities from September 20 through 23 of the same year. This first diplomatic mission was followed by similar meetings among a limited number of divided families. The only people selected for these meetings were the highly educated and the famous (Choon Soon Kim 1988, 107). This procedure was encouraged during the 1990s, after Kim Dae-jung became president and demonstrated a positive attitude toward the North. The meetings of families divided by the thirty-eighth parallel multiplied, especially in 2000 and 2001, when 300 South Koreans selected by lottery were sent to Pyongyang and 300 North Koreans chosen by the government made a trip to Seoul (Foley 2003, 62). The telethon resulted in a series of exchanges between North and South in the 1980s. In 1983, it reunited a South Korean population composed mostly of poor, uneducated people (Choon Soon Kim 1988, 116). The following inter-Korean meetings were largely diplomatic in nature, and the selected families were on display for the state. While the 1983 telethon went unnoticed by the international community, the inter-Korean meetings made the headlines of foreign newspapers.

Ach'im madang's roots in the telethon and its anchorage in South Korean national history elevate its cachet significantly compared with other, similar programs devoted to family meetings that have since been produced.

Reference to the "Ten Million Divided Families"

On *Ach'im madang*, the hosts and the professor suggest that the war is the direct or indirect cause of the participants' separations from their families. The historicized interpretation of family separation is based first of all on a quantitative argument—the number of the "divided families," which is for the most part greatly overestimated. It encompasses not only transnational adoptees but also Korean emigrants. Numbers seem to erase all references to the nature of the separations and to their singularities, suggesting implicitly that all of them stem from the national partition. Family separation is an ideological concept that authorizes the confusion of individual stories with national history. A ready-made expression, the "divided families" has become a familiar leitmotif of all political discourses about inter-Korean relations. But as historian Lori Watt (2009) has shown with the case of "refugees" from Manchuria in Japan, the meanings and uses of such expressions depend on the sociopolitical context of the moment.

It is obvious that all wars generate familial separations, but in Korea, the familiar historical and social phenomenon is tainted with a stronger symbolism due to the ongoing partition of the peninsula. Anthropologist Richard Grinker critically wrote that the issue of the divided families has produced in South Korea an ever-growing social category encompassing people who did not personally experience the war and who are not separated from relatives by the thirty-eighth parallel:

> "Divided families" include even second or third cousins divided from one another.... The category *isan kajok* (divided families) can include people who may actually be living within the same state but who have yet to locate one another; in fact, the term refers to anyone separated from his or her family after liberation, division, or the Korean War, no matter where the person is living. (Grinker 1998, 101–104)

The author stresses the problematic definition and quantitative evaluation of the phenomenon:

> South Koreans, including political leaders, intellectuals, and reporters, rhetorically refer to *ilch'on-man isan kajok*, or "ten million dispersed families." This figure is double the estimated 5 million dispersed family members, emphasizing that one family separated became two separate (north and south) families. (Grinker 1998, 35–36)

For Grinker, the separations involving "nuclear families" are only a minority; most separations involve relatives of several degrees. The ancient extended family is clearly the government's reference. To touch again upon the principle of the three ties believed to define the person in Korean society, the person is the node where the strings of relationships depart or end. The limit to which they extend within kinship is not clear and obviously depends on the context. In the peculiar, idealized discourse on family separations, all the kinship ties are taken into account.

Figures given by historians are also subject to reevaluation, as the terms "separation" and "dispersion" can be used to refer to a very wide range of events. The various macro-events related to the war and larger geopolitical circumstances are vague regarding their dates and their quantification. According to information from official sources compiled and charted by anthropologist Choong Soon Kim, separations "caused by the war" often have nothing in common; they include the military, civilians, the living, and the dead; those who retreated from occupied North Korea, those who were kidnapped by North Koreans, those missing, and so forth (1988, 35). The blurring of distinctions between the living and the dead may well indicate that the categories of "living" and "dead" are not relevant here. We will come back to this important question of representation of the lost and the dead. Despite the official tendency to regard all separations as provoked by external, historical causes, we will see that many of them were and are in fact contingent on the structures of kinship and the micro-histories of ordinary family life and strife.

Fifteen years after Kim, sociologist Foley includes emigrant, diasporic families in the category of divided families, following official South Korean representations (Foley 2003, 57–60). As we have seen, the theorization of the diaspora and its role in the formation of South Korea's national image took place in the 1990s. Because both authors use sources provided by the South Korean government at different times, their texts indicate the evolution of the issue of divided families. Foley's report ends with a chart titled "Koreans Abroad," which leads to an even larger picture (Foley 2003, 59) but adds nuance to the official discourse and calls for a new estimation of the South Korean divided families that would only take into account the "first generation of South Koreans who were born in North Korea" (27, 59–60). The wish to determine an accurate number seems impossible to satisfy, but also irrelevant, since the constant inflation and overestimation have a precise function: they maintain the Confucian metaphor of the nation as a large family.

Dispersal is treated as an extremely negative condition in official discourses. Koreans who live abroad are supposed to share a bitter feeling induced by their separation from the motherland (*moguk*). They are all the more involved in the tragedy of family separation because they are members of the diaspora, which is commonly defined as an oppressed and forcefully displaced population. Themes such as the return of the diaspora naturally echo in family meeting narratives. The expressions "diaspora" and "divided family" evoke a desire for completeness and homogeneity attributed to dispersed Koreans. The whole enterprise consists of creating a need for completeness and a consciousness of a common destiny. The construction of emotions is instrumental to this process. The representation of the suffering, amputated nation would not have emerged without a positive image of North Korea. Perceived as the enemy to vanquish during the Cold War, North Korea has since become a parent nation, starting from the beginning of the twenty-first century, often represented as a younger brother (Em 1999; Jager 2003). In a speech delivered in 1983, President Chun Doo Hwan[5] alluded to the recent telethon and expressed his personal determination in helping the divided families to reunite:

Our sufferings resulting from the forced occupation of the North by the Communists have not lessened even a least bit during the past 38 years.... As our national strength grows stronger so does our resolve to unify the homeland as soon as possible.

The marathon television program of the Korean Broadcasting System which began in June 30 to facilitate the reunion of families separated by the Korean War made us once again realize just how tragic and deep are the wounds inflicted by that war and how strong and sincere are our wishes for national unification.... We should not simply cry and sympathize with the separated families but instead provide all the support and cooperation we can to help them reunite. (Chun 1984, 161)

From the interweaving of humanitarian and political goals, the telethon was born. One television documentary in 1985 recalled the end of the war and closed with images from the telethon. The event was said to have transformed the "individuals' desire for reunion into a right" (*yokkuga anira kwollida*). The documentary concludes with these words: "Our problem [*uri-ŭi munje*] is humanitarian [*indo-jŏgin munje*]."[6] Organized by the South despite the North's hostile attitude, the telethon seems to affirm the superiority of individuals' feelings over political contingencies. The political agenda depends upon the staging of emotions as epitomized by the dramatic scene of tears.

The Scene of Tears: An Icon

The task of "renewing the South Korean nation" independently from North Korea, which was initiated by South Korean television in the 1960s,[7] was replaced by the task of pacifying and unifying the peninsula in the 1990s. *Ach'im madang* was created in 1997. In 1998, the newly elected president, Kim Dae-jung, launched his "Sunshine Policy" toward the North.[8] Kim's presidency was the beginning of a wave of televised family meetings. The Sunshine Policy and the subsequent family meetings within South Korea and between North and South Koreans expressed Kim's Christian ideals of reconciliation. He received the Nobel Peace Prize in 2000 after he met with North Korean leader Kim Jong-il. Compassion implies forgiveness. As anthropologist Sheila Miyoshi Jager has shown, this official conception of the future victory of South Korea (which implies the unification of the peninsula) is less a military victory over an enemy than a spiritual victory over abstractions like discord and conflict (Jager 2003, 144–149). Kim Dae-jung wrote:

We have witnessed the ruin of communism, which called Christianity the opium of the masses that weakened the people's resistance against exploitation by their rulers. History honors those who confess their sins before God, who forgive their enemies and who look after their neighbors. (1998, 173)

This vision of history gives meaning to the nation's suffering and even valorizes it. Many times during the course of my research, I heard South Koreans say that they were proud they had never oppressed other people or other nations in a 5,000-year history. In many respects, South Koreans' victimized representation of their history and their place in the world resembles the role of martyrdom in Christian thought:[9] "Those who have to endure will endure. One fails to endure not because one's suffering is too unbearable, but because there is no higher purpose that gives meaning to this suffering."[10] Even if, on the South Korean side, the political context has changed with democratization, the role of KBS, which is still symbolically located a few hundred meters from the Parliament, consists of producing a homogeneous political discourse.

As we have seen, the scene of tears in *Ach'im madang* is the key moment that awakens the strongest emotions of the public. That moment is carefully prepared, orchestrated, and appreciated for its melodramatic character. Beyond its entertaining quality, the scene of tears transmits a moral message regarding family, as the scenario writer pointed out:

Family should never, never be separated, that's the lesson of the program. . . . Seeing some people younger than me coming up here and telling about their stories made me think of what family is and how grateful I should be to have had a good family. Some people just abandon kids because they can't take care of them. . . . And whatever happens, the family has to stick together. Before the problem was poverty but nowadays, the families separate or divorce or things like that. That's what they learned making this program. What Korean society learned by itself.[11]

If the scenario writer's words were not explicitly political, the program nonetheless uses a type of image that was created in the political context of warming relations between North and South Korea and that embodies politically correct values. If one compares the meeting scenes of *Ach'im madang* with the meeting scenes of North Korean and South Korean relatives, it is easy to see their commonality. The scene of tears anticipated by the audience of *Ach'im madang* repeats similar scenes that occurred more spontaneously during the 1983 telethon. The scene is invariably presented as a close-up on faces (Deleuze 1983, 125–145). By its very nature, the extreme close-up depersonalizes the subject's face, rendering it anonymous even while dramatizing it. This tactic allows the filmmaker to use the face for ideological purposes. The repetitive use of the close-up leads us to analyze all scenes of tears as one unique scene or icon, which is recognized by all and which creates a unifying representation and meaning (Benjamin 2008). The chief characteristic of the icon is its capacity to be reproduced indefinitely without changing meaning or losing its power. Choong Soon Kim's monograph on the telethon displays on its cover a black-and-white picture of two women's faces, one in profile view and the other in frontal view. The women are weeping and tightly embraced. Their eyes are closed in deep wrinkles and their mouths are open in uncontrollable sobs. The author has chosen this picture to show emotion in the most immediate manner. The close-up occupies the whole cover. To Kim, presumably, the display of emotion is self-explanatory and its meaning obvious, but people's emotions are much more ambiguous than they may at first seem.

The assimilation of individuals' fates to the destiny of the nation was illustrated by a fresco displayed for several years in the Sinch'on subway station in Seoul. While waiting for the Line 2 train to Sindorim, anyone could see, among the many paintings that echo the effervescence of the student neighborhood, a collage of two photographs. The top photograph featured the South Korean president Kim Dae-jung shaking hands with his counterpart Kim Jong-il in Pyongyang on June 13, 2000.[12] This picture had been sent out to the world: for the first time since the partition, the two leaders were meeting and discussing the conditions of the reunification. The lower photograph, dated August 12, 1971, featured a man in his fifties embracing a much older woman with white hair who was probably his mother. Both of them were crying. The date does not seem to match the event, as the first inter-Korean meetings did not happen until 1985 (Choon Soon Kim 1988, 107). In fact, the year 1971 corresponds to the beginning of the "movement for reunification" or, more exactly, with the day the "president of the South Korean Red Cross made public a proposal to the North Korean Red Cross for discussions to bring about the prompt solution of purely humanitarian problems" (Choon Soon Kim 1988, 102). The two photographs were the same size, and a single caption referred to both of them: "Meeting" (*mannam*). The two distinct events, one political, the other familial, became one, each implying the other. They did not display names because the people in the top photo are famous, and the people in the bottom photo do not really matter as individuals. They represent their group; all are symbols of their nations (Finley 1981, 69).

The mother figure serves as the metaphor for the nation, the motherland. The Korean nation is represented as a mother who awaits the return of her children. In this society where filiation is patrilineal, the figure of the mother embodies the attachment to the land of origins. The motherland first refers to this physical or organic quality of a land consubstantial of all Koreans. This gendered representation is reinforced by the family meetings and discourses on television. Transnational adoptees who return to South Korea are always asked the same pressing question: "Have you found your mother?" Strangers never inquire about fathers.[13]

Adoptees as Members of the Divided Families

Kim Dae-jung's message of peace and reconciliation was in fact extended to transnational adoptees during his mandate.[14] Those who have suffered must forgive, and witnesses of this suffering must feel compassion. Kim Dae-jung's message has applications at the state level as well as the familial level. During his many encounters with transnational adoptees from Europe and the United States, Kim never failed to deliver the same message on the meaning of suffering:

> A symbolic break occurred in 1998, shortly after President Kim's inauguration, when he invited twenty-nine Korean adoptees to the Blue House and offered them an unprecedented public apology. Along with visa rights extended to adoptees, the opening of the Adoption Center in Seoul in 1999 indicated the government's interest in openly addressing the public stigma of adoption in South Korea. This recognition [was] credited in part to the advocacy and encouragement of . . . First Lady Lee Hee-ho.[15] At the Gathering, presented via a video in Korean with English subtitles, [she] provided a matronly face for the symbolic "motherland," embracing adoptees as a source of pride for adoptive parents, Korean culture, and the South Korean state. . . . "[F]orget your difficult past and renew your relations with your native country in order to work together toward common goals based on the blood ties that cannot be severed. . . . [South Korea is] developing day by day to become a first-rate nation in the twenty-first century. It will be a warm and reliable support of all of you." (Eleana Kim 2005, 62)

By extension, any person of Korean origin who is far away suffers from the separation. That is why South Koreans have the moral duty to help transnational adoptees: they are all linked by a tissue of inchoate compassion. Transnational adoptees must find their birth parents and go back to the society where they were born. This relationship is structurally similar to the one linking South and North Koreans.

As we have seen, transnational adoptees are often won over by official discourses that praise their Korean blood despite their geographic remoteness. The Korean blood, or race, is sufficient to include them in the diaspora. They are de facto members of the divided families category because transnational adoption started as a result of the war. The category of "divided families" and the equivalence between the divided nation and the divided families are constructions. This representation has been passed down to South Korea's citizenry through the media. My grandmother's speech is a good example of how this conceptualization is made manifest in individuals' minds.

To a certain extent, some transnational adoptees who are familiar with South Korean attitudes toward the separation of families accept them as their own, assimilating orphans and transnational adoptees under the same category and considering themselves to be members of the divided families. A documentary shows Sophie Brédier, a French adoptee director, on a quest through Korea in search of the truth about her own adoption.[16] During this quest, Brédier interviews the famous writer Yi Mun-yŏl,[17] who expresses his thoughts about the division of his country and of his own family after the war. As with the professor or Senator Shin on *Ach'im madang*, Yi's literary prestige gives his words authority. Brédier assimilates and reuses his interpretation of family division for the construction of her own identity as a transnational adoptee. Later, she is seen at the KBS studio observing *Ach'im madang* family meetings between orphans or adoptees and their long-lost relatives. She comments on the scene, noting the common points shared by orphans, domestic adoptees, and foreign adoptees. Facing the camera in a brief moment of enthusiasm, Brédier expresses her feeling of "sharing the separation experience with all Koreans." All belong to this community of misfortune, the common fate of those who do not belong to anything. Building on this theme, she validates the South Korean idea that all separations referred to on *Ach'im madang* were caused by the war and that all individuals sharing Korean blood share the same tragic experience. Individual fates in Korea seem to be intertwined with the wider fate of their country. In that moment, the French director agrees to the representation that Koreans have been elaborating, replicating infinitely, and reproducing every week on television over several decades.

The meeting icon created by the media is displayed without historical context. It is a self-evident announcement of a national project that ignores social, political, and economic differences between the two Koreas (Grinker 1998, 66). In the public as well as the private sphere, separations, no matter their nature or cause, are systematically illustrated by the image of two anonymous people who embrace while crying. All these meetings look alike; no separation asks for an explanation other than war and poverty. Yet these examples should not lead us to believe that the whole Korean population subscribes without question to this dominant interpretation. Watching, enjoying, participating in, and using the program do not prevent some from being critical of its message. One forty-year-old South Korean man, who regularly attended the broadcasts in his capacity of volunteer interpreter for transnational adoptees, expressed his weariness at the uniformity of the hosts' and participants' discourse and asserted that this uniformity could not reflect the diversity of experiences:

> Yes, they think it's the same social problem although it is very different. But the other day . . . I was totally sick of the participants' stories: the Korean War, because of the war, right after the war. . . . It is always the same story. These Korean stories are based on the war. Similar stories so many times! Even adoptees . . . . [Transnational] adoption started after the war.[18]

The interpreter did not deny that some separations happened because of the war, but he refused to entertain the idea that the war was the only cause of the divided families. We will see the other causes of family separations in the following chapter.

Similarly, *Ach'im madang*'s scenario writer confirmed that the program generates confusion about the causes of the separations: "My assumption is that even in '83, during the Telethon, not only people separated by the war were present but also people separated for many other reasons. It was not on TV. But then, they tried to accept these people."

"So," I asked, "people who have been separated by the war don't appear today in this program; do they have their own program?"

"We broadcasted them twice in a special *Ach'im madang* but the results were so poor that they stopped. Nobody could find anybody. We have to make the program last. Most people are very old, and they found pretty much all they wanted in '83."[19]

In other words, the scenario writer asserted that attributing all separations to the war is only one possible interpretation among others. As a matter of fact, one participant at *Ach'im madang* explained in his presentation that he first registered for the 1983 telethon in order to find his sister. After the search failed, he decided to contact KBS to appear on the weekly television show.[20] Obviously, participants in the 1983 telethon and participants on the weekly program are not that different: some were separated from their families because of the war, and others were not. Additional evidence for a plurality of causes is the prevailing feeling of responsibility expressed by the reunited family members themselves. About the meetings between North and South Koreans, James Foley reports:

> Perhaps the most commonly reported sentiments, both among those who lived in the South and those who lived in the North, were feelings of guilt and recrimination for perceived failure to fulfil their familial obligations and duties. Despite the fact that the events responsible for their separation, the division of Korea and the subsequent Korean War, were clearly beyond the control of the participants at the reunions, many of the interviewees reported a tendency to personalise the tragedy of their separation from their family members, either on their part or on the part of the family members they met at the reunion, i.e., to place blame on themselves rather than on the turbulent political situation in Korea at the time of their separation. This was especially true in the case of eldest sons separated from their families, parents separated from their children and sons separated from their mothers. (Foley 2003, 127–128)

Foley tends to agree with the official version and deny individuals' agency in the separation of families, whereas his informants express their feelings of culpability in the tragedies that struck their relatives. He notices that culpability is stronger in the case of family members who are expected to take responsibility for the others: mostly men (as opposed to women) and older relatives (as opposed to younger). It appears that even in the case of the division of the peninsula, individuals recognize factors of separation other than the war itself. Therefore, it is all the more absurd to base one's understanding of transnational adoption in Korea solely on the history of the Korean War. The symbolic reintegration of transnational adoptees and their assimilation under the category of "divided families" (*isan kajok*) entail continuous elaboration because the links established among these various categories of families—those divided by the war, emigrant families, and families whose children were sent away for transnational adoption—are artificial. On the one hand, Korean War history is used in official discourses to give meaning to the phenomenon of transnational adoption, which pushes to the foreground its inevitability and mutes all discourses on collective and individual responsibility. On the other hand, since the division of the two Koreas is attributed to the decisions of foreign powers, transnational adoption gives weight to the discourse of victimization that results from the partition.

Several levels of causes contribute to the social phenomenon of family separation: the war, famine, and poverty. But there are also smaller causes that imply actors making decisions and taking actions that led to separation. Other long-term causes belong to the realm of values and practices that are difficult to measure (*longue durée*)[21] but are nonetheless worth examining, as we will see in the next chapter. In other words, the historical causes of family separations were deeply entangled with sociological and long-term causes. Some separations were indeed due to historical factors, others to specific practices within certain patterns of kinship, and still others to certain representations of children and parenthood or to diverse spiritual beliefs. Switching scales will help to deepen the analysis and provide a counterweight to the meaning constructed by the state and the media. By focusing mainly on birth families' stories, we will access the smaller causes such as individuals' decisions, strategies, motivations, and limitations.

PART II

Meeting the Birth Family

6

Stories behind History

I chose open international adoption in the hope that my daughter will come back one day. It is my only hope in life, and I will not marry, like other mothers do, unless my husband accepts my daughter as his own. . . . I write letters to the adoptive parents and I tell them they should make her learn Korean, so that when she comes back we can talk together. For me, it is too late to learn English. . . . Nowadays, many parents send their children abroad, even at a very young age, so that they can study. International adoption is like sending your child abroad to study. That's the way I see the situation.
—Thirty-year-old single mother (interview June 11, 2004)

The meeting program *Ach'im madang* constitutes rich material for the anthropologist: its content sheds light on the reasons and causes of fifty years of parent-child separations. We saw previously that there were historical causes for family separations and transnational adoption. But, as we will see now, there were and still are also other causes related to kinship, family strife, and individuals' strategies and choices. Although there are several cases of siblings looking for each other on *Ach'im madang* broadcasts, we will mostly focus here on participants who look for their parents or who seek a lost sibling on behalf of their parents. The purpose is to better circumscribe the birth parent–adopted child relationship in the context of transnational adoption and the return of adoptees in the birth parents' lives. In this subgroup, however, there is a clear separation between the older Korean participants—approximately forty to sixty-five years old—and the younger Korean or foreign participants, approximately eighteen to thirty-five years old (Dong-won Lee 2000). The older participants were separated from their parents in a few different ways that I call "practices of separation." These practices are related to what social anthropologists have described as "child circulation," that is, child-rearing practices such as child labor, fosterage, informal adoption, and temporary stays at orphanages. In general, anthropologists see these modes of separations as more flexible than the Western style of adoption in that they never completely break the ties between mother and child, creating instead various types of relatedness.[1] Narratives of the later generation of participants at *Ach'im madang* demonstrate the later prevalence of transnational adoption as the dominant mode of separation in urban industrialized Korea. But the very existence and organization of the meeting program, as well as birth mothers' discourse, indicate that transnational adoption can be seen today as yet another flexible practice in South Korea.

Transnational Adoption, Another Type of Child Circulation

The short narratives of parent-child separation given by the older participants on the television show reveal the multiple practices of family separation typical of preindustrial Korea, all of which intensified in the context of postwar poverty.[2] *Ach'im madang* illustrates perfectly how separating from a child through acceptable practices was then common and unquestioned, although of course probably painful.

The program's hosts favored the term "lose" (*ilta*) as it conveniently encompasses—and covers up—all cases. Participants themselves never said that their parents had "abandoned" them or their siblings (*pŏryŏjida, pŏrimbatta*). Instead, they stated: "and that is the way we all got separated" (*irŏkke heŏjyŏssŏyo*), or "it's the way we were all scattered" (*ppulppuri hŭt'ŏjyŏtta*). Their spotty narratives, however, often unveiled the causes of their separation. Although illegal abandonment in a public place such as a train or rail station was common,[3] only two of the thirty-five older participants from a fifty-person sample recalled actually getting *lost* in the usual sense.[4] Three of the participants talked about their parents' "running away" (*tomang katta*), "disappearing," or "going out and not returning." Usually fathers left children after their spouse's death, or for another woman.[5] Four participants gave strange accounts of the way their father or mother—mostly fathers—randomly lost one of their siblings or gave them to an unidentified person, sometimes under the influence of alcohol, which also seems to indicate a willful separation.[6] Willful separations account for less than a third of the older participants' cases, but the majority of older participants revealed in their stories the same process. At the beginning, families tried to overcome the loss of balance caused by the death or absence of one of the parents but soon capitulated and gave up a child or several children. There were many options in these circumstances, including child servitude in a stranger's house, child fosterage by an elderly person, adoption by a relative or acquaintance, or sending a child or children to an orphanage. The word "separation" encompasses different practices and usually implies choices made by female adults—mostly mothers, paternal or maternal aunts, and grandmothers—in the absence of fathers.[7] Before being "separated," children were, in fact, usually taken care of by relatives, friends, or neighbors because parents were in a difficult situation.

Among the many ways that children could become separated from their parents, child servitude in factories and rich households (*puja chip*) was the most common before industrialization.[8] Four participants invoked this practice on *Ach'im madang*, using it to describe their own situations as well as those of the siblings "they lost touch with" because "they did not live at home anymore." Child labor was obviously a good option for large families, put into practice as soon as the child was old enough to work.[9] In his study of *Ach'im madang* participants, South Korean sociologist Dong-won Lee has classified the practice as a kind of begging called *saballongsa* (*sabal*: bowl; *nongsa*: cultivate).[10]

Informal adoption was another solution to poverty, single parenthood, or widowhood. In one case a forty-seven-year-old participant was looking for her father who was a soldier and once remarried after her mother's premature death. He then gave her up for adoption at the age of five to a friend from the same platoon.[11] A forty-six-year-old participant did not remember her name and had no memory of her father. Because her mother worked full-time in a rich household, she gave her up for adoption (*yangŏmŏni taegŭro kage toem*) when she was seven to in-laws of her maternal grandmother, in Taegu.[12] A fifty-eight-year-old participant was looking for her older sister. The two sisters had been adopted into two different families of the Andong region. The participant's sister was adopted into an affluent household. The participant's adoptive family was modest; they left one day for Pusan, and that is how the sisters lost track of each other.[13]

Anthropologists and historians have shown that social status in Confucian Korean society used to be established mostly by one's parents' legitimate union, one's own marriage, and one's having a son to perpetuate the patriline. For a minority, the prestige attached to the passing of official examinations could contribute to status but was most often linked to the family. In theory discouraged by Confucianism, a woman's remarriage after widowhood or divorce made the children illegitimate according to the family law that prevailed until recently. Sending children away was a frequent solution for these situations. As illustrated earlier, in practice, the child must come from a legitimate union,[14] and its status is in fact bilateral although the society is patrilineal. Even if the law permitted a husband to freely validate filiation until 1991, which could lead to disowning a legitimate son as well as integrating any woman's offspring into the legitimate household without the consent of his wife,[15] evidence shows that, in practice, men are not the only ones to decide. Although legally irrelevant, the opinion of a remarried man's wife is generally a major contributor to his separation from children from the previous union (So-hoe Yi, Chŏng, and Kim 1998). The fact that a widower gives his daughter to a friend also shows that adoption between friends can be seen as a gift.

Several cases suggest that though birth parents often considered an adoption to be a secure arrangement, in practice it did not always last. For example, a thirty-four-year-old participant recalled that he had first lived with his parents in the countryside, but they sent him to an adoptive family in Seoul. Since he would always ask his adoptive parents where his birth parents were, his adoptive father said they would go together to see them. The boy fell asleep on the train, and when he woke up, he was alone in the Seoul train station. Some people found him and took him to Holt Adoption Agency, and then he was sent to France.[16] A fifty-two-year-old participant brought sketches of different houses in which he had lived as a child. The second drawing showed the house of the family that had adopted him for a short period. He thought the people were rich because of the tiles on the roof.[17] He did not know exactly what had happened in the adoptive family, but they had sent him back to birth parents' shanty. When he came back, his father was very angry and punished him severely.[18] A forty-year-old participant was adopted by a woman whom other adults called his "twin mother." He did not like her, ran away, and was unable to find his way home.[19]

Sometimes adoptive parents would send back or abandon a child after a trial period, especially if the child was older. These examples of unsuccessful adoptions related on *Ach'im madang* indicate that adoptions of boys are generally more problematic than adoptions of girls. Much is expected from the adoptive son, as opposed to the adoptive daughter, who will leave the adoptive home anyway when she gets married.[20] Nowadays, as we have seen, girls are more often adopted domestically and boys internationally. Ancient patterns of marriage and new trends in kinship are blending in this transitional state of South Korean society. In addition, the case of the French adoptee illustrates the possible failure of domestic adoption versus a definitive transnational adoption.

In some cases, adoption is seen by the birth family as fosterage. The practice of fosterage, in which one person assumes care of another's child without becoming a legal parent, has been studied throughout the world. Fosterage can be formal—supervised by the state—or informal. Because of the informal nature of the practice in Korea until the twentieth century, the birth family often still visited the child after the adoption. Sometimes arguments would start, and the adoptive family would appropriate the child.

A fifty-six-year-old participant was looking for her younger sister, who had been separated from the rest of the family. The mother had died suddenly from a heart attack, and the participant, the oldest of four children, initially had to take care of her two younger brothers and her younger sister. The father sent the two boys to families in the southwest region of South Korea and the youngest girl to a family in a certain neighborhood of their hometown, in the southeast region of the country. The participant herself left for Seoul, found a job there, and got married. After her father's disappearance, she went back to look for her siblings. She first found her two brothers and put one in a hospital because he had epilepsy and the other in an orphanage, since their foster families probably would no longer take care of them. She also found her little sister and started visiting her so often that the foster family moved without notice to lose touch with her. In this way, she lost track of her sister.[21] In another case, a forty-year-old participant did not remember his father. His mother, a traveling merchant, provided for the needs of her two children by herself, with some difficulty. They lived close to the main gate of Yonsei University. Because of the nature of her job, the mother decided to put the older sister in the care of an elderly woman who sold food in the streets for a living and needed help. One day, the old woman disappeared with the girl, and the family never heard from her again.[22] A forty-eight-year-old participant was searching for his sister, who is two years younger than him. He repeated what their mother had told him: "As it was economically very difficult, we sent her to the school director's house. She was adopted there, but we did not hear from them afterwards."[23]

Used by participants and displayed onscreen during the show, terms such as "adoption" (*ibyang*) or "sending" (*ponaejim*) of a child to strangers' houses are ambiguous as to the period of time the child was supposed to be away, the child's status, and the adults' rights over the child. Some of the children sent as labor or as foster children to rich families were later adopted. But those sent to adoptive families could end up being servants.[24]

Temporarily sending a child to an orphanage was also a very common practice (David Kim 2001, 227). Adults in the family kept seeing the child, hoping for better days when the family would be reunited. For example, a forty-six-year-old participant explained that poverty had forced her mother to leave home and work in a rich house (*puja chip*). The participant herself was sent to a relative's home, which was not too far away. Because she kept asking for her mother, her maternal aunt took her to the house where her mother worked. The landlady (mother's employer) took her to an orphanage right away. During that period, only her maternal aunt and the housewife visited her.[25] In another case, a mother, upon meeting her twenty-two-year-old daughter adopted in Germany, explained that giving birth to their third daughter had left her exhausted. Because she was not recovering, she gave her newborn to her own mother for a while. Her condition was not improving, and the grandmother decided to give the baby to someone she knew, who took the baby to an orphanage. Before the mother could react and get her back, the baby had been adopted abroad.[26]

These examples illustrate accepted practices of separation that parents of poor and large families, single parents, widows, and widowers chose in order to survive economically and socially. Most of these practices are common in many rural and preindustrial societies, not only rural Korea.[27] Often the decision of a third party, such as a maternal grandmother, an aunt, or a midwife, the sending away of a child, whether to fosterage, an adoptive family, an orphanage, or a rich family as labor, is not as formal and definitive as the contemporary Western conception might assume. The orphanage example especially seems to illustrate the contradiction between an old, informal practice—sending a baby to an orphanage temporarily—and the new practice of sending children who reside in orphanages to transnational adoption.

The clear demarcation between older and younger participants on *Ach'im madang* shows that in urban and industrialized South Korea, the Western conception of child rearing—one set of parents who take on all rearing functions in a continuous way—came to supersede local practices. The high rate of transnational adoption is obviously linked to the disappearance of the less formal separation practices discussed on *Ach'im madang*. According to Western definitions, the separation is supposed to be final and legally recognized in the case of adoption, and temporary and less formal in the case of fosterage or child servitude.[28] After foreigners opened the first orphanages, practices changed dramatically because of these different views regarding child circulation. Until recently, social workers—foreign at first, then Korean—tried to make Korean birth parents understand that the inconsistency of their relationships with their children was damaging for the children's balanced development. This was a strong argument used to send many children abroad. This conflict of ideas comes from a Westernized definition of adoption held by Western and Korean social workers, which stood for a while in opposition to the definition held by Korean birth parents.[29] This change is reflected in *Ach'im madang*. The younger participants are a minority (fifteen out of fifty participants in the sample group), most of whom were sent abroad via an orphanage.[30]

Like their American counterparts, South Korean social workers recognize the differences between abandonment and relinquishment. These are concepts born out of the institutionalization of adoption. Commonly, to abandon means to give up any rights over something or someone without expecting its return, while to relinquish something or someone implies the regret of an action that may happen against one's will. According to social workers, to abandon a child is to leave it somewhere without information about its background or identity, whereas to relinquish a child is to leave it in the care of an institution. Thus, relinquishment is one's willful and legal separation from one's child as opposed to abandonment, which is illegal. In this case, the parent must provide a justification and have an interview with the social workers of the establishment. The single mothers cared for by institutions who give up their babies legally relinquish them. They still seldom choose to take care of their baby alone and most often choose between domestic adoption and transnational adoption.

During fieldwork I spent time at Aeranwon, an institution that hosts, at no charge, up to forty single mothers. During an interview, the president, Mrs. Han, a South Korean woman in her fifties, recalled that in 1994, social workers from the Holt office in Korea went to the United States and noticed how the methods of adoption differed from those in their own country:

> First of all, contrary to South Korean practice, American adoptive parents do not choose the child they want to adopt; second, they sometimes keep in touch with the birth parents, which is beneficial to all. So, since 1994, open adoption [konggae ibyang] according to the American practice is proposed to birth mothers as well as to American and South Korean adoptive parents. A show like Ach'im madang turns old closed adoptions into open ones [ach'im madang: kŭ sarami pogosip'ta kat'ŭn pangsongi yetibyangŭn konggae ibyangŭro t'aeuda], in the case where birth parents contact their children. It is absolutely positive, because birth mothers can change their minds during their lives.[31]

All transnational adoptions before 1994 were closed, but shows like Ach'im madang have helped to remedy this situation in South Korea. Single mothers whom I met and interviewed at Aeranwon frequently attested to their wish to someday find the child they had relinquished. They regularly watched television programs and read articles related to transnational adoption and were confident that they would meet their child again thanks to the media. When Korean adoptive parents want to engage in open adoption, birth mothers may accept domestic adoption, but if adoptive parents reject that possibility, many birth mothers think closed transnational adoption is a better option: it does not entail regular and often awkward contacts with the adoptive family from the moment of the separation, and it allows the birth mothers to live their lives, while nonetheless maintaining the idea of a possible reunion with the child in the future. So, in practice, birth mothers at Aeranwon really have the choice between closed domestic adoption, closed transnational adoption (Doumeng 2000), and open transnational adoption. If birth mothers choose domestic adoption by Korean parents for their baby, they fear they will remain unknown to their child: except in rare cases, Korean adoptive parents still try to hide their adoptive child's origins. Open transnational adoption does not maintain legal links between birth parents and their child, but only an informal contact based on a non–legally binding contract and goodwill between birth parents and adoptive parents. Closed transnational adoption, which was the most common choice until 2008, allows adoptees to look for their birth parents once they are adults, as their physical differences will make them aware of their adoption no matter how the adoptive parents handle the situation. Therefore, the idea of temporary, informal separations is also relevant in the context of transnational adoption. Because of today's global flows of people and information, transnational adoption can be regarded from South Korea as a contemporary form of child circulation.[32]

A common characteristic of all the practices of child circulation is that women almost always initiate them. Women, and especially mothers, are held directly responsible for the unity of the family: they are at the same time guilty of the separations and accountable for the family reconstitution on *Ach'im madang*. Their status in South Korean society, however, yields questions regarding the validity and durability of these newly reunited families.

Family Ties outside of Confucian Kinship

According to Confucianism,[33] the family ties that count are limited in number and revolve around men: "The six kinship ties considered important to Confucius were the ties between father and son, elder brother and younger brother, husband and wife, and their counterparts: son and father, younger brother and elder brother, wife and husband. The ties between mother and son, mother and daughter, and brother and sister are never mentioned by Confucius."[34] Interestingly, the family ties featured on *Ach'im madang* are many and revolve around women. They reveal a great flexibility regarding child care in times of crisis: mothers, siblings, maternal relatives, remote cousins, and foster mothers. But, on further examination, the multiplicity of caretakers for these children[35] suggests an attempt to compensate for an original loss in the family unit.

Searches for and reunions with siblings occur regularly on *Ach'im madang*. During one broadcast, a participant showed two black-and-white photos attached to a board, part of a display he had assembled himself. One photo had been taken at his older sister's *chŏtdol*;[36] both showed the sister and the brother together, at a very young age. He began recounting memories of their childhood: his protective sister (*pohohaettŏn nuna*) always came to his defense when he was in trouble with the neighborhood kids.[37] Another participant mostly remembered her grandfather, her maternal aunt, and her older brother, with whom she fought and was punished. It was he who taught her how to write. At this dear memory, a tender smile illuminated her sad face.[38]

Participants often look for older siblings, describing them in tender terms. The television show reveals that feelings linked to brotherhood or sisterhood are supposed to stem from physical contact or proximity. To carry a young sibling generates a peculiar tie, as a female participant recalled while standing forehead to forehead with her younger brother, as recounted earlier in the introduction: "I was the one who used to carry you on my back!"[39] Later, the host invited the professor to comment on this tie between younger and older siblings. The professor recalled: "As the older brother myself, I carried on my back the youngest child of the family. When we were refugees during the war, we were walking all day and I carried him that way. He was complaining his belly skin hurt. Even now that he is forty-five, this memory comes to my mind each time I see him."[40] Immediately afterward, the hostess added her own anecdote: "I am the last of five daughters and there is a five-year gap between my second elder sister and me. She used to take me on her back often and today, although I look like a mountain, she sees me the way I was then and tells me I am very cute. No one can forget the affection [*chŏng*] that is related to carrying a sibling on one's back."[41] The hostess named the feeling caused by siblings' physical proximity the "*chŏng* of carrying a younger sibling on one's back." In describing the ideal families in which they grew up, the hosts and the professor established as a norm a relation that was never officially recognized in the dominant Confucian culture, but that nonetheless existed in common representations. Though it lacked judicial value, this type of relation had a strong evocative power and brought back intense emotions. The close bond between elder and younger siblings is common to other societies but provokes a distinctive feeling in Korea.[42] Thus, one fifty-six-year-old female participant on *Ach'im madang*, as the older daughter, took on the mother's role in relation to her younger siblings after their mother's death. At first, she had a confident and energetic voice, but she soon became overwhelmed by emotions and started mumbling and weeping.[43] Looking for those who shared one's childhood is related to the desire of reconstituting the family entity.[44]

Other types of ties, without value in the realm of Confucianism, are also recognized and legitimized by the program. For example, the hostess emphasized the value of the maternal family. After the teary meeting of a female participant and her relatives, the hosts introduced the participant's husband and two sons to her family. The two sides greeted each other. The new grandmother, still weeping, took her daughter's youngest boy in her arms, despite his obvious resistance. "She became a grandmother!" exclaimed the hostess with excitement. "The person one loves the most is indeed one's maternal grandmother, but the grandson does not know that yet!"[45] The hostess referred to a saying that asserts that the closest bond is the one between a maternal grandmother and her grandchild. The ties newly created onstage must appear as idealized, even if the intimidated grandson did not want to be embraced or carried by the old woman. This specific scene well illustrates the construction of emotion related to certain social ties that is undertaken by the program as a whole. A Korean friend commented on the scene that in Confucian patrilineal, patrilocal Korea, a woman lives in her husband's home and must cohabitate with her parents-in-law, who, according to everybody, mistreat the wife. Children, naturally closer to mothers, who take care of them exclusively, witness household conflicts and tend to take the mother's side. A paternal grandmother's presence is experienced as an oppressive one. In contrast, the rare visits to maternal grandmothers are not sources of tension but rather moments of pleasure and peace. The result at *Ach'im madang* is the praising of a tie outside of and against the patriline.

Sometimes the production team allowed a foster mother to appear onstage instead of a birth mother. In the case of a very charismatic transnational adoptee, the woman who met him during the broadcast under the usual applause was not related to him but had been his foster mother. After he was told the truth, the adoptee got upset because he felt that the team had misled him. Because he spoke Korean well and made funny jokes, the scenario writer had told me that many viewers had called the studio to express their sympathy and enthusiasm. The production team had managed to have him back to please their audience. But the event calls for another interpretation: the foster mother figure is in fact part of what social anthropologists have called fictive or pseudo-kinship.[46] In newspapers and on television in South Korea, the negative connotations of transnational adoption have been increasingly counterbalanced by depictions of generous foster mothers who devote their time to babies without the least self-interest.⁴⁷ The ties between children sent abroad and their foster mothers are maintained by adoption agencies like Holt.⁴⁸ During the Seoul International Gathering for the Fiftieth Anniversary of International Adoption in 2004, an article in *Dong-a Ilbo*, a South Korean newspaper, was devoted to foster mothers, who were attributed authentic maternal love and often suffered from grave confusion in the roles they were supposed to play.⁴⁹ The foster mother is the woman who contributes to the child's physical growth for several months. *Ach'im madang* provides an occasion to recognize this fostering tie that seems very strong, although not socially relevant within Korean society. With no rights to the children they raise, foster mother volunteers nonetheless play an important nurturing role in the nation.⁵⁰

In addition to celebrating brothers and sisters, maternal families, and foster mothers, the program also acknowledges remote relatives on both the maternal and paternal sides, especially aunts but also uncles.⁵¹ In many cases, the participant's absent father was represented by a paternal aunt, a paternal grandaunt, or, more seldom, a paternal uncle.⁵² In the case of a thirty-year-old French adoptee, the program featured the older paternal uncle's wife, who spoke more than her husband. The paternal (grand)aunt replaced the father. In these dire circumstances, she seemed to share the attributes of the maternal uncle, who, in many traditional matrilineal societies, represents his nephew's mother (his sister) and precedes the father. Relatives on paternal and maternal sides replaced parents when they were deceased or absent, but also when they had remarried. In the case of meetings during the 1983 telethon, remarriage, which sometimes resulted in a parent suddenly having two partners and offspring from two different unions, obviously posed something of an obstacle to many family reunions.⁵³ In several *Ach'im madang* cases, birth parents' second alliances rendered primary filiations outdated but did not erase them. The participants evoked divorce and widowhood, either of which events can result in one parent taking temporary care of the children until remarriage. Sometimes a relative took care of the children to allow the parent to remarry.⁵⁴ These examples confirm that recomposed families—that is, an adult couple (married or not) with at least one child from a precedent relationship—have been rare in Korea whereas they have been common for several decades in Western countries where they stem from high divorce rates.⁵⁵ Yet in the case of South Korea, where the divorce rate has been one of the highest in the world for more than a decade,⁵⁶ the supposed correlation between the number of divorces and the number of recomposed families does not exist. Although a high divorce rate is usually seen as an indication of changes in the conception of marriage and family,⁵⁷ the ease with which divorces occur in Korea does not indicate a deep change in marriage signification or judicial egalitarianism of genders. For the reasons mentioned earlier, an adult's cohabitation with the child of the spouse's first union, or half siblings sharing the same roof, is an obvious problem. This has led to a high number of children sent to orphanages in the wake of their parents' divorce.

* * *

Fathers appeared onstage and performed the meeting scene at *Ach'im madang* in only two cases in the sample. In the first case, the father was not remarried and wanted to ask his daughter for forgiveness.[58] In the second case, the father was still married to the mother, and the adoption had taken place accidentally.[59] The relative rarity of paternal appearances can be explained by fathers' unwillingness to be seen on television, or the fact that mothers often make the decision to separate from their children when fathers are already missing. It is also possible that, in this specific context, mothers feel free to express their ties to children in a society where these ties do not count. In a way, their meetings with their lost children can be seen as informal. In many patrilineal societies, the maternal tie has its own modes of expression but is denied any power.[60] In a Confucian society, the paternal family has exclusive rights to children, whereas the maternal family has only duties. In societies that commonly practice mother-child separation, one observes the correlation between the two kinds of ties: official patrilineal filiation and strictly private mother-child ties.[61]

Again, mothers are the most valued actors of the televised meetings. We saw earlier that mother-child meetings at *Ach'im madang* were always dramatized as the most central ones, even though they did not represent the majority of the meetings. Usually, legal consanguinity implies the patriline.[62] Here, the emphasis of a feminine consanguinity does not induce any maternal right over the children but seems to be reduced only to a temporary social recognition of their generative role. Thus, meetings do not create or re-create kinship but can stand instead as the expression of compensatory biological ties supposedly based on a cultural, obvious, or primordial fact: blood.[63] The mother-child tie is built on a system that provides symbolic compensation, as it valorizes the mother-daughter relation as opposed to the father-son transmission. On *Ach'im madang*, mothers and daughters were said to look the same, and mothers themselves claimed this resemblance with their daughters but not with their sons. One participant was looking for her younger brother. She and her sister had lived with their mother while the younger brother had been sent to an orphanage. Their mother, sixty-six, was sitting in the second row among the professional public of *Ach'im madang*. When the hosts addressed the mother directly, she said that she had no picture of her son. She added that he did not look anything like her or her daughters.[64] In another case, after a female participant was reunited with her older sister, she learned that their mother had died. The older sister had brought a photo of their mother, who greatly resembled the participant, as the hostess eagerly pointed out.[65] In one broadcast, a young orphan who had grown up in an orphanage with his sister was about to meet with their mother. A flashback reminded the viewers of the poetic letter he had sent to the studio at registration. Among other things, he had written that he was imagining his mother when contemplating his sister's face.[66] A female participant said she thought she might look like her mother, who at the time of filming would be over sixty.[67]

This compensation regarding physical features itself depends on culturally constructed maternal ties. There is an obvious stereotypical discourse on resemblances between mothers and daughters (and, to a lesser extent, of sisters on one side and brothers on the other). In the first example, the mother kept her daughters and sent her son to the orphanage. The symbolic appropriation of daughters by their mothers seemed more natural than the appropriation of the son: no picture of him remained, and his mother denied that he showed any physical resemblance to his female relatives.[68] This was also evident in the case of the father mentioned earlier who seemed embarrassed when facing his daughter and grumbled: "*Aigo!* Really! [*Ch'am!*] You look like your mother."[69]

Until recently, giving birth guaranteed Korean women no rights over their children, as mentioned earlier. Yet the family meetings constitute public events that, first, legitimize a posteriori an impossible tie or, second, provide the apology for the mother's wrongdoing. Mothers are made both innocent and guilty, that is, the perfect tragic figure. The parents-children meeting pattern seems at first to offer the public a uniform interpretation of family separation: the tearful mother figure passionately embracing her child is a recurrent image; sibling meetings do not provoke many comments; the father figure is absent. That is to say, the family reunion generally happens thanks to mothers who seemed to reactivate the ties. This configuration is not without meaningful conclusions. Regardless of the real causes of separation, the ideal mother figure, often dressed in the traditional *hanbok*, is elevated to the rank of a sacred icon. It is upon the traditional mother, the patient and virtuous wife, that the Confucian patriarchal society is supposedly established.[70] So the mother is the instrument of the family reunion, a simple agent of reproduction of the patrilineal chain (Yung-chung Kim 1977; Mattielli 1977; Shu-su Kim 1985). The icon consequently fixes the mother figure as an immutable norm. The traditional mother figure is indeed antithetical to the emancipated woman figure. As we saw earlier, the older separation cases are treated as consequences of the war. But it is well known that any war also causes rapid changes in family configurations, as individuals, especially women, adapt in order to compensate for imbalances due to separations (Choon Soon Kim 1988, 58–84).[71] *Ach'im madang* quickly makes clear that many voluntary separations and single-parent or recomposed families must have resulted from the war. It also appears that many women lost their husbands for different reasons, remaining alone to take care of their children for a certain amount of time until precarious life conditions forced them to separate from one or several of them.[72] Although these examples attest to the difficulties faced by mothers raising their children alone, they also illustrate that some mothers managed to do it nevertheless.[73] But mothers at the head of a family are never praised by the program, which instead promotes conservative readings of the ideal traditional family. Even if the icon, or scene of tears, celebrated the mother figure, it was she who was filmed crying and asking her children for forgiveness. In the father's absence, women are held responsible for the separation.

This ambivalent representation of the mother is reflected in the debates regarding transnational adoption of Korean children, which continued as late as 2008, when the South Korean government triumphantly announced that domestic adoption rates had superseded those of transnational adoption for the first time since 1969, the year South Korea started encouraging its citizens to adopt. As we have seen, women who have given birth out of wedlock have generally been stigmatized as the agents of contemporary family separations. However, surveys have shown that in Korea, as elsewhere, many unwed mothers would keep their babies "if society allowed them to do so." Until 2008, familial or social pressure, enforced by laws, prevented any of these women from becoming the "head of the family" (*hoju*),[74] even in cases of widowhood or divorce.[75]

The family meeting program *Ach'im madang* recalled historic circumstances to explain the different practices of separation or child circulation in poor and large families in the past. But as the media have also exposed via the participants' stories, these practices can in fact occur in any contemporary Korean family after a divorce, a death, or a parent's disaffection. Female relatives and especially mothers figured prominently as the primary actors of family dispersal in the recurrent absence of fathers, which revealed women's structurally weak position in society. Because *Ach'im madang* almost never features fathers, the majority of meetings do not reconstitute families but only secondary ties in this patrilineal society. If most meetings are compensatory recognition of ties that once defined families considered dysfunctional, they reassert a separation of individuals from sound patrilines. As we turn to several meetings' aftermaths, observation of the family configurations at the time of the meetings will confirm that these reconstituted ties are fragile at best.

7

Meetings' Aftermaths

In South Korean director Im's film *Kilsottŭm* (1986), two ex-lovers meet randomly in the context of the 1983 telethon. After the meeting scene that takes place on the staircase of the Korean Broadcasting System headquarters, a short sequence shows the reaction of each of their respective spouses. Both legitimate families suffer in silence, troubled by these ghosts' appearance in their ordinary lives. After their unexpected meeting, the former couple looks for the illegitimate son they abandoned after their families forced them to part. They find him living in sordid conditions with his wife and children. The mother cannot hide her disgust at the sight of her biological son, a drunken, violent man who beats his wife. She also resents his wife's eagerness to claim kinship with them in hope of financial gain. The father is more understanding but also accepting of this helpless situation. They nonetheless decide to take a blood test that, in the end, confirms their ties. The mother rejects the results and leaves the father and the son without a word. Resigned, the father slowly walks away. In the background, the son remains prostrated while his wife bursts out crying as she loses all hope of a better life.

The ex-lovers' final separation from their own child is caused by at least three factors. First, there is the economic gap between the wealthy birth parents and their destitute son, which makes him likely to attempt to take advantage of their reunion. That dynamic is illustrated without ambiguity by the initial eagerness followed by despair of the son's wife. Then, there are the psychological traits of each character that influence their relations with each other: the ex-lovers—the tough woman and the compassionate man—challenge the representations of genders as popularized by the media and seen on *Ach'im madang*. Finally, there is the sociological element: specifically, the marital situation of the parents. These three factors are at play in every meeting.

This film by one of the most famous South Korean directors went almost unnoticed. Its pessimistic warning against vain searches for lost relatives did not fit the general atmosphere of warming relations between North and South Korea. Rare studies focusing on the aftermaths of these 1983 family meetings show that a year after the telethon, one-fourth of the reunited families had only sparse, if any, contact with each other, even though they all lived in South Korea.¹ In the case of those whose relationships endured, nobody knows for how long. There is an obvious contradiction between the collective passions these quests engender and the general indifference regarding the outcomes. One wonders what happens after *Ach'im madang* broadcasts and what the participants do after their initial meeting. One also wonders which conditions promote lasting relations and which are likely to result in only temporary relations.

Viewers can get a glimpse of the meetings' aftermaths through the flashbacks that are usually played during a subsequent broadcast. But direct observation of reunited families over a longer period can help to establish the typical situations that the adoptee participant might encounter while acknowledging less predictable parameters such as individuals' temperaments and life choices.

Happy Endings on *Ach'im madang*

The flashbacks on *Ach'im madang* were typically composed of selected sequences and were intended to share the more intimate moments of the family reunions with curious spectators. In some cases, the first meeting did not occur on a Wednesday in the studio but in another place, depending on the participants' availability. The flashback technique had to convey the same emotion as the live meeting onstage. These slices of postreunion life are of interest less for what actually takes place during them and more for their symbolic value. Through them, *Ach'im madang* dictates to a certain extent proper attitudes and emotions offstage as well as onstage. For this reason, happy endings, which seem to prove the program's legitimacy, are emphasized. Yet no one knows what happens after the "ending." These flashback sequences are constructed and systematically interpreted by the production team through careful selection of necessary moments, partial subtitling of dialogue, the normative comments by the hosts, and a focus on optimistic declarations. The necessary moments are the tearful requests for forgiveness, the happy banquet, the solemn visit to family tombs, and two forms of the happy ending—either the peaceful separation or the optimistic promise of long-lasting relations. Again, these edited suites of moments turn the family meetings into narratives of family reconstruction, a kind of literary fiction to which the hosts and the professor contribute. From what I have seen and based on the program's ratings, Korean viewers clearly find satisfaction in the story line that starts with separations and ends happily, but one may wonder if that is the case for the participants in real life.

Several Meetings outside the Studio

As an interpreter, I occasionally accompanied foreign adoptees for several hours and sometimes over a few days during their first meetings with their birth families. I was therefore able to observe attitudes and listen to discourses for a longer time. Relating these adoptees' experiences and my own, as an adoptee reunited with my birth family, and also referring to examples given by secondhand sources, exposes the typical kinship configurations of birth families. This analysis also evidences the editing work of the production team, which led to the ritualization of actions, discourses, and relations.

In the summer of 2003, I received an emergency call on my cell phone from a social worker at Holt Children's Post-Adoption Services in Seoul. A birth mother had suddenly come to her office to meet her son, adopted abroad, who had returned to Korea and was then present in the office. The meeting had not been organized in advance, and the social worker needed an interpreter. I agreed to come as soon as I could. When I entered the room, the mother was there, red-eyed from crying but calm to all appearances. Her son Mark, thirty years old, was encouraging her with shy smiles. The social worker started asking him questions that I translated. She took notes. Mark repeated several times: "She should not feel guilty. . . . [M]y French parents are very happy I'm visiting Korea right now. They are respectable people, and I like my job."

An illegitimate child, he looked like his father, and she had recognized him at once, the mother related to me later. When her parents passed away, she had almost no resources, and her life had been very difficult. A stressful life had damaged her health, and she had undergone heart surgery several years earlier. Since then, she had to take medication every day. After Mark told her about his life in France, we left the building. The mother invited her son, the social worker, and me to her older sister's home, where she lived. The social worker declined the invitation because of work obligations that evening, so Mark and I accompanied her. The mother's sister's husband had been waiting in a car for the entire duration of the meeting. He obviously did not want to intrude upon the mother-son encounter. He exited the car to greet us and shake hands. We got in the car for a long ride in heavy traffic. The mother's sister's husband told Mark that, as a toddler, he used to play in his house in the days when they all lived in the same neighborhood, before the decision to send him for adoption was made.

Once we arrived at our destination, we crossed a well-kept garden and entered a nice house. While the mother and her sister were preparing dinner in the kitchen, the mother's sister's husband presented his family to Mark by means of a family picture framed in the entrance hall. He had four sons, all of them successful. He added that the youngest one, over thirty, was not yet married and had emigrated to Los Angeles. The mother's sister's husband liked talking about his trips, especially his tour in the United States. Magnets of each visited place were displayed on the refrigerator. Two young grandchildren were playing in the next room. They were called in to greet the "visitors," and the mother's sister's husband introduced Mark as his "friend." "It is not worth telling them about the situation," he declared. I translated, and Mark nodded with goodwill. The mother lived there, and we would go to her room after dinner. Dinner was marked by long silent moments, and the conversation was mostly insignificant. Mark was asked what he planned to do while in Korea. He said he was going to stay for a month so that he could go to Sorak Mountain National Park. At once, the mother's sister's husband declared he would take some days off to go with him. He added that he would pay for Mark's trip. Because he liked traveling alone, Mark was annoyed but did not dare refuse the offer.

The mother asked Mark if he wanted to see her room. They left the table, and at their request I followed them. She lived in the basement. Her job was to make sandwiches for her sister's eldest son's company, which was based in the rich neighborhood of Kangnam. She started praising her sister's husband for all he had done for her for so long. She made him sound like a saint. After Mark left Korea, she had married an old man who was now deeply in debt. They lived separately, and their son was staying with his father in the south. She kept a picture of them on a dresser. Her son was handsome, smart, and a hard worker. He had received several scholarships.

We went upstairs and back to the kitchen to have coffee and dessert. It was then that the solemn discourse began. The mother's sister's husband initiated the conversation; his eyes filled with tears, and his voice became loud while the mother held her face down, lower and lower above her cup of coffee, tears rolling down her prominent cheekbones. The mother's sister's husband declared that the mother had always been smart and pretty, and these qualities put her in difficult situations. The decision to give Mark up for adoption had been terribly hard to make, but the mother could not support him by herself. At these words, Mark was moved and told them not to regret anything; they had made the right decision. Of course, being different had not always been easy in France, but he was happy overall.

It was time to leave. Mark and I wanted to take the subway, but the mother's sister's husband decided to give us a ride to Sinch'on, the Seoul neighborhood where we were both staying. Everybody got in the car, and we arrived at Sinch'on quickly despite the dense traffic. Mark's mother put in my hand an envelope containing 30,000 won (thirty dollars or so). I attempted to refuse the money, but in vain. Mark contacted me once after that day, but I did not go back to that family.[2]

This case reveals a common situation: the illegitimate child is not accepted. As the masculine authority of the house, the mother's sister's husband managed the reunion, explained the circumstances of the separation, and asked for forgiveness in the name of all. It fell to him to accompany Mark in his travels. He embraced this role because he was also obviously the one who had decided upon the adoption. The mother's sister kept quiet while cooking dinner and serving the visitors. The prominence of women during family meetings onstage at *Ach'im madang* seems contradicted by this real-life moment in a private house. The mother was relegated to the role of a minor to whom compliments are given but who works for her sister's family in exchange for room and board. Her marriage is considered a failure, and her indebted husband cares for her legitimate son. More than the economic situation, the marital situation is not favorable to the child's reintegration in the birth family. In fact, Mark does not have a birth family. He just has a birth mother. That is why Mark is called a "friend" by the mother's sister's husband before the grandchildren. There will be no integration, owing to the following factors: (1) Mark's mother gave birth out of wedlock, and Mark has no filiation with his father, who remains absent and unknown—at least, the mother does not reveal anything about him; (2) his mother lives alone, dependent upon her sister's husband whose decisions she must respect, according to traditional kinship patterns;[3] and (3) his mother married and has a legitimate son, circumstances that condemn their relation to secrecy. The mother's relation to her illegitimate son will always be as unofficial as it was in the past. This meeting presents sequences usually covered by *Ach'im madang* camera crews: the tears, the banquet, and the asking for forgiveness, and also the offering of presents. In this case, the present consists of the maternal sister's husband paying for Mark's trip, which will happen with or without Mark's consent. It is more a question of reimbursement for a moral debt than an action taken to make somebody happy. This detail again underscores the idea that the relationship is not socially recognized.[4]

During my fieldwork, I met several foreign adoptees in a similar situation, which suggests it is relatively commonplace. Subsequent meetings with their biological parents usually happen without the knowledge of the spouse or the legitimate children. As on *Ach'im madang*, some adoptees report on reunion websites that they met only with a maternal or paternal aunt. Married or remarried, some birth parents should not be disturbed:

Success Story: [. . .] July 2001, I came to know Separated Family Reunion's website through a newspaper and I became a member, then finally, I could hear my mother's news. My mother has remarried and is well now. She needs her family's understanding first, so we haven't been able to meet yet, however I met my aunt (mother's sister) instead and I heard about my mom's life from her.[5]

In December 1947, Sue was born in Yongsan from a Korean mother and an American father who was a soldier. . . . A Belgian family adopted Sue. Fortunately, her mother's name could be found on adoption forms. . . . In June 2001, Sue came to Korea. . . . Sue was told about Separated Family Reunion's website. . . . Fortunately, she could find and meet her aunt (her mother's sister). From her, Sue found out her mother is now living in Hawaii, and her mother's family doesn't know anything about Sue.[6]

In these two similar cases, filiation is not reconstructed or replaced. The tie with the single parent or remarried parent is not socially valid because, as we have seen, the concept of a recomposed family is still uncommon.

* * *

Later during my fieldwork in 2003, I observed the foreign adoptee from Switzerland whom we discussed earlier meeting her six brothers and sisters after she participated in *Ach'im madang*. The meeting was rendered in a subsequent televised flashback because she had to leave Korea quickly to get back to work. The Korean interpreter called to ask if I could replace him that day, and I accepted. I arrived at 2:00 p.m. at the KBS studio. In the cafeteria, Sarah, her adoptive parents, her boyfriend, and the interpreter were sitting on couches, visibly excited. Miss Ho, the scenario writer, had asked them to come one hour earlier than the Korean family so that, as she said, she could "prepare them mentally." Ho arrived a few minutes later with her associate and a cameraman. She wanted to know what Sarah's mood was, whether she had slept well, what she intended to say, and so forth. After this talk, we all went outside to wait in the shaded alley behind the main building. There were trees and a little wall on which we could sit. We waited in silence while the cameraman filmed Sarah. Sarah's siblings had said they would all come together.

We saw them arriving at half past three. As we saw earlier, the older sister led the delegation. She soon declared that their parents were deceased. The mother had been a fortune-teller, and the father had been a laborer who had loaded train cars in Sihŭng station, on the southern outskirts of

Seoul. The adoptive parents stepped back while Sarah and her older sister embraced before the camera. Both of them wept in silence. Everybody was looking at each other. Each side had difficulties greeting the other. The adoptive father tried to kiss the older sister on her cheek, which made the three brothers laugh. After distributing gifts to Sarah and her parents, the older sister declared that they all should go to Ilsan, the suburb where their mother's ashes reposed. The second and third sisters, who lived in Ilsan with their families, left together early to prepare dinner. The rest of the group—the older sister, the three brothers, Sarah, her boyfriend, the cameraman, and me—went directly to the columbarium. The interpreter would join us in the evening in Ilsan. The adoptive parents were also politely invited, and they accepted, but decided to go back to their hotel first. Someone wrote the address on a piece of paper that they could show to a cab driver in Seoul.

The ride in the van was long. The KBS cameraman was totally silent. He had to film the visit to the columbarium and the banquet only. In the car, the older sister turned toward Sarah and looked at her carefully. She sighed several times and said, "Our mother was always thinking of her two babies.... [N]ow she's an angel [chŏnsa] and allowed us to reunite." She added that she had not been able to sleep the night before. It was a paternal aunt's daughter who had been watching *Ach'im madang* and had first seen Sarah. The older sister suddenly asked Sarah to take off her shoe. She looked at her foot and after a second shouted, "The same feet as our father!" She considered Sarah's complexion and insisted that her skin was dark like the first brother's and the second sister's, although Sarah said she had put foundation on. She also assured us that Sarah's eyes and brows had the same shape and that her face was long like theirs. The siblings in question were all married, except for the first brother, who was once "married to a bad person." Since the end of his marriage, he had lived with their mother until she died.

Sarah learned that she had ten nieces and nephews. The older sister noted proudly that her older daughter now lived in New York with her Korean husband. She took a picture out of her wallet that showed her daughter standing in front of a BMW. Her older son was also married. The younger son was still living at home in Sihŭng and worked at a Jindo dog farm. He would come on Friday. The older sister abruptly asked how old Sarah's boyfriend was. She peered at him. I answered, "He's thirty-four." The older sister asked me in a murmur, "What's his job?" I asked and then told her, "Right now, he's looking for a job." This answer did not please her. That Friday night, when her younger son would ask details about everyone, she would say with irritation: "The boyfriend has no job! [ŏpnae!]."[7] In this case the first portion of the meeting was again devoted to tears and physical contact, to the introduction of all the family members, to the announcement of the parents' death, and to the distribution of gifts by the Korean family to the foreigners.

After the preliminary introductions had taken place, the next important moment consisted of the visit to the parents' tombs (Song 2004).[8] We stopped at a funeral shop on the way to the cemetery. The older sister bought a miniature flower crown to decorate the mother's plaque. When walking up the main alley, the first brother pointed at the traditional tombs, explaining that the mother had been cremated and not buried. After a few minutes spent searching for the way to the columbarium, the older sister found the plaque, removed an old yellow fabric flower crown, and wept calmly: "Mom, your youngest daughter, [Sarah's Korean name], has come back." Sarah knelt down next to her. This moment constitutes an important sequence in the flashback mentioned earlier. After a few minutes of devotion, the older sister said: "Let's go." Everybody left the hall and crossed a yard where plastic tables and chairs were scattered around a kind of tower partially covered with fake flowers. We then went inside a covered rectangular marble hall with one side exposed to the yard. A low marble platform alongside the three walls of the room allowed several families to perform *chesa* (ritual for the ancestors) for the dead on celebration days. For this purpose, traditional tombs often feature a small table and vases allowing visitors to burn incense in front, whereas columbarium plaques have no private space. At the entrance to the hall, a box held several rolled-up bamboo rugs. The first brother explained that people used them to bow and kneel in front of their ancestors' portraits. The older sister had brought ritual food: dried fish, dried fruit, pear, melons, and rice liquor. She had also brought the ceremonial wooden dishes, incense, and candles. The second brother asked what Sarah's religion was. She was Protestant, the same as the second brother, the only other Protestant in the family. As a result, the two of them could not kneel and bow three times like the others but instead had to stand and incline their forehead three times in front of their mother's picture. Both did so before the camera, with the silent approval of the others. Then the older sister performed *chesa*, as did her husband and two other brothers soon thereafter.[9]

The visit to the tomb is, like the celebration of *Ch'usŏk*,[10] an occasion to both worship the dead and include the little sister in the family's ritual life and reunite her with her deceased mother. Although Korean Protestants should not, in theory, worship the dead in the traditional Confucian way, in reality the practices prove to be flexible and consist of performing a different bow. The short filmed sequences of Sarah kneeling before the shrine and bowing toward her mother's picture will be selected for the flashback on the following *Ach'im madang* broadcast.[11] One immediately notices that the mother's tomb is visited first. This choice seems motivated by practical reasons, since dinner takes place in the same location, but also by the presence of the cameraman: the focus of the program is on mothers, and, as we will see, the father's tomb is not presentable. Physical and discursive contact between mother and children is emphasized onstage as well as offstage: the older sister plays the role of the intermediary in communication between the mother and her lost daughter.

The third important moment occurred when everybody gathered and shared a meal at the home of one of the siblings. The invitation to a private house is an honor, a sign of intimacy or integration. As we were approaching their vehicle, the second and third sisters, who had been preparing dinner, called the older sister to ask what Sarah would like to eat. Grilled fish (*ku-i*), sautéed noodles and vegetable (*chapch'ae*), and marinated beef (*pulgogi*) were requested. When we arrived at the second sister's apartment, everything was almost ready. We all sat down on the floor to await the final preparations. The place was quite small and modest. A big fan stood in a corner of what appeared to be the couple's bedroom. A glamorous wedding picture hanging on the wall made me realize that the second sister's husband was absent.

In spite of repeated invitations to join the group, the cameraman stayed in the kitchen during the whole dinner and ate by himself, served by the friendly housewife. The two daughters of the house, around four and six years old, also did not participate in the reunion. The reunion celebrated mainly the mother-daughter and sibling relationship. One of the brothers told me that the siblings had all come this morning by car from different neighborhoods of Seoul. Two of them lived in Sihŭng, where all had been born; two lived in Ilsan; and the others lived closer to central Seoul. We looked at a map of the city that Sarah had brought with her. The brother continued to talk, now in a more confidential tone: he explained that in the past, people had no means of contraception and consequently had many children, sometimes too many.

The interpreter arrived with the adoptive parents, who were somewhat dressed up but who sat on the floor like everybody else. They found a big pillow next to the closet and used it as a banquette. When the Koreans showed them the flat cushions they should have used instead, they answered that they were very comfortable. Dinner then started. The food was simple but very good. The ordinary cheap rice alcohol (*soju*) was replaced by a better-quality and more expensive alcohol, according to the interpreter. Everybody drank a toast to the family with enthusiasm. At this moment, the cameraman came out of the kitchen to take shots of the end of the meal. Before the camera, the adoptive parents spoke first, with simplicity: "We are happy that Sarah has found her family, that's all!" Sarah's declaration was almost the same. I translated the French to English, and the interpreter translated it to Korean for the cameraman.

One of the brothers showed his ID card to Sarah and me and indicated that the first ID numbers on it represented the person's birth date. He explained that this number could provide computerized information, such as former addresses declared to the police at each move or relocation. This way, it would be easy to find their first address, where Sarah was born. He wrote down the names and birth dates of all the family members, arranged by age, and gave the paper to Sarah.

The banquet sequence, which is always conveyed in the flashbacks on *Ach'im madang*, is usually used to constitute the good conclusion and leads to the happy end. Hence, the cameraman intervened only at the end of much eating and drinking to collect optimistic declarations. The dinner was a real feast organized by the Korean siblings to make the most of their sister's short stay. As expected, the flashbacks successively showed the tearful first meeting, the solemn devotion to the family dead, the joyful meal, and the enthusiastic conclusion or happy ending. Spending time together, visiting family tombs together, and eating and drinking together are the essential aspects of any Korean family reunion. The cameraman's role ended here.

Before leaving, Sarah and her siblings discussed the schedule for the following day, which was a Friday. She had to leave Korea on Saturday, and the oldest sister complained more than once that they did not have enough time. The interpreter announced that he had to work on Friday morning to prepare the next *Ach'im madang* with some foreign adoptees and the scenario writer. I promised I would spend Friday afternoon with them as I had language courses in the morning. We left, and I was told to join them after 2:00 p.m. on Friday, at Seoul University Hospital for the DNA test provided by KBS.[12]

That day, I took a cab from the language institute and arrived around 2:00 p.m. at Seoul University Hospital. I entered the forensic medicine building (*pŏbŭihak*), and Sarah arrived a few minutes later, surrounded by all her siblings. Sarah and her older sister got their blood drawn. Then we all left the building, and one brother went to get the car. While we were waiting, the older sister started to make mysterious phone calls. One brother told me that she was trying to locate the other little sister, who, like Sarah, had been taken to the orphanage after she was born. Finding Sarah had obviously triggered this search. After several phone calls, the older sister closed her cell phone, her face altered by emotion. She announced in a strangled voice, "Our youngest sister has been adopted in the United States, in Ohio! What incredible moments we're living!" Sarah remained silent: she was not the last child, as she had thought until that moment. She looked troubled. The car arrived, and we left for Sihŭng. It was hot in the car; everyone was tired, and no one talked much during the ride.[13]

Although the DNA test is the moment that confirms the parties' blood ties, it is never shown on *Ach'im madang*. The so-called reality show seems to reject the only empirical "moment of truth" as unimportant, irrelevant. In fact, while it is relevant to science, the DNA test holds no evocative or emotional power for the public. Unlike the DNA test, the discovery of the adoption of the youngest sister in the United States did attract the attention of the show's producers. The following Wednesday, the hostess would ask for more details from the interpreter.[14]

To complete the puzzle of the past, Sarah decided to go back to Sihŭng, where they had all first lived and where she had been born. After we walked up a very steep street, the first brother distributed cans of plum juice (*maeshil*) and started recounting: "This street paved in concrete was then just dirt. After the war, we were very poor and we ate a kind of gruel [*milkaru*] made of wheat flour mixed with water. On the other side of this hill, where you now see huge apartment buildings under construction, was an American military base. Soldiers would throw chocolate bars and sometimes cans of beer that we drank until our heads spun. At that time, we did not know this type of food. Oh, an old house is still standing there." The house he was pointing at indeed looked to be decrepit. The older sister declared, "We actually lived in that house." One brother expressed surprise, which irritated her. Then she added, "I, I know for I am the oldest!" The white walls of the house looked fragile, but the roof was made of new tiles. The older sister continued: the first house had had a wooden roof and consisted of two rooms. The whole family lived in one room and rented out the other [*hasuk*] to make a little extra money. They moved several times. Sarah asked if they remembered their mother's pregnancy, the delivery and her birth, or any other details of that time. The oldest remembered, but the others had been too young. The older sister had been twenty-two at the time. Everyone admitted that neither of the parents ever spoke about their two last daughters, whom they gave to the midwife to be taken to an orphanage right after their births. While we were walking down the street, the older sister indicated Sarah with a motion of her chin: "She went down this same slope the day she left us." Going back to Sarah's birthplace later that afternoon was the occasion for all the siblings to reminisce about their common childhood with nostalgia. Postwar poverty and the American military presence seemed to compose the most vivid memories. The designation of the surviving old house where they had supposedly lived indicates the desire to fix memory and imagination in solid objects, within a landscape where everything else has changed: these are the same houses, streets, and poor people, they insist. In the absence of parents, the elders share and transmit some of their memories to the youngest.

The father's tomb was in this neighborhood. The second brother warned us, "Well, the tomb is old and messy, sorry." The father's tomb showed the worst neglect. Like several neighboring burials, the earthen mound was cracked, without grass, and lightly secured by netting made of cheap red thread. We had climbed many small platforms displaying perfectly kept tombs in order to find it. There was no path, and the high weeds all around appeared to have never been cut. While slowly ascending the hill, the older sister gathered raspberries and momentarily forgot the purpose of the excursion. This time she had brought less: a dry fish, a pear, a melon, and a bottle of *soju* with plastic cups. She had also brought a garish beach mattress with the cartoon characters Tweety Bird and Sylvester on it. One brother lit a cigarette and placed it on a pebble next to the tomb, "because the deceased liked to smoke." Sarah knelt down this time, because the edge of the platform was so close it could have been dangerous to stand there. The older sister asked who among her brothers would perform *chesa* first. Nobody wanted to start. One looked down at his shoes, and the other smiled vaguely. The older sister got impatient: "Come on, we must do it! Who will start?" Against their will, the brothers carried out the order: it was hot; they had to take their shoes off. I realized that one brother had stayed behind on the road next to the car. I could see him making phone calls to entertain himself. The siblings took a few photos before leaving the tomb. From the elevated setting, we had a view of the surrounding fields and woods. At the edge of the woods was a dog farm, as evidenced by the incessant barking. Old shanties surrounded by wires sheltered poultry. "Forgotten ambience of the countryside . . . it hasn't changed a bit!" said the second brother, visibly amused. But when we left the place, he started singing a sad melody in the back of the car. As we were waiting for the interpreter at Kaebong train station, he confided to me, "Going back to our home was kind of depressing [*uulhada*]."[15]

The interpreter came out of the train station and got in the van. The siblings had asked me to stay for the last dinner, "to do things properly." We were still driving; the rush hour traffic was heavy. We stopped to pick up a young man: the youngest son of the older sister. After greeting everybody, he remained silent. We arrived at the barbecue (*kalbi*) restaurant that used to be the deceased mother's favorite. They all ate there often. I was told to sit next to the older sister and in front of the first brother. The son took a seat in front of his mother. Sarah's boyfriend was entertaining the siblings by eating a handful of hot peppers. The older sister suddenly addressed the waitress, proudly sharing the family story: "This is our little sister who comes from Switzerland; she went on *Ach'im madang*. . . . She does not speak Korean at all. . . . [W]e're having a party." The waitress was attentive and answered politely, "Congratulations . . . she's a beauty!" At the end of the meal, the oldest sister tried desperately to prolong the event with karaoke (*noraebang*), but the other family members decided to put an end to the day, and the older sister reluctantly called a cab. They all decided to meet at 10:00 a.m. the next day at the Inchon airport. Sarah promised her siblings she would always think of them even if she did not write often. They nodded. The older sister, however, would count on her older daughter to communicate with Sarah in English. She said that the next time Sarah visited Korea, her older daughter would come and act as the interpreter for the family. Sarah could then stay longer in each family member's house.[16]

Because she was of the same generation as her Korean relatives, Sarah's status was not problematic. She had a job, a boyfriend, and a well-off family and would never depend on her siblings. She told me before we separated that she was quite happy to go home, felt tired, and did not have any special desires for continued contact now that she had satisfied her curiosity. Except for the pendant, she received no money or other compensation from the family. She was not asked for forgiveness either. Her siblings did not feel responsible for their separation and consequently did not feel that they owed her anything. Unlike Mark and many other adoptees who only meet with one parent or a replacement relative, Sarah could contemplate the idea of visiting and keeping in touch with her siblings. Obviously, the latter expected her to visit again. No one showed embarrassment during the parting, but only joyful anticipation.

* * *

The authentic reconstitution of a family was illustrated on *Ach'im madang* by the previously mentioned case of the young adoptee from Germany who came with her adoptive parents and was reunited onstage with her birth father and birth mother, plus two older sisters. After the tearful meeting, the Korean couple was still crying, not able to say a word. The hosts seemed to respect their sorrow. At this moment, the birth mother started to explain that sending the child for adoption had been accidental. The two older sisters presented gifts to the guests from Germany: two necklaces they placed around the adoptive parents' necks and a traditional outfit (*hanbok*) for the little sister. The latter opened the gift box, and everybody was enthralled at the shiny colors of the fabric inside. As the camera zoomed in, the host addressed the adoptee: "Try it! Do you like it?" He thanked the interpreter, and the reunited family left the stage.[17]

Importantly, the meeting of both birth and adoptive parents signals a reciprocal recognition. There are seemingly no economic or marital obstacles to the maintenance of the ties: the German couple is described by the hosts as successful and handsome, and the Korean couple as respectable.[18] Besides, according to the parents' explanation, the separation occurred against their will, and the complete family assures stability to the status of the child who was found.

Similar situations are sometimes related in search ads sent by birth parents on the Internet, or in adoptee association bulletins like this one, found at Global Overseas Adoptees' Link (GOA'L): "Her birth mother was pregnant in her teens. . . . [H]er mother and father married and are still living together and they really regret losing their baby and have felt guilty. . . . Mother is trying to visit the Netherlands (where she was adopted), if she can find any clue there."[19]

The birth parents' marriage is a strong basis for the maintenance of the parent-child tie that was severed. Yet the relatedness created will be the product of compromise and efforts on both sides. The lack of a common language, among other factors, will create complications and cultural mishaps.

* * *

In 1999, as we have seen, I met my birth mother through the Holt agency, but not my birth father, who had passed away. My parents had married and then divorced, which was the cause of our separation. After I met with them, both my birth mother and my father's sister cried, asked for forgiveness, explained the circumstances of our separation, and told me about all the members of the family. I visited the tombs of both sides' grandfathers, attended both sides' banquets, and received both sides' money and presents.

Longer stays with my family in the following years enabled me to gain a long-term perspective, and I saw that the role of my deceased father had been assumed by my father's sister and her husband. They hosted me in their modest house whenever I visited Korea; my paternal aunt nursed me when I fell sick, cooked for me, and lent me money to rent a studio in Seoul. On the other side, my mother, who never remarried, lives in her mother's house, with her sister, her sister's husband, and their three children. She is replaced in her parental, nurturing role by my mother's sister and her husband. My mother's sister's husband is the one who talks when we have welcome or farewell dinners in restaurants. He also gives the toast. It is always my mother's sister and her husband who treat us at the restaurant, and my mother always gratefully stresses that fact to me. In 1999 and 2000, the tie was first maintained with my paternal aunt through letters in Korean, and then through phone calls with both my paternal aunt and my mother. Each time I return to Korea, I spontaneously visit both sides of my family and participate in family celebrations. They ask about my life, my adoptive family's health, my activities, and my projects. They lend me a cell phone and call me regularly. I feel that they care for me; my presence is not imbued with secrecy, lies, or shame.

In this example, my mother's economic concerns or marital situation—married, divorced, and not remarried—do not prevent a legitimate mother-daughter tie. That said, this first statement does not give any indication as to the quality of this tie. Writing about new kinship forms including adoptees and birth parents reuniting, anthropologist Janet Carsten mentions

> the close-up, experiential dimension of kinship that too often is excluded from anthropological accounts. This lived experience often seems too mundane or too obvious to be worthy of close scrutiny. [It is] clear that kinship is far from being simply a realm of the "given" as opposed to the "made." It is, among other things, an area of life in which people invest their emotions, their creative energy, and their new imaginings. These of course can take both benevolent and destructive forms. The idea that kinship involves not just rights, rules, and obligations but is also a realm of new possibilities is apparent.... I take it as fundamental that creativity is not only central to kinship conceived in its broadest sense, but that for most people kinship constitutes one of the most important arenas for their creative energy.[20]

The kinship configurations of each birth family, and especially the status of birth mothers, determine if ongoing relationships are possible or not. The examples from *Ach'im madang* and firsthand fieldwork experience show that these configurations can take any of a finite number of forms and can be summarized and schematized by order of completeness. Case examinations reveal that sociological causes seem more relevant than economic and psychological ones. In other words, societal pressure and unfavorable configurations in the birth parents' social life condemn the relationship no matter how wealthy or willing to bond birth parents may be. Contrary to psychological and economic factors, sociological factors are in most cases sine qua non factors: favorable sociological factors are the necessary condition that allows ongoing relationships in the first place. Yet they are not sufficient either. Giving sociological factors too much credit for the continuance of the reconstituted ties would reveal a deterministic view on people's ways of handling the blood tie, that is, what they consider as normal kinship.

My ongoing relationship with my birth family, from 1999 to the present, provides insights into the types of family that favorable conditions may allow, years after the initial meetings. Even when ties are possible, they may cease, and when they are maintained, the seeming success of the first meeting is the result of continuous negotiations dependent on the parties' fluctuating and ambivalent feelings toward one another. These feelings, in turn, vary over the years as the protagonists' social and marital statuses change.

8

Evolving Relationship with my Birth Family

You are like my daughter. You see, the word "niece" [*chok'a ttal*] includes the word "daughter" [*ttal*] in Korean.
—My paternal aunt, 1999

Once you are married and you have a job, you will help your mother. Now, your job is to study and finish your dissertation.
—My paternal aunt, 2003

I am not doing well financially right now.... I am sorry we have met only once this past year even though you live in Korea. But, now that you are married, I am not worried about you.
—My paternal aunt's son, 2011

Paternal Side

Almost two hours after I departed from Seoul with the fifty-something Korean women who were introduced to me as my mother and paternal aunt, we arrived in Inchon. We decided that I would first go to my paternal aunt's house. My mother dropped my maternal aunt and me off in a narrow alley that could not fit two cars side by side. My mother's car disappeared as soon as we slammed the door. I discovered my aunt's house for the first time with much curiosity. Later, I would realize that this modest, tidy, and pious interior featuring posters of the Last Supper and a crucifix was the perfect reflection of the lady of the house.

My paternal aunt welcomed me with open arms in 1999. I occupied the tiny bedroom of their son, who was then serving in the army. She and her husband made the exceptional gesture of taking days off from work to take me to the seashore. She also made time to take me to several places in Seoul and Inchon favored by tourists, including a Catholic church where she had been married long ago. She always had a Korean-English dictionary on hand to ease our early conversations. After our first meeting, I went back to

France, and she started writing me letters regularly. Korean friends helped translate them at the beginning. In her letters, she mentioned that she had lost a seven-year-old daughter to heart failure. She explained the Korean expression "Parents do not bury their dead child in the earth but in their heart." My sudden reappearance made her extremely happy, and she considered me as her daughter. She reconstituted the paternal family tree, going from my generation to my grandparents' generation. She wrote down names and terms of address. She looked for the few remaining pictures of my father and explained that his second wife had taken most of them after they had divorced. My father and this woman had a son, but when I asked my aunt if I could meet my half brother, she said that he did not know of my existence and that contact with his mother had been severed.

My paternal aunt and I went together to the mountain where my father's ashes had been spread. The mountain was in fact in a cemetery. I did not know at that time that the Korean word *san* could mean "mountain" as well as "cemetery." I also visited my grandfather's tomb. On the head of the stone stele, my grandfather's name was carved in three Chinese characters reading from right to left (all last names and most first names derive from Chinese characters; they are read with the Korean pronunciation but are written in Chinese in official documents). On the reverse side, several additional names were carved in the same fashion: my father's as the oldest son, my two younger uncles', my paternal aunt's husband's, and one of my grandfather's younger brothers with whom my family had lost contact. Then there were my own and my sister's names, which surprised me very much. My paternal aunt was puzzled at the absence of her own name as well as that of her mother's. That my sister and I were represented on that stone moved me because it was tangible proof of our existence in Korea prior to my return.

After I settled in my cousin's room for my first visit, my paternal aunt made several phone calls, her voice filled with agitation and excitement. My interpreter friend arrived within twenty minutes. Soon after, my paternal grandmother made her appearance. She hurriedly took off her shoes and dashed toward me, bursting into tears. She grabbed my hands and started kneading them. We all sat down, and she would not stop stroking my hands and feet, claiming that the former looked like the hands of her favorite son, who had died of liver cancer in 1996. For a little while she uttered imprecations against my mother. She said that my father's sign was Horse and my mother's Dragon: the two signs were too strong to live in peace together. She grabbed my wrist and thrust an envelope containing about 100,000 won into my palm. She folded my reluctant fingers around the envelope with surprising force for a woman of her age and frail appearance.

While living with my paternal aunt in 2000 and 2001, I once told her that French people give each other presents at Christmas. She told me she knew that, but that in Korea, although people may be Christians, there is no such custom. Still, we agreed we would all go together to the midnight mass despite the cold and the snow. But I fell sick a few days before December 24. My paternal aunt nursed me, performed acupuncture on my hands, bought medication at the pharmacy, and cooked seaweed soup. I stayed in bed and slept to my heart's content. On the night of December 24, the sounds of murmuring and of the sliding door brought me out of my torpor. They were back from the mass. I did not signal my being awake, as I still wanted to rest. All of a sudden, I heard paper being crumpled and cut and excited murmurs. I began to worry; it sounded like they were wrapping gifts, but I had nothing for them. When I finally came out, I tried to explain why I had no gifts on Christmas Eve. But they looked neither disappointed nor surprised; rather, they seemed proud of themselves. During the eight months I stayed at my paternal aunt's house, she and her family categorically refused any money from me, although I wanted to contribute to the household finances. In the following years, they even disapproved of my settling in Seoul, where I paid a high rent to live in lesser conditions, and reproached me for being too busy to come visit them often. In 2003, I occupied a tiny room with no air conditioner in a modest boardinghouse. I shared the bathroom with five other students and took breakfasts and dinners from the lady of the house, who cooked for us as part of the arrangement. One day I was ill, and my paternal aunt came all the way from Inchon to see if I needed anything. When she arrived, she saw my room for the first time. She sat on the bed, at my feet. I could see her face clouding over with sadness. "I am sorry I cannot pay a nice room for you.... This sounds really too expensive for what it is."

* * *

My paternal grandmother is perceived in her family as an extremely impulsive and independent person with no patience. Whereas many older people decide to live with one of their children if they have the chance, she endeavored to live by herself in a tiny rented room until 2008. There was just enough room for a mattress at night and a low cabinet, a small television, a crucifix, and a little statue of the Virgin Mary in front of which she prayed assiduously several times a day. My aunt told me that she went to the mass every morning at six o'clock to pray about various family matters, such as my return to Korea.

In 1999, at the end of the summer, I returned to France. When I came back to Korea a year later, I asked my paternal aunt if we could revisit my paternal grandfather's tomb, where I had seen the family members' names, including my sister's and mine, carved in the stone. The year I had met my birth family for the first time, my paternal aunt had taken pictures of the tomb and given them to me. But I wanted to see it again and ask questions. My request made her uneasy.

She declared, "The tomb does not exist anymore!"

"Why, what do you mean?"

"Because of your paternal grandmother: first, your father died, then, your first uncle died. So, your grandmother thought our family was struck by misfortune. Against our will, she decided on her own to eliminate the tomb, to burn the remains and spread the ashes in nature. Your second uncle and I were opposed to it, but she is the one who decides."

The disappearance of the stone filled me with consternation; my ties to Korea were fragile after all. What I thought was strong and would last forever had simply vanished on my grandmother's whim. But was it a whim? In fact, the inauspicious dead are usually cremated. Looking back, I think that my return had changed her relationship to the dead. I will address this idea in the last chapter.

Toward the end of my visit in 2003, with only two days left before I returned to France, my paternal family had celebrated my departure as usual: we had gone to a good restaurant, eaten well, and drunk alcohol. They wished me a good trip home and asked me to send them news regularly. My aunt had checked to see whether my address in France was still the same and asked me to call her instead of writing, now that I could speak Korean well. We walked to her house to eat watermelon and drink iced coffee. My paternal grandmother, my paternal aunt, and I arrived first. The men were behind us, taking their time. Once in the living room, my paternal grandmother and aunt sat down, and I went to my bedroom to take a nap. When I woke up, everybody was there, eating watermelon, except my paternal grandmother. "Where is she?" I asked. My paternal aunt looked a bit embarrassed but explained, "As you were sleeping and the others were not coming, she got impatient and decided to leave. You know how she is!" "But," I asked, "isn't it the last time I can see her?" My aunt responded, "Yes, I know. . . . Are you pissed off?" I remained silent and thought how quickly my going back and forth to and from Korea had become ordinary to all of us.

* * *

In 2004, expecting my boyfriend to visit, I decided to settle myself more comfortably. As soon as I arrived in Seoul, I found a furnished studio on the top floor of a four-story building. The rental system in South Korea is problematic: either the tenant pays an entire year's rent at once (200,000 won per month), or the tenant pays a substantial deposit at the beginning and owes a higher monthly rent (300,000 won per month) than if he or she had paid all at once. Because I had no savings, I had to choose the second option. But the problem, which I understood too late, was that I did not have enough money for the deposit. I asked the wealthy landlord to wait a day and called my paternal aunt, who agreed to advance me the money. Later, I reimbursed her every month; we would count bundles of 10,000-won bills each weekend I came to Inchon. She kept repeating that she was happy to lend me a hand, but that I had been a bit careless in accepting that studio without checking to see if equivalent studios were available at a lower price. She did not trust the rich landlord, who might have taken advantage of my status as a foreigner. But when she investigated through acquaintances, she realized that the price was typical. Contrary to my relatives on my mother's side who asked about my finances with ulterior motives—either to make sure I would not ask them for money or so that I would help my mother at some point—my relatives on the paternal side took interest in my finances for my own good. They made clear from start that they would never ask me for anything, that they could help me by lending me money, but that I would have to reimburse them. We had real exchanges.

* * *

My paternal grandmother had health issues in 2004—she had sprained her left ankle but could not stand the cast and threatened every day to take it off. Temporarily, she had capitulated and agreed to live with her youngest son and his wife, who is a nurse. The couple had gone into debt to buy a brand-new apartment. It was spacious, well lit, and comfortable, with a guest room where the old woman could be alone if she wanted to be. But cohabitation was still difficult. One weekend, I had come to Inchon to visit my paternal aunt, and I accompanied my grandmother, my paternal aunt, my paternal uncle, and his wife to the hospital where my grandmother had an appointment. The visit lasted for an entire afternoon. I was in the car with my uncle. My aunt had gone with her mother to see the doctor. It was hot and humid. I started expressing my boredom by sighing out loud, which made my uncle and his wife laugh. I just could not stand being in the car any longer, so I got out and sat alone in a little square. After a moment, I saw my aunt and uncle helping my grandmother into the car. As I got up and approached the car, I noticed that they were having a discussion with an old woman I had never seen before; I was told she was my grandmother's friend. I greeted her, got in, and slammed the door. We were about to leave when suddenly my aunt shouted, "By the way, Grandma,[1] look at her, this is Woo-Jung!" Then my aunt turned toward me: "Woo-Jung-a, you know you have a scar on your cheek, right? Well, you were with this grandma when you were hit by a stone on your right cheek. She remembers very well; she took you to the hospital." The old lady was in shock, wide-eyed and open-mouthed in disbelief. She stared at me without a word through the open window. Her eyes filled up with tears, and she grabbed my hand by the open window. I would have stayed longer with her, but the car had already started. We left her behind, standing alone on the pavement. There was a roar of laughter in the car, as if after a good joke. After five years of close contact, my return had pretty much become a triviality.

The evolution of my relationship with my paternal family can be summarized in the following way: I was accepted as a member of the family, as the daughter of my late father, favorite child and brother. Although their resources were obviously modest, my relatives were very generous, and I felt at home at my aunt's place. It was natural for me to call my aunt before I called my mother, to go to her place before going to my mother's, and to stay there longer as well. We exchanged gifts and talked about personal matters such as money, health, and feelings. Whenever it came time for me to leave Korea, I gave my aunt and her husband a present to thank them for their help during my frequent stays. I would also leave behind some objects I needed only when in Korea: summer shoes, umbrella, mirror, Korean language handbooks, dictionaries, and so on. In other words, each time I returned to Korea, a comfortable routine set in within my paternal family. It was not the case with my maternal family.

Maternal Side

During the summer of 1999, my return was also celebrated on the maternal side. My mother was the oldest child, followed by an uncle, an aunt, and another uncle. All were married with children, except for my mother. My maternal grandmother told my interpreter friend to inform me that all of her children were very smart: her second child, my first uncle, had graduated with a degree in law from the prestigious and free Seoul University. He had become a lawyer. Her last child, my second uncle, had graduated from Koryŏ University and had a good office job. My mother and my aunt, her first and third children, did not go to college because they were girls and the family was poor at the time. My aunt, however, was accepted at the expensive Yŏnsei University. My grandmother is most proud of her oldest son, as illustrated by a framed picture in the living room, where he appears in a black gown on the day of his graduation, surrounded by his parents and siblings.

I got to meet my first uncle a few days later. My mother took me to his office at the law firm where he worked. They talked together for a little while before we went to his apartment, where his wife and fourteen-year-old daughter were waiting for us. He repeated several times that I was a very smart child and he was not surprised I was engaged in long studies. I felt flattered by this comment and proudly connected to the most intellectual members of my Korean birth family. In fact, my uncle was speaking like the head of the family: he apologized for the family's wrongdoing in the past and gave me money, CDs of classical music, and a book on law he had written. While we were having lunch together, I thought they represented the ideal Korean family: composed, educated, successful, and happy. But I saw my uncle again that summer in a completely different state: in a tank top, drunk, at a table covered by several empty beer cans. His wife and daughter looked embarrassed and resigned, no longer bothering to oppose his sudden tantrums. I could see that although he was as thin as a rail, he stubbornly refused any food. He had a severe case of diabetes. The first time, he had clearly spoken in the name of the family as the oldest male relative, instead of my mother. After that discourse, he no longer cared about his appearance, and I met him rarely.

That first summer, my second uncle, his wife, his son, and his daughter visited me at my maternal grandmother's home. They brought me several presents as well as a big picture album in which they had already placed old and new pictures of my maternal family. My uncle had created a family tree on his computer, starting from my sister and me, which indicated birth dates according to solar and lunar calendars and the names and professions of all the members of my mother's family. At the top of the page, he had written his name and e-mail address, in case I needed anything. He spoke enough English to make our conversation possible.

One morning in October 2000, as I was sleeping in my mother's bedroom—she always gave me her room and moved to the couch when I came over for the weekend—I woke up to the noise of running steps, hushed voices, rustling paper, and clinking plates. I opened the door in my pajamas and found myself in the midst of a bustling room. Everyone was there, dressed up and awake since early morning, busily preparing the ancestors' rituals: it was *Ch'usŏk*. Nobody had bothered to warn me or wake me up. I got ready as fast as I could in order to participate in the event. My mother lamented that I had not brought my Korean *hanbok*. All my young cousins observed me. Despite my self-consciousness, I was told I was the eldest grandchild in this household and, as such, I had to set an example. At the last minute, my second uncle taught me how to bow three times in front of the altar covered with half-peeled fruit, dried fish, cookies, and incense. There was an empty wooden bowl, which I had to fill three times with water from a kettle. The children bowed after me, then the adults—men and women separately.

We left afterward for the cemetery. On the way to the tomb of my maternal grandfather, my second uncle taught me how to recognize the different religions indicated on tombs, which all had the shape of grassy mounds. In front of most tombs stood a low stone table for offerings and stone vases for incense. Behind these typically stood a stone stele displaying a cross; these crosses were of varying shapes: a simple Latin cross for Protestants, an ornate Latin cross for Catholics, and swastikas for Buddhists. We bought flowers on our way to the tomb, but the ritual was conducted in a simpler fashion at the cemetery than at home. My then-limited knowledge of Korean barely allowed me to ask any questions. My uncle found my interest in the family's tomb strange. He said, with a smile, that I should not be so concerned: I would be buried in France anyway, because that was my country. So, I suppose I was more or less excluded from all funerary concerns. I felt disappointed by his answer at the time.

I spent a semester of Korean language school living in a dormitory adjacent to the institute in Seoul, visiting my paternal and maternal families only on weekends. I alternated nights between my paternal aunt's house and my maternal grandmother's house. At the end of that semester, I accepted my paternal aunt's invitation to occupy my cousin's room while he was serving in the army. I decided to compensate for my choice of residency by visiting my maternal grandmother's house every weekend. During the first summer, I had already felt that my maternal relatives suspected I had a preference for my paternal aunt's house. To make them feel better, I mentioned that my paternal aunt's house was equipped with air-conditioning, whereas my maternal grandmother's house was not. But my relationship with my paternal aunt was much easier because she felt less guilt than my mother. As soon as I had a firm enough command of vocabulary and grammar, I had real conversations with her. During the year between our first encounter and my 2000 return to Korea, it was she who had replied to my clumsy letters in Korean. My mother had just sent a laconic card at Christmas thanking me for my gifts.

During the eight months I spent with my paternal aunt, learning Korean in Seoul at the language school, I visited my mother regularly. Each time, I met with an invisible wall, heavy silences, and contradictory attitudes. After several visits that were unsuccessful due to my failure to contact my maternal grandmother's home in advance, I started calling my mother on her cell phone to ask if she wanted to see me on weekends. She always told me to join her for dinner with my maternal grandmother, my maternal aunt, and her children. But I always found the house empty when I arrived. I knew her job kept her working late at night, but after several failed attempts to visit her, I started wondering whether the house was simply empty or whether it had been deserted on purpose. Sometimes, my fifteen-year-old cousin would be surprised to find me waiting on the couch in the living room and would apologize. Sometimes, my maternal grandmother coming back from the sauna or from a visit with friends would find me there and would mumble an apologetic "*Aigu!*" Sometimes, my maternal aunt would come up from the first floor where she lived with her family and ask me where my mother was, as if I knew. Irritated, I always explained that I had called and that my mother had told me to come that evening to eat with them. Then they would try to call her on her cell phone, only to get voicemail, and hang up with an annoyed expression. Once, as I was just arriving from France and paying them a visit, my maternal aunt addressed me in a murmur: "Why do you keep coming back to Korea?" I was surprised and hurt by her question and, pretending to be simply pragmatic, told her that I had to come back for my studies. She just smiled. In fact, looking back, my tenacious attitude toward my maternal family may have been dictated by the precepts of my field: after all, anthropologists always boast of their ability to get close to their host families, informants, and strangers in general. The only difference is that when strangers and informants are hostile or unwilling to cooperate and sympathize, anthropologists move on and try their luck elsewhere. Here, because of the sense that we ought to have a relationship, I persisted. At that time, the challenge of getting to know my relatives was inseparable from the challenge of embracing Korean society as my chosen topic. In other words, my opting for social anthropology and my actively learning the language were probably the conditions of possibility of our relationship after the first meeting that assessed our relatedness. That commitment on my part was clearly encouraged by my paternal family but not by my maternal family, who at first found it strange and inopportune.

Often, the younger cousins, around five and seven years old then, would walk through the living room in front of me, avoiding eye contact and taking big steps. Instead of playing in the common area, they would take refuge in my maternal grandmother's bedroom and come back to pick up their toys and books. Adults had told them to show respect by bowing in front of me, and the girls were to call me Woo-Jung-*ŏnni* and the boy, Woo-Jung-*nuna*. My youngest cousin, the boy, would dash off a brief bow without breaking stride; it was at the same time heartbreaking and amusing to watch. Once, he and his sister asked a question in a low voice to their mother about my identity and my presence there. She told them I was their aunt's daughter, which was very surprising to them. How could this solitary, blunt, and unpredictable person ever have had children?

Sometimes, embarrassed to serve me an ordinary meal out of Tupperware boxes stored in the refrigerator, my maternal aunt would decide to push her family to the restaurant next door. This often led to muffled arguments with my maternal grandmother, who obviously did not approve of the expense. My maternal aunt clearly felt obligated to take me out for dinner as a result of my mother's absence. Usually, what followed was a lengthy meal with my aunt, her husband, her children, and sometimes my grandmother, often characterized by painful silences. My aunt's husband would try to animate a conversation by asking me, in broken English, the same questions over and over: "How old are you now? When are you planning on getting married? When are you finishing your studies? You should think of making money now." Several times, my maternal grandmother attempted to tell me something with a worried look on her face. I did not understand what she was saying until my fifteen-year-old cousin scrupulously translated in English, in a soft voice: "Your grandmother says that your mother is unhappy, very unhappy, that life is hard on her."

One Sunday evening in 2004, my mother was driving me back to my paternal aunt's house after I had visited her. Staring expressionlessly at the road before her, she suddenly addressed me in a hoarse voice: "I am not a pleasant person because I have no money; when I see you, it puts me in a bad mood because I cannot give you anything." This short conversation confirmed that my presence could be experienced by my Korean relatives as a burden and could lead to a rupture in the long term, unless my own status changed to something other than a child to whom everybody felt they owed something. This feeling did not prevent my mother from showing her affection in a clumsy manner at the most unexpected moments: one stifling summer night, back from work, she dashed into her bedroom where I was sleeping, to tuck me into my bed. After she dashed off, I could not help giggling in the dark.

As a result, I never told my mother about my temporary financial issues. I knew she had her own worries. One day, my paternal aunt revealed that she had lent money to my mother but was never reimbursed. When I expressed my disapproval, she sighed and said that it was a gift. It was also my paternal aunt who lifted the veil of mystery surrounding my mother's recurrent absences late at night. In 2004, I asked my paternal aunt if my mother had a boyfriend. She was shocked that I had offered such a hypothesis and told me, after first extracting a promise of secrecy, that my mother had worked since 1999 in a car insurance company. The company had been struggling since the economic crisis of 1997, so my mother had taken another job to supplement her income: she drove her car at night around the bars, looking for inebriated customers unable to drive home. She did not want me to know because the job sounded scandalous. That, at least, was my aunt's explanation.

The exchange of gifts with my maternal relatives was uneasy, which contrasted with the carefree generosity and constant giving and receiving on my paternal side. In the summer of 1999, as noted earlier, I decided to keep my plans to visit some friends in Japan after I met my birth family. My relatives were a bit surprised, but they let me go. Finding a gift for each family member who had given me money was a headache. I finally gathered all the gifts in two craft bags that I left in a locker at the Osaka train station while I went off to do other things. But I had such a hard time finding them two days later that I missed a train for Kobe, where a friend was waiting for me. I was fuming, thinking this gift exchange did not make any sense and that I had never asked for all this money in the first place. When I came back, I distributed all the little gifts, delicately wrapped. I noticed that my family members were disappointed. I had brought back from the famous Nishiki food market of Kyoto boxes of various kinds of seaweed that are rare in Korea. My relatives barely tasted them and placed the boxes quickly inside the refrigerator. I inferred that Japanese seaweed was no better than Korean seaweed and that food was a somewhat disappointing gift to receive from a person coming back from abroad. Before going to Japan, I had met my mother's godmother, whose condescension and appearance reflected her wealth. My mother had tried to talk about my multiple abilities in front of her, saying I spoke five languages, and so on. The woman replied that all her children were studying abroad. I received a large sum of money from that woman, and I concluded that I had to find her a proportionately bigger gift. I found her a pair of lacquered earrings in the craft museum of Kyoto that I would rather have given to my mother. As soon as I was back, my mother rummaged in my travel pack, searching for her godmother's gift. When I presented her with the little box, she opened it and looked satisfied, if not relieved.

Later on, adults on the maternal side, especially my mother, were in general displeased to receive my gifts. Around Christmas 2001, I used the money I had made from teaching French to buy my mother an elegant, expensive woolen jacket, which I wrapped and left on her bed one evening after I had waited for her in vain. A few weeks later, I saw the jacket on my maternal grandmother's back, mismatched with flashy pants in the sort of large pattern typically worn by the elderly. I got neither explanation nor thanks, which made me very upset. I did not say anything but simply stopped buying personal gifts for adults and opted for collective or children's gifts only.

Matrimonial Concerns

Early on, my relatives on both sides expressed strong interest in my marriage prospects and plans. During one of the first family banquets, which was organized in honor of my return in 1999, my relatives observed me from head to toe, made comments on my complexion and features, asked me many questions, and related to me in detail all the stories connected with my family members. They also gave me a lot of money—in won and in dollars—and fed me expensive meat and fish. At that moment, despite the efforts and devotion of two Korean interpreters, I had a hard time memorizing the nature of the ties that linked me to all these new relatives whose names I kept mixing up.

After my mother and my paternal aunt had brought me to Inchon and I had just settled into my aunt's home, my paternal family gathered and all went to a very good restaurant. We had been drinking high-quality alcohol for a short while. The end of dinner was approaching when my paternal grandmother suddenly started talking in a way that stopped the other conversations around us. A colleague of my interpreter friend whom I had met in Paris several times had come voluntarily to help me out that evening. He had behaved perfectly, spoken in a measured, soft voice, turned his back to the elders while drinking alcohol, and observed all the proper etiquette. After my grandmother had finished talking and was waiting for his translation, he addressed me with a laugh of embarrassment: "Your grandmother asks if we are friends. She thinks I am handsome, well bred, and I live very close by in Inchon, like your family. She adds also that she would like you to get married in one or two years." I could not believe what I was hearing. In front of me, my relatives burst out laughing, watching my reaction. I was quite embarrassed and found an exit. "What is your sign?" I asked him. "I am a Tiger." "Oh, I think I am a Horse. . . . These two signs are very strong signs, a bad combination, I believe. My mother and my father divorced because they were respectively a Horse and a Dragon." My interpreter was speechless for a second, but eventually briefly translated something to my relatives, which made them laugh and change topics. Years later, I was told that my sign was Snake, and that Horse and Tiger actually form a good combination.

Later on, when I was attending the Korean Language Institute of Yŏnsei University in Seoul, I got into the habit of telling my aunt stories about my

Korean and American friends dating and breaking up. She always listened with great interest and would offer comments in a sententious tone such as: "A pot that boils fast gets cold even faster." Or she would try to teach me a proverb: "Men are all wolves." On her side, while driving me around, my mother told me many times with a sarcastic laugh: "Your father was too handsome; from that came all the troubles.... Never choose a too-handsome man. He will have many women."

In 2004, my American boyfriend of Sri Lankan Tamil descent visited me in Korea while I was conducting my fieldwork. Besides typical tourist visits to monuments and the demilitarized zone (DMZ) between the two Koreas, and hikes in a national park on the east coast, I had planned a visit to my paternal and maternal families. The last day of his stay, I organized an outing with my mother and my paternal aunt to Wolmido, a shore area in the city of Inchon. After a long ride on the Line 1 train from Seoul, we got off at the last station and waited for a little while in front of the station building at the colorful, ornate gate that marks the entrance to the biggest Chinatown in South Korea. My mother and paternal aunt pulled up in my mother's car, and we bowed and got in. My mother and my aunt tried a few sentences in English and started to giggle. My mother asked me roughly, "Why did you decide to meet here? It is very far!" "Well," I answered, "we wanted to eat good seafood and see the sunset." She parked her car at the entrance to the sunny promenade along the sea, flanked with restaurants, coffee shops, and street vendors, with an attraction park in the background. Until then, my boyfriend had been left out of the conversation, and I turned to him to ask what he wanted to eat. "Hmm . . . some meat!" he said with an innocent smile. I translated his request with reluctance as we could have obviously had meat anywhere. We went looking for a meat restaurant marked with the Rose of Sharon signaling recommended places. We found one in a location set back from the sea. The dining area was almost empty, and we forgot the sight of the sea and the imminent sunset.

The topics of conversation revolved around my boyfriend's profession, our future marriage, and the place where we would live. My boyfriend asked my relatives if they would come to our wedding. They laughed, eyes downcast, and said while still energetically chewing the meat, "Of course, we will come . . . if you buy us the plane tickets!" My mother explained her preference for the United States, and more specifically California, as the place where we should settle down. She, like any Korean, might have heard that immigrants in Los Angeles do not even need to speak English. And maybe she had the vague hope that one day she would join us, even if she and I did not communicate much. Both my mother and my paternal aunt made comments on my boyfriend's appearance and stated that they had a very good impression. "He has big eyes and a low voice. He must be baritone," said my aunt while playing dexterously on the grill with her chopsticks, distributing the medium-rare pieces of meat. We toasted our future union with little glasses of *soju*. Toward the end of the dinner, my mother felt the need to conclude on a more solemn note. In a manly fashion, using a low tone, she addressed my boyfriend in English: "I entrust you with my daughter. I have confidence in you." We left the restaurant. My paternal aunt paid for everything. We had missed the sunset.

My mother decided to drive us to my maternal grandmother's house so that we could meet the other members of the family. Our arrival provoked an excitement I had never seen there before. My cousins came quickly, forgetting their usual timidity. Their mother, my maternal aunt, came as well, with a benevolent smile. She said in her turn that the young man who stood in front of her inspired her confidence. She added that, in certain ways, we looked alike despite our different ethnicities. My maternal grandmother greeted us with a smile and a plate of diced watermelon. She did not say much this time. But my eighteen-year-old cousin came to me later and murmured, "*ŏnni* [older sister], when are you gonna get married?" I knew that her mother was asking this question through her mouth. I answered in an aloof manner: "First of all, I finish my studies, then, we'll see what happens." "Here, in Korea, when one presents her boyfriend to her family, it means one will get married, *ŏnni*."

After that day, which was entertaining for all, I was asked the same question each time I returned to Korea. I was also exhorted not to wait too long. In 2005, I called my paternal aunt from France. She was not home, and my twenty-eight-year-old cousin picked up the phone. He asked me when I was thinking of getting married.

Changes

Familiarity between my maternal relatives and me set in at the same time I established my economic independence, affirming a social and professional status. It seems to me today that the meeting with my boyfriend at the end of my fieldwork in 2004 was the main reason for this change. That meeting and the prospect of our future marriage were the crucial elements that led to the stabilization of my status within my biological family, and consequently of my relationship with them.

In 2007, I returned to Korea to work on a new project. When I arrived, my maternal aunt, my mother, and my maternal grandmother came to Inchon International Airport. I was pleased by this warm welcome, but I also realized that my maternal grandmother was mostly motivated by her curiosity about the new airport she had seen only in the background of televised dramas. After looking for the car for half an hour (my mother had lost her parking ticket), we got in our vehicle and left for the city. There were some jokes about my growing older and becoming an "old miss," because at the age of twenty-nine I still had not married my boyfriend. I announced that we were going to get married in the summer. First, we would marry at the New York City Hall; then, we would have two weddings, one in the United States and one in France. All my relatives got extremely excited. From then on, my Korean relatives' interest in my fiancé kept growing. My maternal grandmother started praising his supposed qualities and asking whether he had any friends to introduce to my cousins, especially to the one who had fallen for a boy "with no abilities" (*nŭngryŏgi ŏmmŭn namja*). All were truly excited by our future wedding, an event for which they had been waiting for several years, and wanted to attend the event. My mother gave me money to buy two gold rings, although her economic situation had not changed. My maternal grandmother took on the project of ordering four traditional costumes for my adoptive parents and my parents-in-law. I talked her out of it, pointing to the fact that they would probably not wear them often. Several relatives said they "should" go in order to meet and thank my adoptive parents.

In fact, despite my repeated phone calls prior to our wedding in France, in the end my relatives on both sides were reluctant to come because they were not doing well financially. Each time I called, they said they had not obtained passports. I also randomly chose the weekend of *Ch'usŏk* (fall festival that involves ancestors rituals), which gave them the ultimate excuse for not attending our wedding in France. None of my Korean friends came either. If the wedding had happened the way we had imagined, three families would have been united instead of two. But for my Korean relatives, this marriage was also the "sending of a daughter to her husband's house" (*sijip ponaeda*), which would mean my acquisition of definite independence (toward them) and status, which in turn would constitute a separation more legitimate than my having been sent for international adoption. Therefore, it was possible to achieve a subsequent kind of separation that transcended the adoption one and that better normalized my relationship with my birth family.

Because of this announced formal separation, I was suddenly allowed to invite friends to my maternal grandmother's house and to present them to my cousins to possibly help them in their studies and careers. And whereas previously my gifts were not welcome, my promise to buy my mother and paternal aunt plane tickets for our wedding was received with much enthusiasm even if it did not happen.

*　*　*

My relationship with my paternal family has also shifted, along with my residential accommodations. As for me, in 2007, I noticed that my paternal aunt had aged more than my mother since 2004. I thought my mother was going to drop me off at my aunt's, but when I made a move to get out of the car, my aunt said, "No, no, Woo-Jung, go with your mother. Our house is messy these days. I will see you later!" She slammed the door and left without a smile. I was stunned.

Later, in a bar, with a preoccupied look on his face, my cousin revealed his family situation to me: his father had recently spent some time at the hospital and was no longer working. His mother was sick, and there was no real cure for this disease that made her age faster. My cousin, for his part, was struggling to find a job, as he had failed to enter the police academy for the second time. I understood why they could not welcome me anymore in their home and felt this would have an impact on my warm relationship with my aunt. In fact, we are no longer as close and I do not spend time in their home anymore. Most often, I meet my cousin in a public place such as a movie theater, a cheap restaurant, or a bar. As my elder, he used to treat me, but now we pay each in our turn so that he can keep for his own enjoyment some of the money that my aunt gives to him.

In 2010–2011, my husband and I moved to Korea after I accepted a two-year teaching position at the Hanyang University Department of Cultural Anthropology. My relatives on both sides invited us to join familial festivities for *Ch'usŏk* and the New Year holiday but because we were eager to travel throughout Asia, we went to Japan and Sri Lanka instead. They were disappointed, but I thought we would see them on regular weekends. Everyone, however, was always busy with church activities, work, or chores, and in the end we did not spend much time together. My husband and I were considered our own household, so they did not invite us outside of the welcoming or farewell meals and special holidays; they came to our home only once.

*　*　*

Koreans are relieved to hear about what I have accomplished, and my biological relatives consider me part of the family. Although this familial status seems obvious in discourses that constantly emphasize the blood ties of all Korean people, in reality it asks for continuous redefinition, which oscillates between integration and separation. My biological relatives and I were sure that we were "naturally" close and spontaneously attracted to each other, but we were also often tempted to reject this alienating bond, which frequently felt like a bond between strangers.

My fieldwork demonstrated that adoptees' relationships with Korean society and their birth families tend to fluctuate. My marriage—as a proper mode of rupture of filiation, contrary to transnational adoption—ensures a distance from my Korean family. My Korean relatives can exit the one-way debt system they entered when I was adopted abroad. My new status of fully adult daughter permits eased familial contacts and real exchanges on the maternal side, but also diminishing material dependence on the paternal side. Now, time has passed, and I have realized that I had to establish a distance, not physically but within the symbolic frame of kinship, to allow a reciprocal relationship.

Today I say that I have two families to which I relate differently. My old biological ties with my Korean relatives were broken by my adoption. As a replacement, the relatedness created by adoption has grown throughout the years in my French adoptive family. When I first met my Korean family, I felt as if my French identity, life, and relationships were threatened by my discovery of Korea. But my frequent trips to Korea and the time spent with my birth family did not reconstitute our biological ties, and I now conceive my relationship to them as a third kind of relatedness. When I was gone, my birth relatives mourned my absence, and when I returned, they asserted our biological ties while acknowledging the reality of my adoption. Now, I am a married-out daughter, which makes life much easier.[2]

In 2011, when my husband and I were still in South Korea, I announced that I was pregnant, and all my relatives were quite excited. My maternal aunt bought me a handbook on birth and babies and even gave me a lucky charm in the shape of a golden key. She also got a little wooden chair discarded by their neighbors for our future visits, she said. As we left Korea early, everyone was a bit disappointed. Before our departure my paternal aunt gave me $200 to buy anything we would need. After the birth I sent out pictures of our daughter to friends and relatives, including my Korean mother and my paternal aunt. I also sent pictures by e-mail to my paternal aunt's son and my paternal uncle's wife, who replied right away to congratulate us. A week later I was pleased to receive from my mother a package containing baby clothes and a letter. From now on, I will probably call on special occasions and send a letter with pictures of our daughter once a year. When my daughter starts asking me about Korea, I will return with her.

In the case of persons who were adopted domestically in Western countries and were able to reunite with their birth parents—mostly birth mothers—adoption and kinship scholars have found that the resulting relationships are never simple, and only a very few are sustainable for a multitude of reasons. This is the case despite the fact that both parties live in the same country and share a common culture and language, and despite the greater flexibility of kinship arrangements in Western societies than in South Korean society (Modell 1994). What can we infer from these examples regarding South Korean cases? The difficulties met by these domestic adoptees and their birth families surely exist for foreign adoptees and their Korean birth families. To these difficulties, one must add the language barrier and the cultural differences. Moreover, the family configurations are more diverse in Western societies than in South Korea, so options after the meetings of adoptees and birth parents in the former also seem more diverse than in the latter.[3] Therefore, Korean birth parents may have a stronger sense of obligations stemming from their ideas of what good Korean parents and good Korean families should be, and from what the Korean media keep emphasizing. These comparisons are worth exploring further.

For now, we will turn our attention to a question that arises naturally when watching or witnessing the meetings: What are the possible meanings of meetings that do not lead to sustained relationships?[4] Why do parents decide to meet their children even if their familial configuration is not conducive to the maintenance of these ties? Talking about success or failure may not be relevant when it comes to the long-term outcome of the meetings.

9

Management of Feelings

A man ran away after his wife's death, leaving his two daughters alone without resources. They were subsequently sent to an orphanage. To the now fifty-year-old daughter, the hostess says: "Hmm. . . . It must have been difficult for your father after your mother's death."
—KBS, *Ach'im madang*, August 13, 2003

"Transnational adoptees' common point is that they don't know the faces of the people they are searching for, but they all grew up in good conditions and feel no resentment at all."
—Host, KBS, *Ach'im madang*, July 9, 2003

Created after the 1983 telethon and produced since 1997, *Ach'im madang*, with its emphasis on meetings between estranged relatives, may in a minority of cases lead to sustained relationships, but only under certain circumstances. The marital and financial situation of birth parents must be taken into account if one hopes to understand the future of the relationships the meetings seem to restore. Thus, the question is no longer Why did people separate after meeting? but Why do birth parents decide to meet their offspring even when they know they will not be able to sustain that relationship? One may surmise parents' will to meet again with their children was stronger than social conventions, or that they did not realize that these ties were not sustainable. But, here, I suggest that there is another type of explanation to their seemingly irrational actions. Helping separated relatives to find one another and to meet properly is considered a crucial sector of social welfare in South Korea.

Hosts' and Moderator's Other Role

As elsewhere, the different stages of life have been marked in Korea by rites of passage that guide the individual on a standardized journey, providing a sense of norms.[1] Along with graduation from the summer school, the ceremony of marriage, and the coming-of-age ceremony, the meeting with one's family on television seemed to stand for yet another rite of passage for transnational adoptees: it symbolically situated the isolated individual within the realm of family and society. With roots in Korean history and politics, the televised meetings exude a meaning relevant to the nation at large—a forerunner of the reunification with North Korea and a reminder of the value of family. With a commitment to entertaining the South Korean public, the production team and the hosts may manipulate the participants and constrain them to the specific format that has ensured their popularity over the years (Bourdieu 1996). But South Korean citizens as well as transnational adoptees have motivations of their own. During the program, the hosts and the professor not only produced a collective narrative of dispersal but also gave a hand to the families they reunited, trying to influence favorably their potential bonding and future relationship. Let us return to the ritualized meeting scenes of the television show and focus on the figures of the hosts and the professor.

Representing a model of morality and social achievement, the professor—called the "moderator" by the show's production staff—is reminiscent of the master of ceremonies who presides over contemporary weddings (Kendall 1996). The term *churye* comes from the Chinese characters meaning "master" and "rites." The *churye* is a key character for the proper performance of the ancient as well as the modern rite. The future of the ties knotted at that moment depends on him.[2] The master of ceremonies who conducts a wedding must have achieved happiness and success in his own life in order to influence the newlyweds (Kendall 1996, 35–37). This implies that, in theory, virtue leads to happiness. Good relationships ensure a happy and successful life. At first glance, the regular presence of the professor at *Ach'im madang* can find an explanation in his function as the *churye* of the family meetings.

With his white hair and his benevolent smile, the professor Park Dong-kyu radiates paternal authority, erudition, and wisdom. His rank and title command respect from all.[3] Moreover, for many, he is first and foremost the son of the famous poet Mok-wol Park. When I asked a KBS cameraman what Dong-kyu Park's specialty was at Seoul University, he had to check on the Internet because he did not know precisely. But he suggested that the professor was present in the studio at each broadcast "probably because his father was a famous poet." A paragon of illustrious family, the professor sat enthroned in the midst of individuals in search of their parents. It was an implicit display of filiation and filial piety on the show. But the professor obviously lacked the performative nature that characterizes the *churye*'s discourse, which points to the limitation of the comparison between the televised meetings and rituals.[4] The words of the hosts and the professor at *Ach'im madang* did not ensure the reconstitution of families. They mostly joked around and made meaningless chatter. The professor's comments often seemed useless and without apparent relation to the unfolding action. In other words, they lightened the mood. One day the professor was absent—he had taken a vacation, explained the host—and was not replaced.[5] The following week, the host was absent but was replaced by another, younger host.[6] The host was crucial for the process of the show, and he needed to be replaced by a colleague when he went away, whereas the professor's presence was based on his prestige: he was irreplaceable. The usual association of the hosts and the professor confirms the necessity of a third party—or moderator—to facilitate, mediate, and preside over the somewhat uneasy family meetings. The meetings were less about the reconstitution of families than the reconciliation between two parties who, once, were only one. So if reconciliation is the main purpose of the meetings, resuming relationships is only optional.

Shriving Parents

As we have seen, separation stories on *Ach'im madang*, no matter how incomplete, are generally seen to be about family separation rooted in the events of the now near-mythical Korean War. Thus, they normalize the practice of separation. The hosts of the program as well as the participants always emphasize the role of the war in family separation and the role of postwar poverty in the adults' decision to "send away" children. In their narratives, the war is interpreted as the beginning of all familial disarray: "Because of the war . . . " or "After the war . . . "

But other factors were relevant when explaining separations. As mentioned earlier, the modes of separation were many; most implied a thoughtful decision precipitated by dire situations, but a few suggested a lack of consideration on the parents' part of what might happen to the children they abandoned. Participants who were able to meet their relatives onstage often heard versions of the separation story from them. The birth family always provided vague justifications to make parents look less culpable. Upon meeting onstage, a thirty-six-year-old participant was hugging her newly found relatives. While they were crying and tightly embraced, the screen displayed the following text: "Meeting after thirty-one years of separation." The participant's older sister, thirty-eight, said that thirty-one years ago they had all gone to the market with their father. She was carrying on her back her little brother, who also came to the studio. The participant was walking next to her. She must have gotten lost when their father walked away to smoke a cigarette. The older sister speculated, "She must have followed another woman she took for our mother; maybe because she was wearing the same outfit."[7] During another meeting, the older brother of a forty-eight-year-old participant was asked by the hosts what had happened. Embarrassed, he answered, "In my opinion, life was very difficult, that's why." The hosts did not ask for further explanation.[8] On another episode described earlier, the mother of a seventeen- and a twenty-year-old appeared from backstage and looked painfully at her children without embracing them; she did not say anything. Subconsciously, she started to orient her body away from the camera. She bit her lip and mumbled, "It is because of my situation. . . . I don't know what happened to their father." An awkward silence fell on the audience, hosts, and participants.[9]

* * *

These stories functioned as minimal but sufficient explanations on a show that placed every instance of family separation in the same homogeneous category. All meetings were filmed and presented as happy endings by the *Ach'im madang* production team. Parents were excused and forgiven in an implicit manner: either by the words of the mediating hosts, or by the children's proper attitude and silence in the face of embarrassing matters. The solicitous attitude of the hosts and the children's adherence to decorum demonstrated that the relatives—in general, siblings on behalf of their parents—wanted to protect the participants' guilty parents and cover any irresponsibility of the parents by invoking bad luck. There were obviously feelings of embarrassment and shame, especially when the participants remained silent and visibly uncomfortable.[10] But the words and the body language of parents suggested that they appeared onstage often *despite*, not because of, their shame—they were never compelled to do so. Those who were overwhelmed by shame did not face their child; some even called the scenario writer of *Ach'im madang* so that she could tell their child not to look for them.[11] Feelings of guilt were also openly verbalized with parents' and older siblings' frequent use of the word "forgive" (*yongsohada*) and their injunctions to the party whose fate they felt responsible for (*yongso haera*). For example, a forty-five-year-old participant met her seventy-five-year-old father, who had abandoned her and her sister after their mother had fled because he had lovers. The uneasy situation made the father grumble, "*Aigo!*[12] *Ch'am!*[13] You look exactly like your mother. . . . Forgive me!"[14] A fifty-six-year-old participant was looking for her younger siblings, who were all scattered, despite her efforts, after her parents' disappearance. She was asked by the host, "What would you like to tell your sister?" Eyes downcast, the participant turned slightly away from the camera and uttered in a strangled voice, "Forgive me, call me, I will wait."[15] A thirty-six-year-old participant met with her mother again. When the participant's relatives arrived from backstage to dramatic music, the mother, in traditional outfit (*hanbok*), ran to her with open arms and cried, "Forgive me!" "No, you don't need to ask for forgiveness!" responded the participant.[16]

In general, children or younger siblings directly expressed their forgiveness to their elders. Through media technology and the mediation of the hosts in direct meetings with the children, the meeting program relieved those who felt guilt for family separations.

Though the hosts frequently asked their guests what they felt, participants were usually reluctant to answer openly and almost invariably expressed their mixed emotions by weeping. In the case of the German adoptee who appeared in the program accompanied by her adoptive parents, the hosts insisted on their inclusion in the event. "Give the microphone to the adoptive mother [*yang ŏmŏni*]," requested the host. He asked her what she felt. She started talking but, overwhelmed by her emotions, burst into tears, provoking the tears of her daughter. The hostess commented on the scene with sympathy: "The feeling called the *chŏng*[17] is something common to everybody." In the background, an anonymous woman in the audience was weeping and patted her eyes with a handkerchief.[18] In another case, a female participant was about to meet with her long-lost relatives, but the hosts, eager to manage suspense, kept on asking her meaningless questions. "She was always wondering why her older sister and her mother were not looking for her. . . . How do you feel?" "Now, I am fine," answered the participant with impatience. She looked clearly irritated at the hosts.[19] Another female participant was too emotional to answer the hostess's questions. "What did you feel when your brother called you last time?" The participant kept her head down, bit her lip, and wiped her nose. She stepped forward to the center of the stage and sobbed even more. The hosts gave up their questions and finally allowed her to call her relatives: "Well, okay . . . because of emotions, she can't speak." They looked dejected.[20] On another broadcast, the hostess recalled: "And a moment later, we received a phone call for her. . . . How do you feel now?" Emotion prevented the participant from answering; she held back her tears. The host took over from the hostess and tried to ask the participant the same question, but to no avail. She was finally authorized to come forward and call her little brother with a quavering voice.[21] He arrived from the back door.

Feelings arising from the family meetings were often unspeakable and could only be expressed by tears. The adoptive mother, brothers, and sisters were not able to articulate answers to the hosts' questions, which gave the hostess the freedom to rhapsodize about *chŏng* in her softest tones—to discuss the supposedly "natural" attachment generated by the physical closeness of older and younger siblings, and by the adoptive filiation between the foreign mother and her Korean daughter. The *chŏng*, as we saw earlier, is a tender feeling between individuals who share kinship ties or a common life. Tears on *Ach'im madang* were always interpreted in positive terms. The converse was also true: the absence of tears in some individuals was grounds enough to question their feelings, and consequently their motivations and intentions. Bad feelings can never be spelled out on *Ach'im madang*, because the show was meant to emphasize the strength of blood ties and the perfection of family relations across time and despite separation. Yet, as seen earlier, the hosts acknowledged the potential existence of bad feelings by discussing them hypothetically and in the negative. On the occasion of the family meetings, the hosts strove to define and attribute the *chŏng* to participants while tacitly assuming that they might well harbor negative sentiments such as *wonmang* and *han*. These two sentiments are combined in the term *wonhan*, which is often given the same translation as *wonmang*: grudge, rancor, malice, spite, hatred, enmity, animosity, old scores. The term *wonmang* derives from *wonhan*, but its meaning is softer, and its regular use by the hosts on *Ach'im madang* demonstrated their concern for proper attitudes and language.[22] The hosts' recurrent question "What is your feeling now?" confirmed their assumption of hostility. After making comments on and jokes about French food, the hosts asked a French adoptee: "If your parents watch you on television, what do you want to tell them?" In front of the camera, the participant answered, "Mom, Dad . . . dear parents, brothers and sisters, I came back to Korea with a lot of expectation. If you are watching me right now, you should know that I am not angry. The decision is yours, I will wait for your call."[23] The two hosts asked another participant what she would like to tell her birth parents if they were watching her. She said, "I would love to meet them and hear about the rest of my story. . . . I have no resentment, not at all." The host asked the interpreter, "She has no resentment [*wonmang*] toward her parents?" "None," says the interpreter. "Yes, her expression is pristine [*ne, p'yojŏngi palgŭseyo*]," stated the hostess.[24] Another adoptee from the United States just wanted to say to his birth parents: "Long time no see. . . . No hard feelings, you would enjoy meeting me, be proud of me; I want to share my life with you and know about yours." He also wanted to ask them what happened and why he was in this situation today.[25] In another case, the hosts asked a female adoptee what she would like to tell her birth parents. "I have no resentment [*wonmang*], I am lucky, I met good parents," she said, still smiling.²⁶

The hosts' constant questions to Korean participants about their feelings seldom got straight answers and most of the time provoked silent tears. Interestingly, whereas Korean orphans and domestic adoptees were asked what they felt, transnational adoptees were explicitly asked whether they resented their birth parents. This suggests a conscious differentiation of the two groups. While the Korean orphans and domestic adoptees constituted an older generation marked by war and poverty, transnational adoptees were separated from their families for other reasons that may be considered "bad" ones: divorce, for example, or birth out of wedlock. International attention also contributes to the image of transnational adoptees as more victimized than their Korean peers, who at least were not separated from their birth country. As such, Korean orphans and domestic adoptees had a better understanding of their situation and of their birth families. Their familiarity with *Ach'im madang* also allowed them to behave properly and cry during the meeting scene, whereas transnational adoptees' strange smiles tended to depart from the ritualized tears. Korean participants were usually older and had generally married, whereas the transnational adoptees belonged to the vague category of youth who have not settled down. What was at stake in the television show was the management of negative and somewhat dangerous feelings between birth parents and lost children. For this reason, adoptees systematically addressed parents with encouraging and reassuring discourses to make them want to appear on the show.

Parents usually expressed their feelings by weeping, but sometimes they evoked the *han*, an oppressive feeling that mixes resentment, guilt, and powerlessness. As related in earlier chapters, motivated by his restless *han*, a father decided to call in to *Ach'im madang* after he had recognized his daughter. The repentant father said, "The fact that I did not take care of you and your sister generated the *han* in me [*hani toeŏtta*], I could not sleep in peace. I was watching *Ach'im madang* that day; I watch it every day, every day. . . . I waited for forty years for your forgiveness." From the difficult conversation only one phrase, "I am sorry," appeared onscreen, and the hosts' comments covered the father's words several times. The film ended on the daughter's painful smile while the nostalgic piano melody faded. They concluded, "She came from the United States, tense and with a beating heart, and she was able to leave in peace."²⁷

At times, birth parents said they developed the *han* because of a problematic, sad, and frustrating situation.²⁸ Understood as the result of involuntary situations and lack of power more than the result of bad deeds, the *han* does not attribute guilt (*yujoi*) or responsibility (*ch'aegim*) to parents. In this representation, parents are also victims: of a patriarchal society, of injustice, of a bad marriage, and so on.[29] Bad feelings in children as well as in parents are the result of the family separation and attenuate the opposition between the victim and the guilty.

Gladdening Children

During HISS, several participants grew resentful at the social workers' inability to locate their birth parents. As reported earlier, the most rebellious female participant expressed her frustration by performing her duties with ill will and by mocking the instructors and the activities. As we have seen, for the 2004 closing ceremony, she was selected by the organizers to write and read a short, thankful speech in the name of all the participants. A social worker explained to me that because she was an English professor, this participant was naturally regarded as someone capable of good writing and speaking in public. The participant took the request seriously and read her speech enthusiastically, addressing it to the whole Korean team of Holt Post-Adoption Services. But she was also the only one who did not wear the traditional outfit offered by Holt to all participants at the beginning of the course. Her defiant attitude, especially during the long and strenuous tea ceremony, had been observed, and measures had consequently been taken so that she showed signs of acceptance by the end of the program.

The events that took place during the cultural program for adoptees and the family meetings on television all have the shape of integration rites. The proper performance seemed to be more important than the adoptee's adherence to the spirit of the event, and that were constant complaints among the participants. There was in fact a fundamental misunderstanding between both parties: the dissatisfied adoptees would have liked some individualized moral and psychological support from the Korean staff, while the Korean staff kept offering or imposing ritualized collective actions. The same concern over the management of bad feelings seen during the televised meetings is also detectable in the cultural programs for adoptees organized by adoption agencies and the government. The task of turning hard feelings into benevolence is literally a state matter. In 1999, the booklet printed for the closing ceremony of the Holt International Summer School displayed these concluding remarks in broken English on the back page. Although the text is too clumsy to permit elaborate comments on the style, a few expressions or phrases deserve attention.

> **CONCLUDING REMARKS**
>
> Three weeks that sometimes made us to feel long but also whirled away like the current flow of water while muggy summer heat hit us during the rainy season though it didn't rain actually mostly during that period.
>
> Frankly speaking we are afraid of your loving addresses to us, wondering how many fruits on your trees you planted on the first week of July (three weeks ago) are becoming ripe during such a short period of time.
>
> We do hope your wandered and restlessly walked up and down trying to compose yourselves are put together, and try to dry unripe fruits of love with your sunshine of generosity.
>
> Naive love toward human life just like wild flowers in autumn season that secretly scents the air! We would like to give you a big hand and cheers for your such beautiful love praying your small happiness is to be changed to a great pleasure day after day.
>
> Everyone in Post Placement Service Section.

First, the task of the program's organizers, according to the pamphlet, was to make the participants "happy." Then international adoptees are described as being agitated, in disarray, going back and forth, unable to control their emotions during their stay in South Korea. The word "love" is repeated, but no indication is given as to whether its nature is Christian—Holt is a Christian establishment where even employees who are not Christian are required to pray together regularly—or Korean. In the latter case, "love" would be close in meaning to the term *chŏng*. Resentment is described by a metaphor: the green fruit that the concerted action of the organizers has helped to reach maturity. Therefore, the *han* is sublimated and has become the *chŏng*. The text evokes the fear that the whole enterprise may have failed. Only a positive response from the participants can reassure the organizers that the program has truly succeeded.

Participants' responses at the end of the program were usually more or less induced by a strong ritualization, but sometimes they discomfited the organizers. Discontent ran high among the groups that attended the program in 1999 and 2004, and on both occasions complaints were formulated directly to the president of Holt. These complaints were related to a number of issues: the ideological content of many classes featured by the program, the nationalist discourses of certain instructors, and the lack of sensitivity shown by some social workers toward a few participants who needed emotional support. In 2004, asked about her vocation, one younger social worker said with an expressionless face that she had no particular interest in the adoption issue but that it was a job like any other. Hearing this, several adoptees looked dejected, and the conversation ended. According to an adoptee informant, the same scene occurred at the end of the program in 2000. The president reportedly reacted to the recriminations in a very emotional way: abashed, with tears in his voice, he cried, "We did all we could to make you happy during your stay here. I am unhappy to hear your complaints! What else can be done? Should we just stop everything? Let's talk about it with our team." Remembering this incident, the informant grumbled in an undertone, "Koreans say they organize all this for us, but I think they do it for themselves." The adoptee's intuition was right in that either Korean birth families or Korean representatives of the nation or of adoption agencies want adoptees to be satisfied by a warm welcome and seeming efforts to reintegrate them. Behind the organization of the cultural programs lies the idea that if adoptees do everything that is possible to do in Korea, they will be fully satisfied and will not feel the need to come back to ask for more.

In 2004, during the big transnational adoptees' gathering in Seoul, representatives of the state made public apologies to the adoptees on behalf of the nation. Their tone was as dramatic as the tones of parents when they meet with their newly found child. A newspaper reported on this occasion:

> This is the opening keynote by Kim Kŭn-dae, Health and Welfare Ministry, addressed to 430 adoptees who came from 15 different countries and who gathered in the second floor ballroom of the Sofitel Ambassador. . . . The room was filled with applause rather than with sobs. Kim Kŭn-dae said: "I want to tell you that I love you. But I am hesitating. . . . Really, I cannot help being worried: how do I have the pretension to talk to you this way? Imagining your pain and your wounds, it is not easy for me to tell you I love you so lightly. But I have to tell you nonetheless. All of you who are present today, I love you!" Although the messages addressed to international adoptees by our authorities were announced as "Congratulations" or "Encouragements," they all contained apologies. Lee Kwang-gyu, president of OKF, read a message on behalf of Kwan Yang-suk, the wife of the president [who was absent]: "When I think of all of you who found yourselves so young in a foreign land, total strangers, it hurts so much. The closer the moment of my meeting with you, the less words I knew what to tell you. I was afraid of the facial expressions you would show me. . . . " But international adoptees responded in a friendly manner. When they appeared, the program's organizers were welcomed with applause. The event became quickly a big feast. . . . A French adoptee [declared]: "It is the way we are received in our birth country which makes us love our birth country."[30]

This article indicates that the outcomes of the familial meetings, as well as of their political counterparts, are always more or less perceived as uncertain. The language of this article reveals a certain attitude on the part of its author: in particular, a belief that a negative reaction from transnational adoptees toward Koreans is always a possibility. There was more applause than sobs, and "international adoptees responded in a friendly manner." In other words, things turned out better than could have been expected; the event was a success despite the perilous nature of its very premise.

During the four days of the 2004 gathering, the press kept describing the friendly atmosphere; the few critical comments on transnational adoption from the participants barely received any coverage. Toward the end of the event, the press drew conclusions that were mostly positive. Newspapers quoted adoptees as saying they loved and understood their Korean birth parents, as well as their birth country in general: "Mom, Dad, I understand. . . . I love you";[31] "We are leaving with the love of our motherland in our hearts";[32] "Mom, Dad, I understand you";[33] "Our interest in Korea brought us unforgettable memories, thank you."[34] Transnational adoptees are susceptible to feeling resentment because they were once abandoned or rejected. According to the media's rendering, the four-day gathering transformed them into happy young adults who love their birth country and are grateful for the good treatment they received. These optimistic reports were obviously very reassuring for Korean readers.

In fact, these programs are organized in such a way that they surprise the participants with their gratuitousness and showiness. The tour and the stay not only are cheap in comparison to their quality, but, as noted, the costs are often entirely reimbursed if the participant escorts a baby to his or her adoptive country. The luxury accommodations and services suggest a special favor extended by the government, which is not reducible to an economic strategy to ensure South Korea's successful globalization. Moreover, participants receive many gifts from Holt or from OKF, from a tailored traditional costume to history and language books and banquets in the most expensive restaurants. The OKF program in 2004 started with a day and a night at the Ritz-Carlton for a hundred people. All of this sponsorship can be interpreted as gifts, or as ritual offerings serving as compensation for a debt contracted when the babies and young children were sent abroad. In parallel, participants on *Ach'im madang* received department store coupons and free DNA tests in exchange for their participation. This was not the case for their birth relatives, although they also performed onstage. Upon meeting with their children, birth parents themselves offered a large amount of money in the form of cash and presents to their lost children, for whom they also organized a banquet in a good restaurant.[35] This special welcoming implies gifts and offerings; it also entails ritualized moments such as the meeting itself, the visit to the ancestors' graves at the family cemetery, the rites of passage to adulthood, or the wedding ceremony.

Along with the various ritualized actions in which transnational adoptees took part and the discourses offered by past governments to adoptees to include them in the Korean diaspora, the televised meetings were devices to gladden children who may host bad feelings toward their birth country and birth parents. Beyond their abilities to potentially renew interrupted relationships, the televised meetings gain a new meaning through the analysis of the emotions provoked, tamed, and interpreted during the broadcast.

The management of children's emotions ultimately aimed at relieving Korean parents' uneasy feelings and stemmed from modern representations of childhood mixed with ancient societal values and organization that are not unique to Korea. This was a crucial element of *Ach'im madang* that further reinforced the idea that the acknowledgment of biological kinship alone does not spontaneously resume familial relationships after a long separation. To the contrary, that moment was the recognition and acceptance of what had been lost: whatever the blood ties usually entail. By performing meetings and ritualized actions, both sides acknowledged their belief in the blood ties that once linked them but also recognized that without society and ritualized actions, these blood ties do not lead to anything meaningful and communicable.[36] The blood ties are eminently social constructions that necessitate a public display or expression. That ambivalence of blood ties between separated kin is not without similarities to the ties between living and dead kin. The final chapter will develop this comparison.

10

Meeting the Lost and the Dead

When I returned to South Korea and found my birth relatives in 1999, I learned that my father had passed away in 1996 at the age of forty-five. Weeping, my paternal grandmother explained that this premature death of her second-oldest son had been followed shortly by the death of her third son in 1998. After these two deaths, my return was a real consolation; my relatives interpreted my renewed presence in their lives as a sign that bode well for the fate of my entire paternal family, as my paternal aunt expressed in a letter she sent to me in France after my departure: "When you came back last summer, your grandmother's *han* was half relieved. It was as wonderful as meeting again with her first son who was left behind in North Korea before the war. But she will find peace only when your younger sister comes back as well." In 2003, as related earlier, I spent considerable time with my paternal aunt, who welcomed me in her house for several months. Once, she reported my father's words on his deathbed:

> He said many times to your grandmother and to myself that he had no regret: he had done all he had wanted, loved the person he wanted . . . but his only torment was that he had left you and your sister at the orphanage. So, he thought that he was dying early as a punishment from God. . . . (Silence. She wipes her eyes) He had become very religious toward the end.

These words from my paternal grandmother, my paternal aunt, and my father reveal a representation of the lost or abandoned child that lies close to the representation of the malevolent dead. The abnormal deaths of her two sons left my grandmother disconsolate and worried for the rest of the family. She has gone to a Catholic church to pray to Jesus and the Virgin Mary every morning since her conversion in the 1980s. My aunt told me that before, my grandmother frequented shamans' houses with the same assiduity (*yŏlsimhi katta*). My return as a transnational adoptee has occasioned a great deal of relief. The correlation between the two deaths and the two lost children left at the orphanage is suggested by my aunt's evocation of the *han*. In my aunt's letter, the equivalence of the two children left at the orphanage and the child left in North Korea with relatives is made explicit.

* * *

The representation of resentful, potentially dangerous children in the South Korean context can be understood by establishing relevant comparisons with cases from other regions of the world and other times in history. Lost children and dead children are two close categories in their birth parents' minds, which suggests that there is a lingering spiritual element to the entire enterprise of inviting transnational adoptees back to their birth country. But the conflation of a lost child given up for adoption with a dead and dangerous child is not incompatible with the real wish to reintegrate the child in the family, as we saw earlier in the discussion of family and kinship.[1]

Different Types of Mediation

Infanticide, child abandonment, and child circulation are the three options available to adults who have to deal with unwanted children in large families and children outside of the patriline. Historically, the unwanted children have tended to be daughters.

The widespread issue of abandoned children in Korea has been handled in a variety of ways through the centuries, but it was never considered as critical as in the late twentieth century, when it provoked solicitude and scrutiny from other nations. There is established evidence that foundlings of premodern Korea were provided care by the state and by Buddhist monks in temples until they were old enough to work (Jung-woo Kim and Henderson 2008). In modern Korea, foundlings have been cared for by Christian institutions and by foreigners, due to the development of transnational adoption by American missionaries after the Korean War. But it was not until three decades after the war that the children lost to transnational adoption became a public issue in South Korea. The fact that birth parents only recently became visible in the public sphere does not mean that they were less sensitive about the issue in the past.

It also seems likely that infanticide was committed for social and economic reasons not only in ancient Korean society but also probably during modern Korea's direst periods, such as the Korean War and the postwar era.[2]

Contemporaneous with the steep increase of transnational adoption was the explosion of abortion rates in the 1980s. Although abortions in Korea never reached the drastically high level as those in China following the implementation of its "one child" or "one boy" policy, family planning policies in South Korea were implemented and the ideal of the nuclear family promoted in the 1960s. If the promotion of the nuclear family succeeded, it did so in an unexpected fashion: abortion became the most efficient method of contraception.[3] Most abortions were selective, as parents were willing to limit the number of their children while at the same time ensuring the patriline by giving birth to a son. As a result, the South Korean government grew concerned at the imminent demographic imbalance and began passing laws limiting the conditions under which abortions could be performed and punishing doctors who provided the illegal service.[4]

The case of abortion sheds light on the evolving structures of feelings between parents and children in South Korea. Catholic and Protestant churches were the first institutions to call for a better handling of abortion issues by the government, and for an awakening of consciousness of the value of fetal life in the 1970s. Following the changes in abortion law passed by the government, South Korean Buddhist monks[5] addressed the subsequent guilt related to abortion by creating rituals for aborted fetuses in the mid-1980s, after the Japanese cult for the *mizuko-kuyo* (LaFleur 1992):

> An awakening of concern for aborted fetuses occurred among Buddhists in Korea in early 1985 with the work of Venerable Sok Myogak... [who] incited great interest among a group of *posallim* (female supporters) in Seoul when he introduced them to a first draft of his Korean translation of some selections from a Japanese book regarding *mizuko kuyo*. The book's depiction of the fears and suffering of the spirits of helpless, aborted children and their attempts to seize the attention of their parents through dreams and misfortunes (interference) in their daily lives resonated deeply among these pious Buddhist women. It obviously brought to the surface feelings of uneasiness and guilt they had experienced for years but could or would not identify and provided a justification for certain life problems. "We grieve over the death of our pet animals and even bury them. How much more so a baby in the womb which is aborted! We cannot ignore them," to quote a *posallim* on a local radio broadcast this spring.... The *posallims* encouraged Myogak to continue his translation which they eventually published as a paperback at their own expense in 1985. It is evocatively entitled "*Agaya, yongsŏhaedao*" which can be translated as "My Dear Baby, Please Forgive Me!"... The book's readership quickly spread from Seoul to Taegu and Pusan.... the book also spread among the ordained clergy.... The monks began to offer rites for aborted fetuses on their own,

modeling their rituals on what they learned from Myogak directly and through their reading of his translation. (Tedesco 1996)

These rituals for the aborted fetuses grew in importance because Buddhist monks in Japan and Korea were drawing on ancient folk beliefs that previously had seldom emerged in public. It seems that the 1980s marked a period of transition in the way children were represented in South Korea. On the one hand, there is an ancient folk belief that children are close to nature, and if they die they may be born again quickly (LaFleur 1992). Unlike the death of an adult, the natural death of a child is not sullied with impurity; the child's body can dissolve in nature, in accordance with the Buddhist ideal. According to anthropologist Janelli, "Children who die before adolescence, say informants, do not afflict the living, even in later years" (Janelli and Yim Janelli 1982, 160). Therefore, prior to the 1980s, there was no Confucian funeral for children.[6]

On the other hand, this belief in the harmlessness of the young dead is clouded by the other belief that those who have not used their allotted life span can turn into dangerous spirits. The blurry demarcation between children and adolescents or even young adults may reflect the evolution of the status of the child in society.[7] That is why until recently cremation was reserved for the young dead as well as for the inauspicious dead (Hong 1994; Taeho Park 2006; Prébin 2012).[8] That is also why some families include offerings for their inauspicious unmarried dead, or "humble ancestors" (Janelli and Yim Janelli 1982, 151). Within families, the thought of these peculiar dead seems to have always been present. Shamans have always recognized the power of dead children, including them in the pantheon of their divinities,[9] pacifying them with offerings (Janelli and Yim Janelli 1982, 160), or even taming their spirits for their own empowerment.[10] Not unlike these shamans, the Buddhist monks who launched the rituals for aborted fetuses claimed that the willful termination of a child's life is the kind of pollution that makes children potential restless spirits.

Shamans' clients are mostly women in their forties and over who are also mothers (Janelli and Yim Janelli 1982, 149). Mothers whose children had died have consulted shamans because society used to offer no other venue for the open expression of their grief.[11] I tried to interview two female shamans about this specific subject, but my questions were quickly dismissed with defensive hostility, which interrupted our otherwise friendly chatting. Nobody wanted to talk about this, and it was a bad topic of research, they said.[12] One male shaman (*tangol*) whom I met during fieldwork defined the mother-child relationship as organic and inalienable because mothers give birth to children and care for them the most:

The relationship of mothers with their children is special [*t'ŭkch'ulhan kŏt*].... As they lend their bodies to their children, as they feed their children, they are the ones who feel the *chŏng*, in contrast to fathers who only lend a little bit of their energy [*ki*] to their children.... The child looks for his mother because he just wants to go back to his "home."[13]

The mother is held responsible for her children's health and well-being:

It is the duty of the parents to raise children; when a mother is possessed by her child, she is expressing her own pain for not being able to fulfill that duty. We see very ambivalent emotions—a mixture of mutual love and hatred, affection and guilt—projected onto the spirit of the child.... The spirits of children often express their grievances through the speech of shamans they possess, with statements like "Mom, I couldn't have enough of your milk." (Ch'oe 1998, 97)

The shaman defined the mother-child relationship in terms of *chŏng* and *han*:

The *chŏng* and the *han* are the same. The *han* starts in the *chŏng*. Because the *chŏng* has roots in the *han* and this can't change.[14] If there is no *chŏng*, there is no *han*, right? And if there is no *han*, there is no *chŏng*. For example, what you feel when you are alive is the *chŏng*, right? After death you call it the *han*.[15]

The shaman's role is to untie the knots of the *han* between the dead and the living. For this purpose, the shaman must call the dead, help the dead to communicate grievances to the living, and please the dead with ritualized, sympathetic words and offerings of food and money. When satisfied, the dead speak to announce their departure from the world of the living. The client can live in peace until the next domestic crisis. Each side is separated, in its own place again (Kendall 1985, 1988; Jae-hoon Lee 1989; Jung Young Lee 1981; Hee-kyung Lee 1995; Seong-nae Kim 1989).

This cultural interpretation of the complex relationship between mothers and dead children also characterizes the relationship between mothers and lost or abandoned children. Because their separation is recalled as involuntary and due to social pressures, and because mothers are ignorant about whether their child is alive or dead, this situation is also one of *han*. In many respects, aborted fetuses, lost children, and dead children share many characteristics worth examining. Although fetuses were not yet children when they were aborted, parents imagine them as toddlers (Moskowitz 2001; LaFleur 1992). The same applies to adult adoptees, as we have seen. In addition, parents can only imagine the latter as inhabiting a "somewhere," an "elsewhere," or a transitional "placelessness" (Pentikäinen 1968, 52). A few years ago, a documentary on overseas adoptees on South Korean television was entitled: *Mom, I Am Here*.[16] Although all birth parents may not experience these uneasy feelings, or at least do not express them in words (Janelli, 1982, 154–155; Kendall 1988),[17] there is ample evidence of their expression.

The fate of lost children, whether orphans or adoptees, is usually uncertain. They may be alive or dead, and if they are dead, there is often reason to think they have died in a state of frustration (Kendall 2003).[18] Because their premature and possibly unknown death is a distinct possibility, lost and abandoned children may be regarded as the causes of disasters striking their birth mothers' families. The absence of proper rites may provoke their hostile return. During fieldwork in 2004, a Korean social worker of Holt Children's Services asked me to edit her English translation of several letters that Korean single mothers addressed to their babies adopted abroad. The letters would be published in a book. One mother had written, "Grow up well; later, come back and have your revenge." The shaman I interviewed not only mentioned his work with spirits and dead children but also spoke about the frequent visits of mothers anxious to know about their lost children's fate: "Many mothers come see me. Those who lost a child ask me if he is still alive and if they will be able to see their child again. . . . So, I evaluate if yes or no they will." Parents who seek help from a shaman usually express the wish to know whether or not the child is alive. If this practice does not necessarily imply the desire to meet the child in the flesh, it does point to a need for an intermediary. A mother who asks a shaman about her lost child may seek ways to separate rather than to reunite, because shamans provoke meetings to allow a ritualized separation. A bad separation must turn into a good separation. Today, along with the ancient but still-active shamanistic traditions of reading the future and contacting the afterlife, parents—mostly mothers—have other efficient means to find their lost children: newspapers, television, adoption agencies, and so forth. These different institutions seem to organize the integration of lost children within their families, but as we have seen, the extent and duration of this integration are often limited.

In fact, anthropological literature abounds with examples of integration rites that do not do what they pretend to do: most often, they stage the creation of ties between the living and dead to better separate them. For example, the aim of the posthumous marriage, as practiced in Korea, China, and Japan, is not the legitimate union of a man and a woman but the passage of the frustrated dead person to a superior social status in the afterlife, which will ensure the deceased's transmigration and definite separation from the living (Takeda 1990; Ch'oe 1998, 98; Jordan 1972). This type of separation ritual in East Asia has its Christian equivalents, such as the posthumous baptism and the posthumous burial in traditional European societies. The same phenomenon of dead children tormenting their mothers is what led the church to institutionalize expulsion rites.[19] These rituals for lost children stand for reversed rituals, that is, separation rituals. The comparison of lost children to the potentially malevolent dead is illuminated by a comparison of the television meeting program *Ach'im madang* with a shamanistic ritual of separation: the goal of each is to entertain, to make people cry,[20] to promote the expression of feelings that are repressed in everyday life, and to manage emotions that are harmful to individuals as well as society. The program takes care of children without parents just as the state has taken care of the dead "with no ties" or no descendants. The hosts describe their job as an act of welfare on behalf of society. For example, one day the host said: "We must relieve these people whose entire life is sorrowful." The host called for the audience's compassion: "Try to imagine the life of these people, who for thirty or forty years have not known their real names."[21]

The maintenance of relationships after the staged meetings is not the meetings' ultimate purpose. In this context, even parents who are not able to reconstitute formal filiation agree nonetheless to the brief encounters in order to express their recognition of marginal consanguinity. At the same time, these events confer meaning on a reality that can be difficult to grasp: transnational adoptees are neither different nor similar, neither strangers nor relatives, neither present nor dead, neither children nor adults. For the majority, they are sons and daughters of their mothers, but not of their fathers. The seeming integration of the staged meetings is a means of affirming this reality despite its ambiguity. It is a necessary and ephemeral stage that definitively sends the adoptees abroad, a metaphor for departure to the other world. In other words, I argue that the meetings reveal structural parameters and past actions that cannot be fully redressed. The understanding of others' circumstances and the soothing of painful feelings are conducive to peaceful partings.

The integration that is performed must ensure a separation without risks. The status of overseas adoptees as potential inauspicious dead calls for remedies usually applied to the actual inauspicious dead: localization, identification, allocation of relatives, genealogical integration, welcoming, offerings, and rites of passage. In these circumstances, organizing the meeting of lost children with their birth parents resolves their respective *han*. These ritualized events reveal a manifold symbolism. The welcoming of overseas adoptees by the South Korean state and society is dictated not only by economic or political strategies or feelings of guilt in birth parents but also by this threatening representation of the lost child. Gifts and money from parents and honors from the state are ritualized offerings and compensation for the debt. To find parents for lost children, to submit them to rites of passage and to give them gifts, is to convert them to future benevolent ancestors.

* * *

In the case of Korea, as in Japan or Taiwan, business is not the main motivation for the creation of rituals for aborted fetuses; the rituals address a real social need. Like Japanese society a few decades earlier, South Korean society has expressed its awareness of the problem, which was not only demographic, political, or economic but also ethical and psychological. Some researchers argue that in Japan, guilt and fear were provoked in women by Buddhist monks willing to make money by selling rituals for the aborted fetuses at their temple (Hardacre 1999). Others argue that Buddhist temples, while indeed creating a new market, were nonetheless responding to psychological or religious needs that had previously been imperfectly met by other and more ancient systems of beliefs, such as shamanism.[22] Moving forward with the second interpretation, these new rituals do indeed respond to the needs of women who underwent abortions and provide them with a way to express their "uneasy feeling" in a larger public context. This public aspect is crucial, as it gives recognition to private suffering. The "commodification of sin" (Moskowitz 2001, 166–170) through rituals flourishes where modern technologies generate new social practices and issues, and where social welfare is still weak.

The representation of children evolved in similar ways in pagan Europe with the propagation of Christian doctrine and the institution of baptism for newborns as a guarantee of their status as Christian sons and daughters of God (Delumeau 1983; Héritier-Augé and Copet-Rougier 1996; Fine 1987; Buchet 1997). Studies demonstrate that abandonment, exposure, or infanticide of babies in northern Europe began to be judicially sanctioned when Christianity was implemented. New expressions of preexisting guilt over an old practice were inspired and encouraged by the law and relieved by new rituals created by the church (Pentikäinen 1968; O'Connor 1991). Eventually, feelings of guilt and welfare systems developed in such proportions that the practice of child abandonment and infanticide itself decreased.

Drawing on psychological concepts such as mourning and melancholia,[23] one sees the obvious relation between aborted fetuses and abandoned children.[24] In both cases, the separation can be properly mourned by birth parents through meetings, either through ritualized mediation or in person. Meetings are the occasion to face one's loss. While open adoptions are still rare, the meeting program helps birth parents to deal with separation and find forgiveness and social recognition of their suffering. More than creating a need, media technology has given meaning to familial rupture and provided a venue for the ritualized expression of grief. Its efficiency, however, is not all retroactive and does not serve only parents.

The individual and collective acknowledgment of the loss attributes importance to children. It generates new structures of feelings that contribute in their turn to the evolution of family and society. It has had a positive impact on the development of social welfare and the evolution of the status of children in South Korea. Two cases at *Ach'im madang* attested to these changes. In the first case, a twenty-year-old participant and his seventeen-year-old sister were looking for their parents. She attended high school while he worked to make a living for both of them, as they lived together.[25] In the second case, a twenty-six-year-old participant told the hosts that she and her twenty-four-year-old brother had lived with their mother, and their father visited them from time to time. At some point, they left their mother to live with their father. But when he remarried, he sent them to an orphanage. After growing up in an orphanage, they established their household and started working.[26] These younger South Korean participants belonged to the same generation as transnational adoptees, but they were too old to be adopted when their parents left them in an orphanage. They nonetheless illustrate the improving social welfare programs for sibling orphans, called "youth-headed households," within South Korea (Jung-woo Kim and Henderson 2008).

This chapter has traced the evolution of the structures of feelings related to the issue of lost children in the context of the changing social landscape of South Korea. Anthropologist Ruth Benedict, in her seminal examination of Japanese culture *The Chrysanthemum and the Sword*, first published in 1946 (Benedict 2005), theorized the opposition of a "culture of guilt" versus a "culture of shame" and posited that Japanese society, unlike Western Christian societies, had developed a culture of shame. Most social anthropologists have challenged this theory since the release of Benedict's famous book. But instead of arguing against similar assumptions regarding Korea, analyzing the historical and sociological articulation of shame and guilt in the context of child abandonment may be more useful. Even though expressions of personal guilt appeared after the expression of collective shame, collective shame over transnational adoption, and the South Korean government's demographic concerns, led to the creation of a mass-mediated social service that allowed feelings of guilt, which until then had been restricted to the private sphere, to be absolved in public.

Brief Meetings at the Border

When I went back to South Korea in 2006, my paternal aunt told me that my paternal grandmother had been contacted by the South Korean Red Cross right after she had turned eighty. The Red Cross offered the following service: a filmed interview about her family that would allow her to deliver an ultimate message to her relatives who had stayed in the North. One copy of the video would be hers, and the other copy would be sent to a video center in her hometown, where she expected her relatives to have remained. This center shelters visual documents sent by South Koreans to their North Korean relatives, with whom they have had no contact for fifty years. I had the opportunity to watch the video: my grandmother is dressed up, and she smiles while recalling her hometown memories. She describes in detail her "very pretty first son who had very wide eyes." Then she cries with a tired expression. She asks her son and her parents for forgiveness because she was not able to care for them: "If you are still alive, I hope you're well. . . . I am really sorry." Suddenly, she giggles and nods, saying, "Of course they are dead! Haha! They would be over 105 years old!" Because of her age and because of the lottery system the government employs to organize meetings, my grandmother has very little chance of seeing her North Korean relatives again. Media technology allows for a new kind of ancestor ritual: the video will make up for the impossible meeting.[27]

This conception of a binary world, separated between the living and the dead, is even stronger in the context of the peninsula partition. Impassable for most, the frontier inspires various ritualized practices that all have the same objectives: to ensure the forgiveness of the departed and lost relatives, and to find peace. The performance of these rituals for the dead is the main purpose of these family meetings. This concern is at once national and familial, public and private. The televised meetings always take a recognizable, ritualized form, whether the meeting occurs between Korean orphans, transnational adoptees, North Koreans, or South Koreans, because they treat the same familial reality: the problem of separation and the need to pacify the potentially malevolent dead "before it is too late."[28]

In the North-South context, many meetings organized by the two states in 2000 and 2001 generated awkward situations, when individuals who were supposedly of the same blood realized their fundamental differences. The use of the term *ijilgam* (*ijil*: heterogeneity; *kam*: feeling) seems a dominant sentiment of many participants in the 2000 and 2001 meetings:

[*Ijilgam*], literally, *sense of difference*—is the Korean term employed in South Korea to describe the ideological, psychological and social differences which have grown between the two Koreas' citizens as a result of living for over half a century in the states with diametrically opposed socio-politico-economic systems. (Foley 2003, 124)

Numerous South Koreans quickly realized the cultural and psychological gap between their northern relatives and themselves.[29] For some families, communication was very difficult to establish despite the shared language, and the normal expression of emotions was dwarfed. Several informants reported their dismay:

> Also, my younger sister who is just below him (in age) is not very well off. She felt very awkward. She had knitted him a sweater with her own hands for him to wear in winter. He said: "I can't wear this. It's too good. I'll give it to National Defense Commission Chairman Kim Jong-Il." So, my poor sister's face changed colour on hearing those words. (Foley 2003, 125)[30]

> It was a shocking meeting. Also, the daughter I had missed so much for so long... apart from meeting her, there was nothing. On that subject does anything more need to be said?... To be honest I didn't cry... couldn't cry. Why? I've lived and owe everything to Kim Il Sung, that sort of thing. The fact that it's still like that up there, that it hasn't changed means that you can't really have a discussion. Our brothers and sisters, wife, daughter... all aged now... they can't say what they think... in that place, it wasn't a place for loving small talk. The atmosphere was not good. In the North, not because they were being watched, but because our ideologies are so different, how could we express our feelings. I couldn't speak.... My first words were: "It must have been hard. How have you managed?" They answered coolly: "Thanks to our great General we have lived well and without hardship." At hearing these words, I was so upset. (Foley 2003, 125)

> In the three nights and four days I carefully collected my thoughts and prepared myself emotionally. We were alive, so we had to go back and live on, because if reunification comes, then that will be the day we meet again. Whether it was because of the fact that I didn't cry, I don't really know, but others thought our reunion was a little cool. Because of that I hardly featured at all in the television coverage.... I was crying inside though.... People weeping, people crying out emotionally, they were the ones the television coverage showed. (Foley 2003, 124–125)

These quotes suggest the importance of the display of proper emotions. Foley uses the term *ijilgam*, or "sense of difference," to summarize all the emotions evoked by the informants, but they talk instead about feeling awkward and upset, about shocking meetings and cool attitudes. An unhappy informant attributes a reproachful attitude to the daughter he met in 2000: "At first, the first words, without even crying or recognising each other. . . . I called my daughter's name. Without rushing to greet me, she looked at me reproachfully, bowed and said, "Father, why have you come?" (Foley 2003, 130). The author reports that his informant suffered a "nervous breakdown" after the traumatizing meeting. These examples, taken from different sources and contexts, indicate that *wonmang* is attributed to the children separated from their parents through international adoption or by the thirty-eighth parallel. These feelings are opposed to *chŏng* (attachment), as they do not provoke tears. The references to "cool" meetings confirm the idea that the expression of emotions in public is compulsory and their management by intermediaries crucial. The intermediaries can be the organizers, the television hosts, or even the viewers. What is at stake in the proper expression of emotions onstage is the empathy and communion of all parties and actors. If expressed properly, the scene of tears allows the emotional contagion of all viewers. Emotion is "not clearly separable from its intended purpose" (Armon-Jones 1986, 35). If tears fail to flow properly, the encounter can have devastating consequences.

The frontier is not exclusively a place of confrontation and violence, as one might assume from the barbed wire and the ubiquitous military forces. Christian, Buddhist, and shamanistic altars are erected in the observatories along the demilitarized zone. Observatories are not merely tourist-oriented places where South Koreans and foreigners can observe the North from a distance, visit museums that reconstitute the supposedly backward houses and classrooms of North Korea, buy products manufactured in North Korea, and hear North Korean defectors speaking about their experiences. They are also religious spaces where members of divided families perform rituals for ancestors, mostly on the Harvest Festival. Hamlets containing hotels and motels are located a few miles away and allow the pilgrims to rest after a long trip.

In one of the first scenes of the blockbuster film *T'aegŭkki huinallimyŏ*,[31] the main character, an old man, is shown in his house. He receives a phone call from a team of archaeologists at a dig site who have just uncovered the remains of his older brother. The attentive viewer may notice a detail on the wall of the room: it is the picture of a meeting between tearful northern and southern relatives that was cut from a newspaper. One can infer from that detail that the old man is very interested and feels deeply involved in these events. Although he knows his older brother died on the battlefield to protect him, the rest of his family survived and stayed together.

In a flashback, the viewer is immersed in the war. After a misunderstanding between the two brothers, the older brother joins the Communist North Korean side out of spite, while the younger brother stays on the South Korean side. The older brother is depicted as a simple and generous man who has fallen victim to the wrong ideology. The postmortem meeting and the mutual forgiveness of the two enemy brothers is symbolic of the future national reunification. With the exception of one battle scene, in which a multitude of counterattacking Chinese soldiers covers the entire screen, all figures of foreigners are banished from the film. The real actors in the war are the Koreans. Although seen as the decisions of foreign powers, the Korean War and the reunification are ultimately family matters.

The juxtaposition of the first and last scenes leads to the conclusion that meeting the dead belongs to the same category of events as meeting long-lost relatives: it is as important and as emotional. In the last scene, the main character is seen kneeling at the dig site, an old battlefield close to the frontier. In a broken voice, he reproaches the skeleton for not having come back as promised. Then he bends over, touches his head to the skull, and cries. The older brother is one among millions of young soldiers who died without descendants. The younger brother, now an old man, will bury his remains, perform the ritual for ancestors, and find peace in accomplishing his duty. This is the end of the film.

* * *

Touching upon the varied aspects of meetings facilitated by media technology, we have seen that televised family meetings serve a political agenda, entertain viewers, contribute to the changing of people's views on orphans and adoptees, provide a historical interpretation to all family separations, create a sense of community based on nostalgia and the collective memory of prewar Korea, feed birth mothers' hopes for reunion with the babies they send abroad to transnational adoption, and allow individuals to acknowledge and assert their relatedness and, in some cases, to build relationships. In the cases where the reunited families only acknowledge their relatedness without investing in a relationship, the meetings soothe ambiguous feelings between parents and children to help them resume normal lives. The idea that the meetings aim at new, acceptable partings is further reinforced by implicit assimilations of the lost with the dead. This is an instance where media technology, through the reproduction of the iconic scene of tears, provides people with the material for "magic contemplation" (Benjamin 2008, 26). In other words, the mediation operated by media technology confers religious or ritualistic quality on the meetings. Media technology and rituals are both techniques that make social life and build the nation.

Conclusion

Anthropologists of kinship and gender have framed the first half of the transnational adoption process—first-world, educated parents choosing to adopt a foreign child—within the category of global ideologies of reproduction (Ginsburg and Rapp 1995; Strathern 1992). This book has shed light on the second half of the transnational adoption process that only a few can experience and fewer have talked or written about: the moment of recognition and reaffirmation of ties between children and their birth families that international laws and regulations have in most cases denied. The type of relatedness created by the return of the adoptees to their birth country is possible because of globalization as a general state of the world in which a growing number of individuals have the material means to travel between places, communicate with anyone, choose temporary places of residence, make the best use of flexible citizenship, and do, undo, and redo relationships at will. In this second half of the process, adoptees and birth parents reclaim agency. This is able to happen not only because of material means but also because it has become morally and psychologically acceptable (Volkman 2009). There is a growing collective understanding that these modes of living and relating to one another across cultures are part of an all-encompassing neoliberal modernity where even the family is no longer a sacrosanct, immutable value prescribed by cultural traditions (Ouellette 2009).[1]

In these circumstances, transnational adoption is, as some young South Korean single mothers recently separated from their babies seem to consider it, another practice of child circulation, though on a much wider legal, technological, political, and temporal scale. Because it changed in fifty years from a barren land into a rich, developed nation, South Korea has achieved the means to turn irrevocable adoptions into flexible and informal relatedness between children and birth parents despite Western laws, diplomatic intricacies, old social restrictions, cultural differences, economic and gender inequalities, and time. Upon their return to South Korea, transnational adoptees are given the means—by both adoptive and birth countries—to create relatedness with their birth families.

The meeting moment facilitated by the media sparks a limited range of options in terms of relatedness between the adoptees and their birth families. In that way, these meetings contribute to changes in many adoptive and birth families in the world and to the way their members represent themselves. Adoptive families may want to engage in a relationship with regular exchanges with adoptive childrens' birth parents; adoptees may represent their family tree differently upon the discovery of their birth family; a destitute birth mother may start relying upon her child after their meeting; reunited siblings may contemplate their future reunions and anticipate visits with excitement. But if meetings augur well for the future, good relationships in the long run do not always ensue. Even if the conditions of possibility of relationships seem favorable, the first moment of recognition of the blood ties can lead to aborted, on-and-off, or ongoing relationships. This book has illustrated some of the limits and difficulties that arise in the wake of the meetings and will hopefully encourage further research on postmeeting relationships between adoptees and their birth families from different sending countries.

* * *

Scholars of adoption studies have recently pointed out that the experience of the return to the birth country is ambiguous and seldom leads to closure for the adoptees. Returns are never real returns to an original past; they always destabilize the returnee's identity before, perhaps, providing the ground for the creation of a renewed identity (Yngvesson and Bibler Coutin 2006). Meeting one's birth parents is often as much a conclusion as a new beginning. Does this statement apply to birth parents as well?

This book has conveyed the meanings of the return of adoptees for South Koreans in the context of highly staged and ritualized first meetings of transnational adoptees with their birth country and birth families. It has analyzed in a different light many South Koreans' discourses on and attitudes toward transnational adoptees that are often considered simplistic, fake, or manipulative. The first part of this book has depicted adult adoptees who return to South Korea going through a series of ceremonies and ritualized performances that, supposedly, make them pass from the status of unwanted Korean orphans to that of diasporic overseas Koreans valued by the South Korean government; from the status of foreigners to that of Korean people inscribed in a national history of war and partition; and from the status of wandering, resentful children to that of stable, happy, and independent adults. Koreans intend to make sense of adoptees who come back as "matter out of place" by offering them partial integrations and meaningful redefinition of their identity within South Korean society. These partial integrations seem to become complete when adoptees meet with their birth families. However, they cannot simply reconstitute biological families. As the literature on transnational adoptees' experience in their birth countries has pointed out, returns do not undo the departures, and meetings do not mend ruptures. Instead, I argued that returns and meetings aim at making departures and ruptures acceptable, and sometimes open a space for relational possibilities. So, partial integrations and family meetings lead to a certain type of closure while allowing in certain cases the emergence of new relationships and identities.

This book complicates the dichotomies between integration and separation, acceptance and rejection, and biological kinship and fictive or ritual kinship that usually sprinkle and cloud discussions on adoptions and returns. Like other countries that have sent many children abroad via transnational adoption, South Korea creates spaces where adoptees can reclaim parts of their previous citizenship, identity, and family ties, on different levels of relatedness. The cultural camps, the television meeting program, and the family meetings are such spaces. Many birth families reclaim their relatedness to lost children in order to move on as they finally accept their absence. By succeeding in reuniting individuals of different nationalities and cultures, the program *Ach'im madang* seems to confirm that biological relatedness is a human need while conceding that the maintenance of relationships is contingent if not optional, depending on a multitude of parameters that make every social life a different story.

* * *

In the context of transnational adoption from South Korea, the media have been instrumental in changing the lives of many people who were divided from their family members for various reasons. The media have helped to create yet another form of relatedness in addition to two categories that have been traditionally opposed in the anthropology of kinship: biological kinship versus so-called social kinship. In fact, I found that seeming "reintegration" of transnational adoptees to the birth country or the birth family is not organized against adoptive citizenship and adoptive families. The South Korean televised meetings create a moment that helps to define a type of transnational relatedness in historically and culturally acceptable terms. Problematic because they are past and yet present, lingering and yet severed, inalienable and yet unacceptable, blood ties are turned into a middle-ground alternative, a relatedness that combines and accepts a plurality of belongings and fluidity of identities (Yngvesson 2002)—no matter the outcome of the meeting. By looking at the South Korean side of transnational adoption, one realizes that meetings are valuable not only for Koreans but also for adoptees and adoptive families. Once acknowledged, relatedness exists.[2]

If biological birth is the thesis and adoption the antithesis, the return-meeting is the synthesis, since it takes into account both realities of biological birth and adoption. It does not undo adoptions but does not reconstitute birth families either. Opening up a dialogue between Korean birth parents and former children, this synthesis offers a way of conciliating opposites in order to allow for dialectical dynamism and movement in adoptees' and birth families' life narrative and in intergenerational transmission.

* * *

The meetings of transnational adoptees with their birth families generate a type of relatedness that is hard to conceive and define because it is based on both blood (seen in the Korean context as noncontingent or necessary) and choice (seen as contingent). Families in the world are assuming different shapes, and more and more of them come into existence through choice, reproductive technologies, and political economy. The relatedness from adoption and the relatedness from the meetings between adoptees and birth families look similar because in the end they both depend on choice and on political economy. However, they involve different actors within the adoption triad, and the relatedness from the meetings is not about reproduction: mothers may have other children who are legitimate; or they may not want to have children; or there may be no fathers.

Influenced by the common metaphor that describes anthropologists as being adopted by their informants, I often had the impression of being "adopted back" into my birth family. Discordances made me first doubt that we were a family again, and then realize that we were building and negotiating other kinds of ties, by choice. My birth family also thought for a while that we were resuming our natural biological relationship, but they felt relieved when I married. By expressing their relief, they demonstrated the longevity of the Confucian idea that daughters who get married join their husband's family and, therefore, separate from their birth family. Contrary to the separation from a daughter through transnational adoption, the separation through her marriage is legitimate and positive. At least, that is what my relationship with my birth family has taught me.

My relationship with my birth family has also led me to rethink and reevaluate the ties I built with my adoptive family. Whereas in the past I could only compare my adoptive relationships to biological relationships, I can now put them in relief to the relationships I have created with my birth relatives after adoption and meeting. On the one hand, the choice of engaging in a relationship with my birth family taught me that blood alone does not create a relationship. It involved time and effort, and still does. On the other hand, the knowledge of my birth family's history and my own preadoption history paradoxically legitimized my adoptive parents' decision to adopt me, whereas before their choice looked arbitrary. So, in the end, my experience over time challenged the idea that biological birth produces noncontingent or necessary ties and that adoption produces contingent or free ones.

By exploring the birth parents' side of the meetings, this book contributes to our understanding of South Korean perceptions of the return of adoptees and helps to defuse potential confusion and misunderstandings that stem from the inevitable cultural gaps between transnational adoptees and their birth families. It can also help adoptees rethink their adoptive ties in comparison not only to imagined biological ones—as common representations have taught them to—but also to concrete postmeeting ties with birth families.

* * *

Social phenomena are born at certain times in history and are reproduced over the years because they provide relevant representations and actions that respond to a myriad of lasting or changing social issues. Many social phenomena are embedded in ancient systems of beliefs that cannot completely disappear or be replaced. This book has highlighted a combination of historical and cultural approaches, enhanced with comparisons of Korean society to other East Asian or European societies whenever relevant. Social facts are multilayered not only because they involve different spheres and actors but also because the same individuals may harbor different and sometimes contradictory motivations to engage with them. South Korean televised family meetings are a perfect example of this unavoidable human complexity that social scientists ought to explore.

Notes

All translations are the author's unless otherwise indicated.

NOTES TO INTRODUCTION

1. Harry Holt founded his international adoption agency in South Korea in 1956 (two years after the South Korean government opened the Child Placement Service). His story will be told at length in the next chapter. Hereafter, I will refer to the Holt International Summer School as HISS. I will return to HISS through an analysis of its activities in chapter 3.
2. "It was, in fact, adult Korean adoptees who transformed the view of international adoption as a one-way journey from 'sending' to 'receiving' country into a two-way transit" (Eleana Kim 2010, 13).
3. Korean names are pseudonyms except for mine, my sister's, and those of famous people.
4. A tender interjection usually used to address children.
5. The deep bow is reserved to elders and ancestors.
6. I will go back to *Ach'im madang* in detail in chapter 4.
7. On adult adoptees' agency in the South Korean social and political landscape, see Eleana Kim, *Adopted Territory*.
8. "There is a substantial literature on adoption, including novels, autobiographies, and a variety of case studies. In these, adoption is treated as a personal event, not unreasonably, but without attention to the social or cultural context. The few exceptions that do exist here can be found in social science and in history" (Modell 1994, 12). I discuss my intellectual itinerary, the translation process, and some of the differences between French and American academia through the prism of adoption studies in Prébin, "Towards a Franco-American Self-Ethnography."
9. Hübinette, *Comforting an Orphaned Nation*.
10. Media productions are usually divided into two categories—fiction and nonfiction—but it is obvious that the delimitation between these categories fluctuates and the definition of "fiction" has become loose. I do not, however, subscribe to the enlarged definition of "fiction" as a term indicating any written epics—including anthropological texts. On this specific subject, see Clifford, "Introduction," in Clifford and Marcus, eds., *Writing Culture*, 1–26; Colleyn, "Fiction et fictions en anthropologie."
11. "[Most works in the 1970s and 1980s] were based on reports about the children by their adoptive parents and focused on 'adjustment' and 'self-esteem' while studiously avoiding issues of racialization" (Eleana Kim 2010, 9).
12. "In our personal lives we have come to this topic in different ways. Some (although not all) of us are adoptive mothers, but no one occupies the two other positions in

what has come to be known as the 'adoption triad' of birth parents, adoptive parents, and adopted children. We are acutely aware that the voices of birth parents and adoptees are largely absent from the academic literature on this topic, as they have been, until recently, from most representations of adoption" (Volkman 2005, 2).
13. Eleana Kim, "Our Adoptee, Our Alien."
14. Two notable examples are films by Korean adoptees: Chu, *Resilience*; and Liem, *First Person Plural*.

NOTES TO CHAPTER 1

1. Since 2005, every eleventh of May, a procession leaves from the Kanghwa gate and crosses Seoul with signs and banners to promote adoption. It is indicated in the national calendar as "Adoption Day."
2. See further Holt's life story and the conflicts within the institution between Americans and South Koreans in the 1970s.
3. See the quote in the epigraph (Rothschild, "Babies for Sale"). International adoption peaked from 1983 to 1987, and adoptions in the United States account for a third of them.
4. Chira, "Babies for Export."
5. "Korea Still Suffers from Image of Orphan Exporting Country," *Korea Times*, 07/25/97; "Korea Still Main Source of Adoptions in America," *Korea Herald*, 03/03/01; "IMF Economic Pinch Increases Number of Abandoned Children," *Korea Herald*, 03/03/01; http://www.koreanadoptees.net/KADfacts.html;http://en.wikipedia.org/wiki/International_adoption_of_South_Korean_children#Statistics.
6. Holt video no. 40: KBS 01/29/89.
7. Holt video no. 43: KBS 12/13/90.
8. Holt video no. 146: KBS 04/20/97, *60 Minutes* follow-up.
9. There were 2,899 Korean children adopted abroad from 1953 to 1959; 6,166 from 1960 to 1969; 46,035 from 1970 to 1979; 66,035 from 1980 to 1989; 22,925 from 1990 to 1999; and 18,129 from 2000 to 2008. From 1958 to 2008, out of 161,364 Korean children adopted abroad, 29,975 were abandoned, especially from 1958 to 2000; 28,956 came from a broken home, especially from 1958 to 2000; and 102,433 were born to single mothers, with peaks in the 1970s (17,627), 1980s (47,153); and 1990s (20,460). See Eleana Kim, *Adopted Territory*, 20–25. Although the total number of transnational adoptions has diminished, the proportion of children adopted from and within South Korea is today as high as it was during the 1980s, in relation to the total birthrate.
10. See the collection of videos recorded by employees of Holt Children's Services since 1983 and available at the headquarters in Seoul. The common themes of these videos are international and national adoption, orphans and lost children, and social welfare and its institutions. There are commercials for different domestic and foreign adoption agencies, amateur films on internal events at Holt, and, above all, debates, documentaries, and family search and meeting programs recorded on national and private channels since 1981. The whole collection reflects the history and evolution of more than twenty years of adoptions in and from South Korea. See especially Holt video no. 68: MBC live program 05/09/92, "Confessions of a Single Mother"; Video no. 72: KBS 1993, "Where Is the Respect for Human Beings in Our Society?

Abandoned Children"; Holt video no. 102: MBC 05/31/94, "The Month of Family"; Holt video no. 106 11/1994, "Abandoned Angels"; Holt video no. 148: SBS 04/21/97, "I Want to Know: Teenagers' Sexual Education"; Holt video no. 180: KBS 07/26/99, "News Today: Emergencies: Abandoned Children."

11. Although domestic adoption began to be promoted in the media soon after the 1988 crisis, laws regarding adoption did not begin to change before 1990: "The Family Law enacted in 1958 adopted the tradition of 'the best interest of the family' principle by specifying that the primary purpose of adoption was providing means to maintain family lines and estates.... Since the passage of the Family Law of 1958, child welfare reformers pressed the law to recognize the 'best interests of the child'.... Through several revisions of the law, most recently in 1990, the Family Law has moved slowly to incorporate the 'best interests of the child' principle as a basis for adoption.... The first major national legislation influencing the adoption of homeless children was the Special Adoption Assistance Act of 1961. Its primary goal was to promote international adoption in order to find permanent homes for Korean Civil War orphans and children abandoned out of destitution.... Today, there is a government policy goal to reduce international adoption by 5 percent each year. With the goal of reducing and ultimately ending international adoption, there has been a continued effort to increase domestic adoption. Revision of the Special Adoption Assistance Act in 1994 represented such effort" (Joo-lee Lee 2007, 192–193).

12. Holt video nos. 74, 76: MBC 12/07/93.

13. Holt video no. 176: KBS 04/02/99.

14. The institution will subsequently be referred to as Holt.

15. "Holt has eleven branches in the whole country and approximately 400 employees. Holt is 20% financed by the government. The rest comes from adoption fees (around 6,000 euros per child) and from national and international patrons. Two agencies, one in the United States and one in Europe, link together adoptive parents and the parent company" (Bourbon-Parme and Tourret, 2004, 76).

16. "As in any war, civilian casualties outnumbered those of the military, there being one million civilian casualties and three hundred thousand military. In South Korea, in addition to two hundred thirty thousand wounded, the war created some three hundred thousand widows, three hundred thirty thousand permanently handicapped, one hundred thousand orphans, and one million tuberculosis cases" (Choong Soon Kim 1988, 3). See also Eckert and Lee, *Korea Old and New*, 345–356; Cumings, *The Origins of the Korean War*; Middleton, *Compact History of the Korean War*, 230; Republic of Korea National Red Cross, *Dispersed Families in Korea*, 71.

17. Many have compared Korea's situation to that of Germany, another nation divided from 1945 to 1989 that suffered from comparable human traumas. See, for example, Myong-kyu Kang and Wagner, *Korea and Germany*; Metzler, *Divided Dynamism*.

18. See the anecdote reported by anthropologist Laurel Kendall: "There was an American GI with a Korean wife, and we gave [our baby girl] away to them. She would have a good life.... I cried and cried, and they took her away. We heard the taxi drive away, and a little while later we heard the taxi come back. The GI and the woman had quarrelled. He said that no one would believe this was his child, not with her tiny little black eyes. He wasn't going to go through with it" (Kendall 2005, 174).

19. On the success of Protestantism in developing, urban South Korea, see Ryu, *Reading the Korean Cultural Landscape*, 66–75; Chung-Shin Park, *Protestantism and Politics in Korea*. On postwar American capital investment, see Eckert and Lee, *Korea Old and New*, 394–399.
20. See, for example, the National Origins Quota, part of the Immigration Act of 1924, the War Brides Act of 1945, the Immigration and Nationality Act or McCarran-Walter Act of 1952, and the Refugee Relief Act of 1953.
21. The Holt adoption agency, as an independent organization, came under a lot of criticism from rival agencies in the United States for practicing and promoting proxy adoptions directly in South Korea instead of following a minimal procedure. See Choy, "Institutionalizing International Adoption," 25–42. Today Holt has offices in many other countries, including India, Vietnam, and Colombia. See www.holt.or.kr.
22. See Ministry of Health and Welfare, quoted in "200 000 Adoptees Live Homesick for the Country Which Has Abandoned Them," *Dong-A Ilbo*, 08/04.
23. Holt video no. 41: 01/29/89, *News Vision*.
24. For other examples of attacks on transnational adoption agencies in a climate of growing concerns about the well-being of children, demography, and fluctuating nationalisms in sending countries, see Fonseca, "Transnational Connections and Dissenting Views"; Khabibullina, "International Adoption in Russia."
25. Holt video no. 56: SBS 04/30/92.
26. Following the economic and social reforms launched by Park Chung-Hee, "the average number of children per family in South Korea . . . dropped from nearly six in 1960 to less than two in 1990. This equates to an average reduction of two persons per family per one generation. The crude birthrate was over 40 per 1000 in the population in 1960 but fell steadily in the last thirty years to 16.2 in 1990 and it has reached below replacement level in the last decade." See Tedesco, "Rites for the Unborn Dead," 61–74. See also Tsuya and Bumpass, *Marriage, Work, and Family Life in Comparative Perspective*.
27. Holt video nos. 151–152: 12/13/97, Live "Seeking Happiness" I and II.
28. Holt video no. 202: KBS 05/09/99, "We Raise Our Children Ourselves."
29. Holt video no. 72: KBS 1993, "Where Is the Respect for Human Beings in Our Society? Abandoned Children."
30. Holt video no. 204: 04/05/2000, "A Wide World: Adoption Grows Love."
31. Holt video no. 254: KBS 05/26/2002, Special Saturday Broadcast: "Domestic Adoption: A Beautiful Choice."
32. Holt video no. 307: KBS 05/06/2004, "People in the World."
33. Holt video no. 94: 04/18/94, "The Era of Mankind."
34. Holt video no. 295: KBS 12/21/2003, Selected documents 4321: "To Practice Love through Adoption."
35. Holt video no. 256: 07/24/2002, "Domestic Adoption System, We Must Change the Culture of Adoption Now."
36. Holt video no. 286: KBS 02/14/2003, 9 p.m. news.
37. Holt video no. 304: YTN 04/22/2004, International Overseas Korean News.
38. Norimitsu Onishi, "Korea Aims to End Stigma of Adoption and 'Exporting' Babies," *New York Times*, 10/09/08, http://www.nytimes.com/2008/10/09/world/asia/09adopt.html?_r=1&oref=slogin.
39. Janelli and Yim, "The Transformation of Filial Piety in Contemporary South Korea"; Sang-Hun Choe, "Where Boys Were Kings, a Shift toward Baby Girls," *New*

York Times 12/23/2007, http://www.nytimes.com/2007/12/23/world/asia/23skorea.html?_r=3&oref=slogin&oref=slogin.
40. Holt video nos. 212–213: SBS, KBS news 07–09/09/2000; Holt video no. 216: KBS 08/29/2000, "People in the World: Bertha Holt, She's Been Planting Love in South Korea for 50 Years"; Holt video no. 219: SBS 2000, "I Want to Know: Bertha Holt's Life."
41. Holt video no. 185: KBS 08/21/99, "Thank You Sister Molly"; see also Holt video no. 6: KBS 12/05/83, "Let's Meet at 11"; Holt video no. 216: KBS 08/29/2000, "People in the World"; Holt video no. 285: ITV 12/29/2002, "Good Mood Morning"; Holt video no. 291: MBC 02/14/2003, "A Good World."
42. Overseas Koreans Foundation, *Community 2004: Guide to Korea for Overseas Adopted Koreans*, 14. These figures are based solely on the number of adoptees who visit adoption agencies (as children and as adults). The secretary-general of GOA'L reported that he had 40 active names of adult adoptees on his group list in 2004, and 100 names in 2005, and that 150 adult adoptees had attended the Christmas party of 2005. These figures may be more relevant because they reflect the growing adult Korean adoptee community in Seoul. See Eleana Kim, *Adopted Territory*, 184–185.
43. See www.back.or.kr, http://iecef.org; www.koroot.org.
44. See, for example, International Korean Adoptees Associations (IKAA): http://ikaa.org/en/.
45. "The Big Gathering of International Adoptees," *Chosun Ilbo*, 08/06/04.
46. *Chosun Ilbo*, 08/06/04.
47. *Chung An Ilbo*, 08/06/04.
48. *Seoul Kyungjae*, 08/06/04.
49. *Chungang Ilbo*, 08/06/04.
50. *Maeil Kyungjae*, 08/06/04.
51. *Chosun Ilbo*, 08/09/04.
52. *Dong-A Ilbo*, 08/02/04.
53. *Dong-A Ilbo*, 08/02/04.
54. *Dong-A Ilbo*, 08/07/04.
55. *Dong-A Ilbo*, 08/09/04.
56. "Korea Still Main Source of Adoptions in America," *Korea Herald*, 08/16/03.
57. "200,000 Adoptees Live Homesick for the Country Which Did Not Take Care of Them," *Dong-A Ilbo*, 08/02/04.
58. *Dong-A Ilbo*, 08/02/04.
59. http://www.koreaembassyusa.org/.
60. For an interesting comparison with repatriation and reintegration in Japan, see Tamanoi, "Overseas Japanese and the Challenges of Repatriation in Post-colonial East Asia," 217–235; Watt, *When Empire Comes Home*.

NOTES TO CHAPTER 2

1. Standards have changed over the past ten years. Now, most girls wear miniskirts and tank tops in the summer and display bare legs.
2. Many Korean words are based on Chinese characters but transcribed in Korean alphabet with a Korean pronunciation. They are formed by two syllables that correspond to two Chinese characters. There are many homophones, so one guesses the meaning of these words either from the context of the sentences or because the

Chinese characters are written between parentheses after the words. After reaching a certain level of proficiency in Korean, students learn the basic Chinese characters in order to better understand and memorize the Korean vocabulary.

3. The school tie is essentially hierarchical: especially among male students, a junior student (*hubae*) must greet an older student (*sŏnbae*) as soon as he sees him on campus, even if he is more than a hundred feet away. This civility will be rewarded in the future in terms of finding a job and getting promoted. In fact, the soil tie supplants the school tie in the political sphere. See Nam-Hee Lee, *The Making of Minjung*.

4. Personal notes, 2003.

5. Holt video no. 75 MBC: 10/29/93.

6. Adoption of babies and younger children is the priority in Korean institutions. In today's orphanages, children older than six have only a small chance of being adopted abroad. In addition, the law forbids children to be adopted after they reach the age of fourteen.

7. Saint Don Bosco (1815–1888) was an Italian Roman Catholic priest and educator who devoted his life to the poor and delinquent youth.

8. Interview with Molly Holt, 08/19/03.

9. Ibid.

10. "Arirang" is the title of a traditional ballad that has many versions. The lyrics are about love and resentment caused by separation and abandonment. For this reason, the destiny of the Swedish Korean adoptee is linked to the destiny of the heroine of the song: "Arirang, Arirang, Arirang, he's now crossing Mount Arirang. The one who leaves me and goes away will have sore feet within a mile."

11. See Kil-su Chang, *Susanne Brink's Arirang*.

12. See Ki-duk Kim, *Address Unknown*.

13. Dog meat is considered a rare, expensive dish reserved for men or the sick because of its nutritional value. The dog butcher is considered a member of a lower social class in traditional Korean society.

14. The minority Koreans in China do not use the term *kyop'o* but the self-designation *chosŏnjok* (the people of Chosŏn).

15. Personal notes, 2003.

16. Studying—more so than living—in Europe or the United States is also enviable because most of those in the Korean elite were educated abroad.

17. In the past couple of years, South Korean universities have hired English-speaking faculty to globalize their curricula.

18. Yet another category, education emigrants (students who left South Korea to attend schools abroad, usually with their mother but sometimes alone) have been recently despised for fleeing the demanding South Korean education system in hope of graduating from a minor American college. See Abelmann and Lie, *Blue Dreams*.

NOTES TO CHAPTER 3

1. This chapter has been previously published with minor differences as Prébin, "Three-Week Re-education to Koreanness."

2. "On the weekend of April 17, 18 and 19, 1998, with the support of the Korean Consulate in San Francisco, and with funds raised by the Korean American community in Sacramento, leaders of the adoptee-adoptive parent community . . . discussed the need to cultivate closer connections to Korean communities and to Korea. We

formed Korean American Adoptee, Adoptive Family Network (KAAN).... The network will encourage and expand the sharing of resources. There are 140,000 adoptees in the United States. If you count approximately 15 extended family members and friends, that is over 2,000,000 people with connections to Korea. If they travel to Korea, buy Korean products, feel positively about Korea and serve as unofficial ambassadors, they are benefiting Korea and the Korean American community as well. I believe that Korea has recently begun to see adoptees as a resource. This recognition can begin to define a reciprocal relationship to the benefit of all with adoptees and adoptive families both giving and getting" (www.kaanet.com).

3. "Mom, Dad, I Love You," *Chosun Ilbo*, 06/08/04. "The government began to nominally address the increasing adoptee presence with provisions in the 1995 Special Act Regarding Adoption Promotion and Procedure . . . that stipulated the establishment of programs and services to help returning adoptees. Programs, including cultural education, language training, preferential job recruitment, and birth family reunions, were further outlined in 1996, and over the past decade they have been slowly realized by adoptee advocacy goups such as GOA'L and a handful of recent NGOs" (Eleana Kim 2010, 184).

4. This program for childlike ill-adjusted adults illustrates well Foucault's terminology of state technology, deviance, and discipline. This program can be seen as one manifestation of the South Korean government's apparatus of control over subjects, who must be standardized to fit its definition of the diaspora. Foucault, "The Political Technology of Individuals"; Foucault, *Discipline and Punish*.

5. In South Korea, Protestant crosses are simple and straight, whereas Catholic crosses are ornamented at the extremities. This may reflect the fact that Protestantism and Catholicism are regarded as separate religions. See Clark, "Protestant Christianity and the State."

6. The former president of the Overseas Koreans Foundation (OKF), Lee Kwang-kyu, is also considered the founder of Korean anthropology. He is the author of numerous books, mainly on kinship but focused lately on overseas Koreans. See Reinschmidt, "Interview with Professor Lee Kwang-kyu."

7. "Due in large part to the quality of our care and adoption programs, Korean children adopted internationally are doing very well. . . . without the firmness and discipline of parental control, and without a hopeful future that a family can help provide, there would undoubtedly be higher levels of anti-social, if not criminal, behavior in store for Korea from these children" (Holt Children's Services 2002).

8. Capping no longer exists in South Korea. It used to directly precede marriage, when the groom-to-be would simply tie his hair in a bun and start wearing the hat for married men. See Ch'oe, "Belief in Malevolent Spirits," 95–110. See also description in Harvey, "*Minmyŏnuri*."

9. In line with or against the South Korean government's attempt to build the Korean diaspora through these programs, adoption scholars and adoptees consider that today's Korean adoptees constitute an effective community and report a rise in the number of Korean adoptee couples among their acquaintances. The 2004 OKF tour's brochure displays the word "community" and a picture of two adoptees dressed as traditional bride and groom.

10. The baby escort is generally only carried out by adoptees, but the opportunity is occasionally offered to Koreans or to foreigners who go voluntarily to one of the

main adoption agencies in Seoul and present the required criteria. In this case the practice has no symbolic meaning and is merely a way to finance one's plane ticket. I met in 2003 a Korean student who had chosen this option to visit her Korean American fiancé. His mother had heard of the practice at her Protestant church and asked her to do it.

11. Overseas adoptees are not the only group to encounter the motherland's imperialism. Studies have already evidenced similar characteristics in OKF programs for overseas Koreans such as Koreans living in ex-Soviet Central Asia. See Chung and Dibble, *Koryo Saram*.

12. "Since the early 1980s, indigenous and minority peoples have begun to take up a range of media in order to 'talk back' to structures of power that have erased or distorted their interests and realities. Faye Ginsburg has called this kind of work 'cultural activism,' to underscore the sense of both political agency and cultural intervention that people bring to these efforts, part of a spectrum of practices of self-conscious mediation and mobilization of culture that took particular shape beginning in the late twentieth century." In Ginsburg, Abu-Lughod, and Larkin, *Media Worlds*, 7–8; the text refers to Ginsburg, "Aboriginal Media and the Australian Imaginary."

13. "Emphasizing the failure to address class and gender differences in particular, Anthias (1998) points out that in the analysis of diasporic populations generally, theorists tend to take an overly homogenizing view of populations who may be very different, according to the time and circumstances of their departure and the conditions of their lives in different countries" (Agnew 2005, 151).

14. Like anthropologist Dorinne Kondo, who participated in and described a fairly harsh "ethics retreat" for Japanese workers, I was surprised to observe mostly obedience and consent in participants, although they were all foreigners and entitled, I thought, to misbehave or express disagreement with the treatment and speeches addressed to them. See Kondo, *Crafting Selves*.

NOTES TO CHAPTER 4

1. Naver Celebrity Search: Park Dong-kyu, http://people.naver.com/search/people_detail.nhn?frompage=nx_people&id=10032 (accessed 10/10/12).

2. Born in 1947, Lee Sang-byŏk attended Hongik University in Seoul and was a radio announcer at the beginning of his career. http://people.naver.com/search/people_detail.nhn?frompage=nx_people&id=3593 (accessed 10/10/12). Born in 1966, Lee Kŭm-hŭi studied political science and communication sciences at Yonsei University in Seoul. She started her career at a radio station and later became a hostess for television and a university professor. See http://people.naver.com/search/people_detail.nhn?frompage=nx_people&id=2283 (accessed 10/10/12).

3. KBS video no. 43-2-13378, news 9, 09/20/97. Korean Broadcasting Sytem changed from a governmental to a public broadcasting station in 1973. But until today, KBS's ties to the government are strong.

4. *Ach'im madang* was ranked number 17 in February 2005, and 14/15 in February 2009 and is no longer in the top twenty in 2012.

5. Many students whom I met in Seoul affirmed that their parents, who were Korean emigrants, had cable in Germany or the United States and loved *Ach'im madang*. One of my Korean American students in the United States told me her parents

rented recorded videos of *Ach'im madang* broadcasts at local Korean stores as regular entertainment. See KBS, *Ach'im madang*, 06/04/03, 8:56.
6. Personal translation of notes given by *Ach'im madang*'s scenario writer after her speech at the Global Overseas Adoptees' Link (GOA'L) Fifth Anniversary Conference, National Assembly (08/16/03).
7. There are thirty-five Koreans and eleven transnational adoptees.
8. KBS, *Ach'im madang*, 07/09/03, 8:30.
9. KBS, *Ach'im madang*, 06/04/03, 8:49.
10. Ibid., 8:45; Ibid., 9:19.
11. KBS, *Ach'im madang*, 08/06/03, 8:50.
12. KBS, *Ach'im madang*, 07/10/03, 8:54.
13. KBS, *Ach'im madang*, 06/04/03, 9:14.
14. See interview with the scenario writer Ho Yŏng-sŏn, 08/13/03.
15. KBS *Ach'im madang*, 07/30/03, 8:33: In fact, in my sample only one male participant is introduced by the hosts as a single man "living by himself," somewhat negative information for a forty-year-old man. The fact that the hostess insists on this detail shows it is an exception.
16. KBS, *Ach'im madang*, 08/06/03, 8:50.
17. Ibid., 8:36.
18. KBS, *Ach'im madang*, 06/04/03, 8:33.
19. Ibid., 9:01.
20. Ibid., 9:04.
21. In general, national audiences prefer locally produced programs to foreign ones. I submit that this is true also for at least first-generation emigrants abroad: "International trade in television programmes, while impressive in terms of its value, is nevertheless dwarfed by the overall volume of television programmes that only receive domestic circulation.... A series of national researchers working independently ... have shown that where national audiences have a choice they usually prefer television programmes produced nationally or in the national language" (Moran and Keane 2004, 4).
22. "The diasporic public spheres ... are part of the cultural dynamic of urban life in most countries and continents, in which migration and mass mediation co-constitute a new sense of the global as modern and the modern as global" (Appadurai 1996, 10).
23. http://www.findparent.or.kr/main_e.htm. The website is closed as of 2012.
24. http://www.koreanadoptees.net/KADfacts.html; http://www.reunion.or.kr/eng/family-search/search2/list-2asp (accessed 10/10/12).
25. Eastern Child Welfare Society, Holt Children's Services, and Korea Social Services. See http://seoul.usembassy.gov/acs_finding.html (accessed 10/10/12). The website also indicated other means of search, such as "Missing Persons Office" at the Seoul police headquarters; ads in the main newspapers *Hankook Ilbo*, *Dong-A Ilbo*, *Korea Times*, and *Korea Herald*; and various websites. *Ach'im madang* used to be described as the most efficient option, but as of 2012 this is no longer the case.
26. This is my translation of the scenario writer's notes for her presentation at GOA'L Fifth Anniversary Conference (08/16/2003).
27. Since the creation of the program, the hosts' personalities and private lives were the subject of gossip. The host Lee Sang-byŏk had the reputation of a bon vivant. "He

likes alcohol and consumes it without restrictions," revealed an interpreter. Middle-aged and older Korean women, who constituted the majority of the audience, found his humor immensely appealing. His retirement in 2005 provoked a flood of letters and e-mails on the KBS website. The hostess Lee Kŭm-hŭi was well known for still being single despite her good looks. In 2004, KBS studio corridors resonated with people's comments on her having put on weight. In 2005, a Korean friend who knew of my interest in the program told me that the hostess had been on a diet and was now back in shape. This revelation was the subject of much discussion online. During the broadcast, the host often overdid his paternal and jovial character, whereas the hostess was younger, overly maternal, compassionate, and an archetype of femininity. Their fame obviously added to the appeal of the program.

28. For similar reactions in audiences of Indian series, see Punwani, "Portrayal of Women on Television,"; quoted in Mankekar, *Screening Culture, Viewing Politics*, 7.
29. Ho's notes for her presentation at GOA'L Fifth Anniversary Conference (08/16/03).
30. KBS, *Ach'im madang*, 07/09/03, 9:26.
31. KBS, *Ach'im madang*, 06/04/03, 8:36.
32. KBS, *Ach'im madang*, 07/30/03, 9:14.
33. Ibid., 9:22.
34. A study reported that "1000 to 2000 dynamic [*hwaltonghanŭn*] married women (*ajumma*)" earn between 6,000 and 12,000 won per hour as a remunerated public. They typically hear about this income possibility through acquaintances (*arŭm arŭmŭro*). They most often attend programs with their friends or neighbors: first, to have fun, and second, to make a little money—between 50,000 and 100,000 won each month. See Sŏn-mi Kim, *Kugyŏng* (Watching).
35. Video KBS no. 43-2-18885 04/02/87 documentary: "*Kŭ sarami pogosip'da: nunmul-ŭi hyŏnjang*," or "scene of tears."
36. KBS, *Ach'im madang*, 07/16/03, 9:16.
37. KBS, *Ach'im madang*, 08/06/03, 9:09.
38. KBS, *Ach'im madang*, 06/04/03, 8:38.
39. KBS video no. 43-2-13378, news 9, 09/20/97, "The scene of tears."
40. Used only when referring to a man, the adjective *muttukttukhada* means laconic, severe, grumpy, blunt.
41. KBS, *Ach'im madang* 06/04/03, 9:19; KBS, *Ach'im madang* 08/13/03, 8:36; and KBS, *Ach'im madang* 07/30/03, 8:40.
42. KBS, *Ach'im madang* 06/04/03, 8:39; and KBS, *Ach'im madang* 07/16/03, 9:10.
43. KBS, *Ach'im madang* 06/04/03, 9:19.
44. KBS, *Ach'im madang* 07/30/03, 9:01.
45. KBS, *Ach'im madang* 08/13/03, 8:36.
46. KBS, *Ach'im madang* 07/09/03, 8:42.
47. Ibid., 9:05.
48. KBS, *Ach'im madang* 06/04/03, 9:04.
49. KBS, *Ach'im madang* 07/30/03, 9:01.
50. KBS, *Ach'im madang* 08/13/03, 8:36.
51. KBS, *Ach'im madang* 07/09/03, 9:17.
52. KBS, *Ach'im madang* 07/09/03, 9:08.
53. "Cultural nationalism has emerged to overcome the difficulties caused by the rapid globalization in the 1990s. *Sint'obulli*—'body and earth are inseparable'—and since

Korean bodies consist of food from Korea, Koreans should only eat Korean food—a recently popularised rallying phrase in Korea attempts ideological protection for Korean products" (Jeong Duk Yi 2002, 26).
54. KBS, *Ach'im madang*, 07/16/03, 8:59.
55. KBS, *Ach'im madang*, 06/04/03; 9:04.
56. KBS, *Ach'im madang*, 07/09/03, 9:21.
57. Ibid.
58. *Drama* is today a Korean word derived from English. It was first used by the Japanese to designate dramatic television fictions—as opposed to sitcoms, which depict mainly family stories.
59. "According to statistics, the country which produces the largest number of dramas in the world is India, then, it is South Korea" (Dong-won Lee 2000, 359). On television and series in India, see Mankekar, *Screening Culture*.
60. After the title of one chapter in Dong won Lee, *Taejung Maech'ewa Kajok*, 324: "I want to see this person again: the divided families' stories, more dramatic than dramas."
61. In his analysis of the mechanism of modern consumption, Appadurai establishes the difference between memory, a reconstruction that still refers to the past, and nostalgia, which is a recent strategic process observed especially in marketing. See Appadurai, *Modernity at Large*, 76–78.
62. Dong won Lee, *Taejung Maech'ewa Kajok*, 340.
63. "Nostalgia has become more evident in the global-human condition. In other words, nostalgia has increasingly assumed a global-cultural significance, quite regardless of its ontogenetic importance as a natural part of any individual's autobiography or lifestyle. . . . Fred Davis's definition of 'collective nostalgia' is relevant here: 'Collective nostalgia . . . refers to that condition in which . . . symbolic objects are of a highly public, widely shared, and familiar character, those symbolic resources from the past that . . . can trigger wave upon wave of nostalgic feeling in millions of persons at the same time.' . . . Davis provides a sociological account of the conditions that are producing collective nostalgia" (Davis 1979, 31–71; quoted in Robertson 1992, 160–161).
64. For Kalulis, this type of ritualized commemoration allows the living to be reminded of their dead by evoking the names of the places they used to occupy, as well as their relations with them. See Munn, "An Essay."
65. KBS, *Ach'im madang*, 06/04/03, 8:30.
66. Historians acknowledge the diversity of biographical genres and forms. For example, Kadar includes in that category the transcription of family recipes in the context of deportation and internment in concentration camps. See Kadar, "Wounding Events and the Limits of Autobiography," 81–104.
67. KBS, *Ach'im madang*, 06/04/03, 8:30.
68. Ibid., 8:32.
69. Ibid.
70. KBS, *Ach'im madang*, 07/30/03, 8:30; KBS, *Ach'im madang*, 06/04/03, 8:30; KBS, *Ach'im madang*, 07/09/03, 8:33.
71. The young and the old alike may know *Ach'im madang*, but as sociologist Dong won Lee explains, reception of the program undoubtedly differs depending on the viewer's age and generation. See *Taejung Maech'ewa Kajok*, 329.
72. KBS, *Ach'im madang*, 08/06/03, 8:38.
73. KBS, *Ach'im madang*, 06/04/03, 8:39.

74. KBS, *Ach'im madang* 07/09/03, 9:17.
75. See http://www.senatedemocrats.wa.gov/senators/shin/biography.htm (accessed 10/10/12).
76. "To define one's belonging to a generation through history and selective history (an event or a remarkable phenomenon) is part of a discourse and of social practices that contribute to the production of memory and history" (Attias-Donfut 1988, 172).

NOTES TO CHAPTER 5

1. Technically, the talk show *Ach'im madang* can be categorized as a program format or as an adapted copy of an original. See Moran and Keane, *Television across Asia*.
2. For a brief history of Yŏŭido, see Nelson, *Measured Excess*, 33–68.
3. KBS video no. 41-2-02862, 05/29/85, "Special Program: A 40-Year Separation."
4. The current main building of the Korean Broadcasting System was built in 1976.
5. Mandate: 1980–1988.
6. KBS video no. 41-2-02862, 05/29/85, "Special Program: A 40-Year Separation."
7. "It was not until the early 1960s that the Korean television industry began to be regulated. This was a time when Korea began to put every effort into modernization. In 1961 the military regime founded KBS-TV, the national broadcasting system, to 'cure the citizens' sick minds' and to display an image of 'the renewing nation'" (Donghoo Lee 2004, 38).
8. The Sunshine Policy was the foreign policy of South Korea's former president Kim Dae-jung toward North Korea. The name of the policy was inspired by one of Aesop's fables: The sun and the wind bet that they have the power to undress a human. By making the man warm, the sun wins, whereas the blowing wind makes the man put on more clothes. By showing a friendly attitude toward North Korea, Kim Dae-jung achieved cooperation in business and humanitarian enterprises.
9. Kim Dae-jung is seen as a martyr (because of continuous persecutions by his predecessors Park Chung-hee and Roh Tae-woo) or linked to miracles, as his nickname *indongch'o* indicates: *indongch'o* refers to a type of grape that produces fruit even in the winter. See Jager, *Narratives of Nation Building*, 147.
10. Ibid., 182.
11. Interview with Ho Yŏng-sŏn, 08/13/03.
12. See also http://redcross.or.kr (accessed May 2009).
13. Although my research has led me to assimilate historically and structurally the meetings as seen in the weekly meeting programs and the reunions between North and South, one can note a slight variation in these representations: whereas the weekly meetings mostly stage mothers and daughters, the sporadic inter-Korean meetings valorize the mother-son pairs. This seems to indicate that in the first case, the reunions are more or less voluntary, and separations from daughters are more natural. In the second case, separations from sons are depicted as involuntary and more dramatic. (I owe to Nancy Abelmann this insight.)
14. Mandate: 1998–2003.
15. "Kim Dae-jung's personal interest in the adoption issue may well go back to his own family background as the alleged extramarital son of a second wife and widowed mother in impoverished Chŏlla province. This specific familial, social and regional background and belonging . . . has made him instinctively aware of marginalized

and stigmatized groups and individuals in Korean society. In addition, after the premature death of his first wife, [he] married Lee Hee-ho [a professional social worker] who more or less adopted his two sons as her own" (Hübinette 2005, 96).
16. Brédier, *Corps étranger*.
17. Born in 1948.
18. Interview, 07/02/03.
19. Interview, 08/13/03.
20. KBS, *Ach'im madang*, 07/09/03, 8:50.
21. Expression first used by French Annales school historian Fernand Braudel (1902–1985) between the two world wars.

NOTES TO CHAPTER 6

1. Anthropologists also tend to oppose adoption and fosterage, which demonstrates the difficulty of thinking about certain dynamics of kinship that cannot belong to one category or the other, as well as the difficulty of finding a satisfactory definition for all these child-rearing options that could apply to all societies.
2. This section is based partly on some of the data I used in a previously published article. See Prébin, "Looking for 'Lost' Children in South Korea."
3. In fact, many sources confirm that child abandonment has been a major social problem ever since the end of the Korean War, though it was far from nonexistent before. "Three successive changes of government within a period of eleven months [after the Park Chung-Hee assassination in October 1979] wrought chaos and economic instability in Korea. More and more unemployed moved into Seoul and other big cities seeking jobs. The number of abandoned babies increased, particularly in Seoul. . . . Most of the 800 orphanages in the country were in Seoul or nearby cities. Eighty thousand children were accommodated in these institutions. It would be easy for the parents to bring their babies to one of them. But for some reason, people chose to leave their babies on the doorsteps of individual homes, bus stations, train stations, or marketplaces where the babies would be spotted by those who passed by. Whoever found these babies usually reported it to the nearby police station or brought them to the city children's department. The police would initiate an investigation to identify the person who abandoned the child. Abandonment was a criminal offense with a prison sentence of up to eight years. Because of the heavy penalty, abandonment was done discreetly. The police were almost never successful in finding the parents" (David Kim 2001, 227).
4. KBS, *Ach'im madang*, 07/30/03, 8:47; KBS, *Ach'im madang*, 08/13/03, 8:41. Cases of abandonment were less common than other forms of separation on *Ach'im madang*, because those who had been abandoned were less likely to have enough information to locate their birth families and, consequently, had less of a chance to appear on the television show. For figures on adoption circumstances, see Eleana Kim, *Adopted Territory*, 25.
5. KBS, *Ach'im madang*, 06/04/03, 8:45; ibid., 8:56; KBS, *Ach'im madang*, 08/13/03, 8:48.
6. KBS, *Ach'im madang*, 08/06/03, 8:43; KBS, *Ach'im madang*, 07/30/03, 9:17; KBS, *Ach'im madang*, 08/06/03, 9:14; KBS, *Ach'im madang*, 08/27/03, 9:02.
7. Until 2008, in theory, the family missing a father—the only possible "head of the family"—was not recognized by law. In practice, there have been and there are more

and more families led by mothers. See Soo-jin Kang, "Change in the Family Structure and the Family Law."
8. On child labor in the colonial period, see Janice Kim, *To Live to Work*.
9. KBS, *Ach'im madang*, 06/04/03, 8:45; ibid., 8:49; KBS, *Ach'im madang*, 07/30/03, 8:47; KBS, *Ach'im madang*, 08/06/03, 8:57.
10. Dong-won Lee, *Taejung Maech'ewa Kajok*, 335–337.
11. KBS, *Ach'im madang*, 07/30/03, 8:42.
12. Ibid., 9:09.
13. KBS, *Ach'im madang*, 08/27/03, 8:55.
14. Seungsook Moon, "Begetting the Nation."
15. "The pre-1991 version of family law granted the husband as the provider of his family a series of rights over family members—i.e., the right to accept or refuse one's entry into the family register, the right to expel a family member from it, the right to decide a place of residence, and the right to exercise primary custody over children in case of divorce. . . . the husband is even entitled to admit an 'illegitimate' child he begot with another woman into his family register without his wife's consent!" (Seungsook Moon 1998, 53).
16. KBS, *Ach'im madang*, 06/04/03, 9:04.
17. Before industrialization, a tiled roof, as opposed to a thatched roof, was a sign of wealth in the countryside.
18. KBS, *Ach'im madang*, 07/16/03, 8:50.
19. KBS, *Ach'im madang*, 08/27/03, 9:12.
20. The same arguments can be said to apply to Chinese adoptive families. See Johnson, Huang, and Wang, "Infant Abandonment and Adoption in China"; Johnson, *Wanting a Daughter, Needing a Son*.
21. KBS, *Ach'im madang*, 06/04/03, 9:14.
22. KBS, *Ach'im madang*, 07/09/03, 8:50.
23. KBS, *Ach'im madang*, 07/30/03, 8:40.
24. Interview with Molly Holt, 08/19/03.
25. KBS, *Ach'im madang*, 08/06/03, 8:50.
26. KBS, *Ach'im madang*, 08/13/03, 8:57.
27. Lallemand, *La circulation des enfants*; Etienne, "Maternité sociale, rapport d'adoption et pouvoir des femmes chez les Baoulé"; Bowie, *Cross-Cultural Approaches to Adoption*; Leinaweaver, *The Circulation of Children*.
28. For Brazil, see Fonseca, "Patterns of Shared Parenthood among the Brazilian Poor," 142–161.
29. Based on a certain idea of children's welfare, this Western definition of adoption is increasingly criticized by adoption scholars. See, for example, Ouellette, "Social Temporalities of Adoption and the Limits of Plenary Adoption," 69–86.
30. KBS, *Ach'im madang*, 06/04/03, 8:04; KBS, *Ach'im madang*, 07/16/03, 9:10; KBS, *Ach'im madang*, 08/13/03, 9:08; ibid., 9:14.
31. Interview, 06/03/04.
32. For more detail on my interviews with several birth mothers, see Prébin, *Adoption Internationale*; Prébin, "Korean Orphans, Domestic Adoptees."
33. Because there is a large and established literature on Confucian Korea, I do not feel the need to review and revisit it, and instead invite the reader to consult the bibliography on that topic.

34. Maurice Godelier, *Métamorphoses de la parenté*, 518; see also Gernet, *La Chine ancienne*.
35. Théry, *Recomposer une famille, des rôles et des sentiments*; Théry, *Couple, filiation et parenté aujourd'hui*.
36. There are two celebrations for a baby. After a hundred days (*paegil*), the baby's life is supposed to be secured. Parents and relatives gather to conduct a ritual that greets the child. On the child's first birthday *chŏtdol*, relatives celebrate the child again and make him or her grab an object that is indicative of his or her future: a pen for a scholar, money for business, and so on. This tradition is still alive in contemporary South Korea, and most large hotels host the event along with weddings and sixtieth and seventieth birthdays.
37. KBS, *Ach'im madang*, 07/09/03, 8:50.
38. KBS, *Ach'im madang*, 07/16/03, 8:43.
39. KBS, *Ach'im madang*, 06/04/03, 8:39.
40. Ibid., 8:44.
41. Ibid.
42. Fonseca, "Patterns of Shared Parenthood," 143–161.
43. KBS, *Ach'im madang*, 06/04/03, 9:18.
44. On siblings' relations in recomposed families, see Martial, "Partages et fraternité dans les familles recomposées."
45. KBS, *Ach'im madang*, 07/09/03, 8:42.
46. "The term pseudo-kinship designates social relations which are expressed in kinship terms (address or reference terms) without necessarily building real kinship ties like consanguinity or marriage. It is not the only term to be used, as quasi-kinship and fictive kinship have the same meanings" (Fine 1992, 195). See Bonte, "Pseudo-parenté." According to Fine's definition, "The terms pseudo-kinship, parallel kinship, fictive kinship, artificial kinship, and ritual kinship [designate] ties between persons who, modeling after filiation, germanity or alliance, create these ties by means of rituals different from birth or marriage."
47. Holt videos, no. 73: 09/93, "Children of the World, Foster Mothers Visit Norway"; no. 111: 05/08/95, KBS1 9 o'clock news, "A Foster Mother's Love"; no. 154: 05/03/98, Sunday Magazine, "A Foster Mother's Story"; no. 203: 03/07/2000, Pohang MBC, "Foster Mothers Volunteering"; no. 228: 2000, KBS1, "In the World: Foster Mother Park Young-ja's Eighth Farewell"; no. 244: 2001, Happy Saturday, "Pop Star Ha Li-su Becomes Foster Mother"; no. 247: 11/25/01, KBS Selected Files 4321, "A Feeling Stronger Than the One of Giving Birth—A Foster Mother's Story"; no. 287: 05/31/03, Opening Channel, "My Thirteenth Son: A Foster Mother's Story"; no. 288: 04/03, MBC program, "Foster Mother Chae Song-hwa upon Her Child's Departure"; no. 314: 11/25/01, KBS ITV Selected Files 4321, "How to Become a Foster Mother: Adoptees Return" ; no. 315: 2004, MBC Midnight Special, "To Be a Foster Mother."
48. "As part of the overseas training program for long-service foster mothers, Holt Children's Services sent two foster mothers, Ms. Yoo (who has cared for 72 babies) and Ms. Kim (who has cared for 52 babies) to Europe on June 5. This overseas training included 11 days of visiting overseas cooperating agencies in Norway, Denmark and France, meeting adoptive families and having a meaningful reunion with children the mothers had fostered" (Holt Children's Services 2003, 13).
49. "Although they decided to become foster mothers, many women stop their activity because raising a child is more difficult than they would have thought, especially

when after a few months they must separate from the child they got attached to. This pain is so unbearable that they stop fostering. . . . Hong, 53: . . . when my child departs, I seek refuge in a corner to cry my heart out. . . . Lee, 65: . . . when I see my child go, the child I want to keep with me, I feel emptiness in my bosom and I have to sit down. When I miss my child's odor, I cover my face with one of the little clothes he/she wore." In "It Breaks My Heart When People Accuse Me of Raising a Child to Sell It Later," in *Dong-A Ilbo*, 2004. A 1990 documentary indicates that Holt foster mothers are all volunteers who receive approximately 3,000 won (three dollars) per day for each baby. See also Holt video no. 43: KBS 12/13/90, "Children Still for Sale."

50. The figure of the foster mother in South Korea is not unlike that described in Abreu, "Baby-Bearing Storks," 138–153.

51. KBS, *Ach'im madang*, 06/04/03, 8:38; KBS, *Ach'im madang*, 08/13/03, 9:14; KBS, *Ach'im madang*, 08/09/03, 9:02; KBS, *Ach'im madang*, 08/27/03, 8:36.

52. The younger brother of one female participant was adopted in the "elder house" (house of the head of the lineage—oldest living male relative on the father's side) after the parents' death. The elder house's representative, a cousin, came onstage with the brother. See also KBS, *Ach'im madang*, 07/09/03, 8:58.

53. In his ethnography of the 1983 telethon, Choong Soon Kim finds that remarriage is one explanation for the absence of fathers during the reunions. Choong Soon Kim, *Faithful Endurance*, 119–120.

54. KBS, *Ach'im madang*, 07/30/03, 8:42; KBS, *Ach'im madang*, 08/13/03, 8:48; KBS, *Ach'im madang*, 08/27/03, 8:42; KBS, *Ach'im madang*, 08/06/03, 9:14.

55. Meulders-Klein and Théry, *Les recompositions familiales aujourd'hui*.

56. "Divorce in South Korea: Striking a New Attitude," *New York Times*, 09/21/03, A19.

57. Théry, *Le démariage, justice et vie privée*.

58. KBS, *Ach'im madang*, 06/04/03, 8:56.

59. KBS, *Ach'im madang*, 08/13/03, 8:57.

60. The Kamanos of New Guinea practice closed adoption: "Food creates the flesh of the individual. A woman can claim she 'made' the baby she breastfed, but this nutritive generation does not suffice" (Lallemand 1993, 98–99).

61. "Paradoxically, when the type of filiation tends to minimize women's importance in the family, they insist on the specificity of their being pregnant, their delivering, their fostering to be recognized socially, even when they haven't gone through these stages. The overemphasis on their biological tie to the child is a compensation, which sounds like a perpetual complaint about their denial of any social status. As they themselves claim that their rights come from the very nature to which society relegated them, they get even further from the less natural but far more tangible prerogatives given to men" (Lallemand 1993, 100–101).

62. "Kinship systems cut the field of genealogical consanguinity in many different ways . . . in ensembles where the social quality of consanguinity differs according to the degree of proximity between individuals" (Héritier 1981, 14).

63. See also Meillassoux, *Mythes et limites de l'anthropologie*, 13–83; Godelier, *Métamorphoses de la parenté*.

64. KBS, *Ach'im madang*, 08/06/03, 9:14.

65. Ibid., 8:37.

66. KBS, *Ach'im madang*, 08/27/03, 8:36.

67. Ibid., 9:08.
68. The descriptions of family resemblances by family members are often the result of interpretation, motivated by either ideological or material interests—especially in cases where inheritance or succession is concerned. These resemblances are often stereotypical. See Vernier, *Le visage et le nom*; Medick and Sabean, *Interest and Emotion*.
69. KBS, *Ach'im madang*, 06/04/03, 8:56.
70. In the Confucian state, "Deviation by women from prescribed sexual mores . . . would lead not only to the disruption of the agnatic line and paternal power but would undermine the foundation of the national sphere as well." Jager, *Narratives of Nation Building*, 68.
71. Choong Soon Kim invokes Confucian ideals of the virtuous wives in his interpretation of the faithfulness of couples separated by the war with several life stories. But he attests indirectly to the phenomenon of women's emancipation in postwar Korea: a mother successfully supports her family by herself and chooses not to remarry. For comparisons, see Reuben Hill, *Families under Stress: Adjustment to the Crisis of War Separation and Reunion*.
72. KBS, *Ach'im madang*, 07/09/03, 8:50; KBS, *Ach'im madang*, 07/30/03, 9:17.
73. See American adoptee Katy Robinson's biographical story: Sunny, her "auntie," is a biological daughter of Katy's grandfather, who left his legitimate wife (Katy's grandmother) under the pretext that she caused their son's death. Sunny was raised by her mother, then by a maternal aunt when her mother left to work in Japan for fifteen years. Looking at each other, Sunny and Katy mutually contemplate what they could have been as an adoptee living abroad or as a Korean without a father. See Robinson, *A Single Square Picture*.
74. In Korea, the term "head of the family" (*hoju*) refers exclusively to a man. "Reflecting the principle of primogeniture, the legal order of succession of household headship moves down from the first son, to the first son's first son, to the second son. When there is no male heir, the first daughter can assume the domestic authority of the household head, but only on a temporary basis, until she marries. . . . Yet the revised family law still prohibits marriage between persons with the same family name and ancestral seat and the formal succession of household headship" (Seungsook Moon 1998, 53).
75. The "head of the family" system has been maintained since 1957, despite successive reforms in family law, but it changed in 2008. The disappearance of the *hojuje* and the implementation of an individual register imply (1) gender equality that makes the saying "a married daughter is no better than a stranger" outdated, and puts an end to the practice of discriminating against children because of their parents' divorce; (2) that a child can take the family name (*sŏng*) and the name of the place of origin (*pon*) of either the father or the mother, even in case of divorce or birth out of wedlock; (3) the inclusion within the family of people who were not considered as such until 2008: daughters-in-law, sons-in-law, parents-in-law, siblings of one's wife; (4) the facilitation of adoption of a child younger than fifteen by parents married for at least three years. That child will have the same rights as the biological children of the adoptive father. If one child follows one of his or her divorced parents and that parent remarries, the new spouse will have the option of adopting that child after a year of marriage. See Korean Broadcasting System, *Family Relation Register*, http://english.kbs.co.kr/mcontents/zoom/1499518_11689.html (accessed 10/10/12).

NOTES TO CHAPTER 7

1. "From April 1 through May 25, 1984, a team of social surveyors from Korea University and the *Hankook Ilbo* newspaper studied the adjustment problems of reunited families. An analysis of a sample of 336 families revealed that only a few reunited family members were living together (2.1 percent) and that among the others contact was less frequent than expected: 74.1 percent met once a month, but 9.3 percent met less than once a month or irregularly, and 14.5 percent had had no contact since their reunions" (Choon Soon Kim 1988, 119).
2. Fieldwork, 03/22/03.
3. A female *ego* calls the older sister's husband *hyŏngbu*, whereas he simply calls her by her first name, as there is no address or referential term for this side of the relation. Kwang-kyu, Lee *Kinship System in Korea*.
4. In the Korean context, presents are often given to ensure prestige (to save face: *ch'emyŏn sŏda*), for the symbolic reimbursement of debt, or as an overture to establishing relations.
5. http://www.reunion.or.kr/eng/family-search/search2/list-2asp (accessed 2005; site no longer exists).
6. Ibid.
7. Fieldwork, 07/10/03.
8. With the continued migration to the city and the high population concentration in South Korean conurbations, the lack of space to bury the dead in traditional ways has led to an increase in prices and to the adoption of other funeral practices. Traditionally, "information about a tomb typically includes its location, the direction in which the coffin was buried, and whether a husband and his wife had a shared burial mound (*happu*), separate mounds placed side by side (*ssangbun*), or mounds located in the same tomb site (*tongwŏn*)" (Shima 1998).
9. Fieldwork, 07/10/03.
10. As already mentioned, *Ch'usŏk* is the harvest festival during which Koreans gather in their hometowns with their relatives to visit the tombs of their recently deceased relatives. Sometimes, when the family extends to the clan, all parties go to the place where their common remote ancestor was supposedly buried. See Janelli and Yim Janelli, *Ancestor Worship*.
11. KBS, *Ach'im madang*, 06/16/03, 8:59.
12. Fieldwork, 07/10/03.
13. Fieldwork, 07/11/03.
14. KBS, *Ach'im madang*, 06/16/03, 9:04.
15. Ibid.
16. Ibid.
17. KBS, *Ach'im madang*, 08/13/03, 8:57.
18. KBS, *Ach'im madang*, 07/09/03, 9:21.
19. See GOA'L, *The TOAK: GOA'L Newsletter: A New Beginning*; see rubric: "Birth Families Searching for Children," 31.
20. Carsten, *After Kinship*, 9.

NOTES TO CHAPTER 8

1. Generic term used for older women, related or not.

2. The difficulty of my own relationship with my relatives gave me essential insights into other adoptees' relationships with their biological families after the first meeting. I am not familiar with the case of male adoptees' return and building of relationship with their birth families, but the few I have met were living in Korea, some were married to a Korean woman, and most seemed to endorse their role of sons fully, taking care of their mothers or parents. Several told me they were sent to transnational adoption to get a better education but in the hope they would come back and help their birth parents. As in the case of domestic adoption, these examples suggest that the reasons boys were adopted abroad and are able to rebuild relationships with their birth parents if they meet them do not apply in the case of girls.

3. At least in discourses reported by Modell, American birth parents try to accommodate the existence of the child they parted from according to a wide range of options: "Birthparents tried a variety of models, including friendship, extended kinship (becoming another member of the family), genealogical parenthood (a tie of biology, not of conduct), and social parenthood (involvement in the adopted person's life). Always, however, the practical details of establishing a relationship compelled a reconsideration of the meaning of parenthood" (Modell 1994, 187).

4. As mentioned earlier, Carsten has shown evidence of the benefits and the profound meaning of meetings for adoptees, even if the initial reunions with their birth parents do not lead to a strong, long-term relationship and even provoke painful feelings. Here, my concern is with birth parents' rationale for meeting their children.

NOTES TO CHAPTER 9

1. "The notion that good rituals make better people stems from Korea's Confucian heritage wherein all demonstrations of propriety (*ye*, in Chinese *li*), including the correct performance of critical passage rites, are seen as fostering harmonious human relationships and a well-run social order" (Kendall 1996, 10).

2. "The *churye* who accomplishes the marriage is a thoroughly secular figure, a respected elder who is invited by the groom's side to preside at their son's wedding. In this, the new wedding follows solidly upon a tradition of Confucian family rites for which there is no designated clergy. Instead, knowledgeable and virtuous elders ensure that the procedures are carried out according to the teachings of the sages. [The *churye* is] someone who has a reputation for virtue and whose family is flourishing" (Kendall 1996, 35).

3. Until the beginning of the twentieth century, the highest class in Korean society was the *yangban* class. Following the Japanese annexation and colonization of Korea, which lasted from 1910 to 1935, Korean intellectuals accused the *yangban* class of causing Korea's backwardness by preferring Chinese culture over the Western influences that led Japan to power. But to this day, the pride of contemporary Korean families is still to have a doctor, a lawyer, or a university professor among their members, which comes from the emphasis the *yangban* class placed on education. Korean families do not hesitate to spend their savings in financing doctoral studies for one of their members.

4. "The spatial positioning of the master of ceremonies, commanding the wedding hall from behind a podium, suggests a Christian minister, as does his oratorical style. As primary officiate, the *churye* performs the critical work of wedding ritual . . . he

"does things with words," proclaiming the couple as husband and wife. "The *churye's* speech (*churyesa, churyeŭi malssŭm*) is the most significant contribution to the wedding" (Kendall 1996, 35–37).
5. KBS, *Ach'im madang*, 08/06/03, 8:31.
6. KBS, *Ach'im madang*, 08/13/03, 8:33.
7. KBS, *Ach'im madang*, 07/09/03, 9:41–42.
8. KBS, *Ach'im madang*, 07/30/03, 8:39.
9. KBS, *Ach'im madang*, 08/27/03, 8:36.
10. Sociologist Hosu Kim argues that the meeting scene expresses feelings of shame, which have mainly to do with questions of self-representation in front of others, or matters of face. Hosu Kim, "A Flickering Motherhood: Korean Birthmothers' Internet Community," http://www.barnard.edu/sfonline/blogs/ (accessed May 2009).
11. Interview, 08/13/03.
12. An interjection expressing lamentation, complaint, or pain. Could be translated as "alas!" or "aaah!"
13. An interjection expressing embarrassment, frustration, or anger. Could be translated as "Jesus!" or "God!"
14. KBS, *Ach'im madang*, 06/04/03, 8:56.
15. Ibid., 9:14.
16. KBS, *Ach'im madang*, 07/09/03 8:38.
17. See earlier discussion on *chŏng* in chapter 4.
18. KBS, *Ach'im madang*, 07/09/03, 9:21.
19. KBS, *Ach'im madang*, 06/04/03, 8:36. See introduction.
20. KBS, *Ach'im madang*, 07/30/03, 8:36.
21. KBS, *Ach'im madang*, 07/09/03, 8:56.
22. "In Korea, people do not express their suffering or their desire of revenge; . . . they abstain from talking about it by fear that it provokes terror in the audience, and that it constitutes an antisocial act. . . . Thus, all suffering and the desire of revenge are repressed. It is only in the space and time of a particular rite, with the help of the dead, that the *han* generated by the repression is revealed in its integrality" (Hee-kyung Lee 1995, 129).
23. KBS, *Ach'im madang*, 06/04/03, 9:04.
24. KBS, *Ach'im madang*, 07/16/03, 9:05.
25. KBS, *Ach'im madang*, 07/09/03, 9:01.
26. Ibid., 9:21.
27. KBS, *Ach'im madang*, 06/04/03, 8:56.
28. "The elaboration of *han* and resentment depends less on the individual dispositions than on certain human 'situations.' The form of these 'situations' already presents a certain potential of *han* or of resentment" (Hee-kyung Lee 1995, 126).
29. Sometimes the process of developing *han* is described differently. The description starts from anger that explodes outside and points at an external cause separated from the self before being repressed and becoming reflexive: "[*Han*] also envelops the individual in self-blame. . . . unlike simple anger against others; [*han*] is reflexive" (Schwartz and Kim 2002, 214).
30. "Mom, Dad, I Understand . . . I Love You," *Chosun Ilbo*, 08/06/04.
31. *Chosun Ilbo*, 08/06/04.
32. *Dong-A Ilbo*, 08/09/04.

33. Ibid.
34. Ibid.
35. The power of children and young people at certain ritualized moments of the year in societies where they usually do not have prerogatives is a social phenomenon explored by Lévi-Strauss in his famous article on Christmas festivities. Lévi-Strauss, "Le Père-Noël supplicié," 1575–1590. See also Sorlin, "Children as War Victims in Postwar European Cinema," 104–124.
36. This resonates with what has already been written about family search, meetings, and their seemingly contradictory outcomes in Western settings: "While the act of seeking out birth relatives appears in a very obvious sense to underline the primacy of birth ties in the culture of British kinship, in other ways these adopted people simultaneously disturb that primacy" (Carsten 2004, 150).

NOTES TO CHAPTER 10

1. I use the term "lost" in the same way that the media uses the term "separation." It encompasses all kinds of separations, including death, abandonment, domestic or international adoption, fosterage, child labor, or the real loss of a child in the words and minds of birth parents. See chapter 6.
2. In fact, infanticide occurs in developed countries and does not always coincide with a society's poverty or material decline, or with a specific social threat: "Infanticide is still a fact in the United States and Western Europe (Hobbs and Wynne 1996).... both child abuse and neglect deaths are likely to be concealed within the diagnosis of sudden infant death syndrome (SIDS)" (Einarsdottir 2000, 167).
3. Norgren shows how Japan's successive contradictory policies regarding abortion and contraception were mainly a question of lobbyists willing to protect their source of income and the state trying to regulate its population in quantitative and qualitative terms. Like the issue of transnational adoption in South Korea, which was first raised by foreign journalists during the Olympic Games of 1988, the issue of abortion in Japan was tackled by the media during the Olympic Games of 1964, pushing the Japanese government to react. In both countries, concerns about demographic imbalance and about labor shortage, respectively, contributed, along with international opinion, to the revision of laws and the change of policies. For a history of abortion in Japan, see Tiana Norgren, *Abortion before Birth Control*.
4. "According to the Korean Penal Code, articles 269 and 270, induced abortion is illegal. The government did not immediately legislate more liberal laws regarding abortion when it began its family planning campaign, however. Two attempts were made to legalize induced abortion with the pressure of Protestant religious groups and politicians in 1966 and 1970, but they were defeated. A Maternal and Child Health Law, however, was passed in 1973 by the Extraordinary State Council (martial law authority) which set out conditions in which abortions could be performed. According to the law, a physician is only permitted to perform an abortion, with the consent of the woman and her spouse, in case of hereditary defect of the fetus and certain infectious diseases, when the pregnancy results from rape or incest and when from a medical point of view, the continuation of pregnancy will be detrimental to the health of the mother. It did not permit abortion on socioeconomic grounds although the government had intended to do so in the earliest preparation

phase of the law. It did not do so because of religious protest from Catholics and a few politicians" (Tedesco 1996, http://eng.buddhapia.com/_Service/_ContentView/ETC_CONTENT_2.ASP?pk=0000766823&sub_pk=&clss_cd=0002180012&top_menu_cd=0000000808 (accessed 10/10/12). See also Peterson, *Korean Adoption and Inheritance.*

5. One-quarter of South Koreans call themselves Buddhists.
6. A Korean proverb expresses the private nature of children's death and the absence of a conventional public event for this occasion: "A parent is buried within a mountain, but when a child dies, it is buried in the parent's heart." "When children die, their parents ritually weep in the same way as when an adult dies, but no funeral is held and no formal burial mound is built. If the corpse is buried, the place of internment is marked with a simple stone only. The corpse of a child may also be either thrown away or hung on a tree. . . . Moreover, dead children are not commemorated in Confucian rituals thereafter. . . . All these actions carry the meaning that children who have died are not considered full-fledged persons" (Ch'oe 1998, 96–97).
7. "It is not easy to draw a sharp line between a child and an adult in terms of age. According to the *Li-chi* (Treatises on Ceremonial Usages), *sang* ["death of children" in Confucian terms] applies to death under the age of nineteen. Death under the age of seven is especially designated as *sang* without mourning dress. In Korea, a person under the age of seven is definitely considered a child. In the past, a man was considered an adult after he had held an initiation ceremony, usually during the teens. Since such initiation ceremonies are no longer held, further investigation is needed regarding the age at which a person is no longer considered a child in relation to death rituals" (Ch'oe 1998, 106).
8. Possibly with the Japanese colonization and the implementation of cremation as the most hygienic way to dispose of the dead, the young dead were exclusively cremated in modern South Korea until the government started promoting cremation for everybody as the most economical and ecological solution to the lack of land. Cremation instead of burial has long been considered the proper funerary practice for the abnormal dead. But representations of the different categories of dead may change, as cremation is already practiced by up to 60 percent of the population (Prébin 2012).
9. *Doryŏngnim* is the spirit of a boy who died at home before reaching the age of five. *Sanma Doryŏng* are two divinities usually represented together as a young boy and a young girl. See Yŏl-su Yun, *Searching for the Origins of Folk Religion.*
10. For Taiwan, see Moskowitz, *The Haunting Fetus,* 150–165. For extreme cases of criminal seizure of young children's power by shamans, see Ch'oe, "Belief in Malevolent Spirits," 96–97.
11. In South Korea, people say about a woman whose husband or children die before her that she is "bad"; her in-laws especially accuse her of having "eaten" them (*mŏkta*). She is indeed viewed as responsible for their health and therefore for their death.
12. I, however, heard specialists of Korean shamanism speak about their experiences of shamanic rites during which shamans are visited by the spirits of dead infants whose voices then became so shrill it made their audiences shiver.
13. Interview with shaman (*tangol*) Park In-o, 07/04/04. About dead children in Taiwan trying to accomplish reincarnation by going back to their mothers' womb, see Moskowitz, *The Haunting Fetus.*

14. "The dark side consists of *won* (enmity, vengeance), *won* (written differently in Chinese characters and meaning 'false accusation'), *sorum* (sorrow), and *t'an* (lamentation, regret, grief). The bright side consists primarily of *han* as *chŏng*—*chŏnghan*—by which *chŏng* literally means 'attachment,' but more generally means the conversion of resentment into creativity, love, and commitment" (Grinker 1998, 80).
15. Interview with shaman Park In-o, 07/04/04.
16. Holt video nos. 310–311: MBC production 08/04, "Special Fiftieth Anniversary of International Adoption: 'Mom, I Am Here!'" I and II.
17. Janelli evokes the reluctance of informants to speak about ghosts and malevolent spirits of dead kin out of context, which means outside of the shamanistic ritual *kut*. Older women do not talk about their lost children. They sometimes evoke the subject during interviews but only briefly. Younger women, like the single mothers I interviewed, were willing to soothe their anxiety by meeting an adult adoptee and confiding in someone.
18. Death far from home (*kaeksa*) used to be considered as inauspicious as suicide or violent death. The same spirit is invoked in the three cases during the shamanistic rite *kut*.
19. "Expelling rites for dead children . . . may be divided into two groups according to whether the rite is intended 1) to subdue the being momentarily or 2) to destroy it definitively by confirming the status of the dead child among the dead, which it temporarily lacks. . . . [The rites can consist of] 1) prayer, the word of God; swearing; questioning formulae; command to kill mother; expelling words: go away etc.; Lord's prayer backwards; stroke or thrust; shooting; crossing running water; encircling the being; sign of the cross; steel; knife; going to a field; going to cross-roads. 2) baptism, name-giving; burial in haunting place; taking body to the graveyard; throwing or shrouding cloth; revealing crime or parents" (Pentikäinen 1968, 357).
20. "One shaman boasted of her abilities by telling us that she could make a lot of people cry; evidently, eliciting the emotions of participants is seen by shamans as a major goal" (Janelli and Yim Janelli 1982, 154).
21. KBS, *Ach'im madang*, 07/30/03, 8:52.
22. On Taiwan: "It would not be possible to promote this practice for profit were it not fulfilling fundamental psychological and social needs that are not being met in other religious beliefs and practices" (Moskowitz 2001, 40).
23. Mourning is the public expression of grief. Grief is the personal reaction to the loss of a loved one. Melancholia refers to a state where a person is unable to put an end to grief and exit the period of bereavement. The impossibility of verifying death after someone's disappearance, the interdiction of public mourning, and the feeling of responsibility for someone's death are common reasons for melancholia.
24. "Many have suffered the loss of older children—children who have been chronically ill, murdered, or killed in accidents; others have lost children at birth or just after birth (neonatal deaths); others have had children who were stillborn; others miscarried; others surrendered their children for adoption. All of these losses share a common tragedy: the uniquely grievous loss of a child" (Savage 1989, 2). See also "A Flickering Motherhood: Korean Birthmothers' Internet Community," http://www.barnard.edu/sfonline/blogs/ (accessed May 2008).
25. KBS, *Ach'im madang*, 08/27/03, 8:36.

26. Ibid., 8:42.
27. South Korean television uses the videoconference technique to let some transnational adoptees "meet" with their biological family. See Holt video no. 184: 08/03/99 "Looking for Our Lost Families."
28. This is the main argument given without further explanation by those who promote the reunions of the divided families. See Chung-in Moon and Steinberg, *Kim Dae-jung Government*.
29. Grinker warns against the illusion of the reunification at the end of the 1990s: "One way in which South Koreans seek to resolve their ambivalence is to assume the metaphorical role of colonizer, transform the north, and reintegrate (unify) Self and Other. In doing so, they define and affirm North Korean's otherness. . . . The idea that North Koreans have to transform themselves, or be helped to transform themselves, is strikingly similar to the ideas of evangelists and colonists at the turn of the century, and it presents us with the disturbing recognition that a form of colonial discourse on unification is beginning to emerge" (Grinker 1998, 64–66).
30. Issues of identification between West and East Germans and their disillusion have been described by sociologist Andreas Glaeser, *Divided in Unity*.
31. A film by Je-gyu Kang (2004, 147 minutes). The title has been translated in English as "Brotherhood of War." *T'aegŭkki* is the Korean flag informally created and used for the first time in Japan in 1883 by a Korean diplomat. According to the Chinese characters, *t'aegŭk* means "cosmos" in reference to Taoism; *ki* means flag. See Schmid, *Korea between Empires*, 78–80.

NOTES TO CONCLUSION

1. About the myth of a more stable mononuclear family in the previous centuries, see Carsten, *After Kinship*, 17.
2. "Here I draw on Strathern's (1999b) argument that, in Euro-American contexts, acquiring certain kinds of knowledge about one's ancestry implies acquiring identity. Strathern also argues that this kind of knowledge has an immediate effect—once obtained, it cannot be rejected or put aside: 'knowledge creates relationships: the relationship comes into being when the knowledge does (1999b: 78).' This is the case, she suggests, whether one admits the relation or not. The immediacy of these effects is quite apparent in the accounts of reunions that I collected. But one might add that these effects are already prefigured by the decision to search for birth kin and the process of undergoing such a search" (Carsten 2004, 106).

Bibliography

Abelmann, Nancy, *The Melodrama of Mobility: Women, Talk, and Class in Contemporary South Korea* (Honolulu: University of Hawaii Press, 2003).
Abelmann, Nancy, and John Lie, *Blue Dreams: Korean Americans and the Los Angeles Riots* (Cambridge: Harvard University Press, 1997).
Abreu, Domingos, "Baby-Bearing Storks: Brazilian Intermediaries in the Adoption Process," in Diana Marre and Laura Briggs, eds., *International Adoption: Global Inequalities and the Circulation of Children* (New York: NYU Press, 2009), pp. 138–153.
Abu-Lughod, Lila, "Finding a Place for Islam: Egyptian Televisions Serials and the National Interest," *Public Culture* 5, no. 3 (1993): 493–513.
———, "The Object of Soap Opera," in Daniel Miller, ed., *Worlds Apart: Modernity through the Prism of the Local* (London: Routledge, 1995), pp. 190–210.
———, "Modern Subjects: Egyptian Melodrama and Postcolonial Difference," in Timothy Mitchell, ed., *Questions of Modernity* (Minneapolis: University of Minnesota Press, 2000), pp. 87–114.
Agnew, Vijay, *Diaspora, Memory, and Identity: A Search for Home* (Toronto: University of Toronto Press, 2005).
Alford, Fred C., *Think No Evil: Korean Values in the Age of Globalization* (Ithaca: Cornell University Press, 1999).
Anderson, Benedict, *Imagined Communities. Reflections on the Origin and Spread of Nationalism* (London: Verso, 1983).
Anthias, Floya, "Evaluating 'Diaspora': Beyond Ethnicity?" *Sociology* 32, no. 3 (1998): 557–580.
Appadurai, Arjun, *Modernity at Large: Cultural Dimensions of Globalization* (Minneapolis: University of Minnesota Press, 1996).
Armon-Jones, Claire, "The Thesis of Constructionism," in Rom Harré, ed., *The Social Construction of Emotions* (Oxford: Basil Blackwell, 1986), pp. 32–56.
Attias-Donfut, Claudine, *Sociologie des générations: L'empreinte du temps* (Paris: PUF, 1988).
Bai, Tai Soon, "Korea's Overseas Adoption and Its Positive Impact on Domestic Adoption and Child Welfare in Korea," in Kathleen Ja Sook Bergquist, Elisabeth M. Vonk, Dong Soo Kim, and Marvin D. Feit, eds., *International Korean Adoption: A Fifty-Year History of Policy and Practice* (New York: Haworth Press, 2007), pp. 207–220.
Baptandier, Brigitte, ed., *De la malemort en quelques pays d'Asie* (Paris: Karthala, 2001).
Beach, Dwight E. (Gen.), "Marching Together, Korea and the United States," in In-Hah Jung, ed., *The Feel of Korea: A Symposium of American Comment* (Seoul: Hollym, 1966), pp. 17–23.
Benedict, Ruth, *The Chrysanthemum and the Sword: Patterns of Japanese Cultures* (Boston: Mariner Books, 2005).
Benjamin, Walter, *The Work of Art in the Age of Its Technological Reproducibility, and Other Writings on Media (1935–1936)*, edited by Michael W. Jennings, Brigid Doherty,

and Thomas Y. Levin; translated by Edmund Jephcott, Rodnay Livingston, Howard Eiland, and Others (Cambridge: Belknap Press of Harvard University Press, 2008), pp. 19–55.

Bensa, Alban, and Daniel Fabre, eds., *Une histoire à soi: Figurations du passé et localités* (Paris: Editions de la Maison des Sciences de l'Homme, 2001), pp. 103–117.

Bhabha, Homi, *The Location of Culture* (New York: Routledge, 1994).

Bishoff, Tonya, and Jo Rankin, eds., *Seeds from a Silent Tree: An Anthology by Korean Adoptees* (Glendale, CA: Pandal Press, 1997).

Blanchot, Maurice, *L'écriture du désastre* (Paris: Gallimard, 1996).

Boëtsch, Gilles, and Christoph Wulf, eds., *Hermès*, vol. 43: Rituels (2005).

Bonte, Pierre, "Pseudo-parenté," in Pierre Bonte and Michel Izard, eds., *Dictionnaire de l'ethnologie et de l'anthropologie* (Paris: PUF, 2000), pp. 550–552.

Bordes-Benayoun, Chantal, and Dominique Schnapper, *Diasporas et Nations* (Paris: Odile Jacob, 2006).

Bourbon-Parme, Tristan (de), and Nathalie Tourret, *La Corée dévoilée, 15 portraits pour comprendre* (Paris: L'Harmattan, 2004).

Bourdieu, Pierre, *Esquisse d'une théorie de la pratique, précédé de trois études d'ethnologie kabyle* (Geneva: Droz, 1972).

———, *Distinction: A Social Critique of the Judgment of Taste* (Cambridge: Harvard University Press, 1987).

———, *Sur la télévision* (Paris: Liber, 1996).

Bowie, Fiona, ed., *Cross-Cultural Approaches to Adoption* (London: Routledge, 2004).

Buchet, Luc, ed., *L'enfant, son corps, son histoire*, Actes (proceedings) des Septièmes Journées Anthropologiques de Valbonne, 1–3 juin 1994, CNRS, Centre de Recherches Archéologiques (Sophia-Antipolis: Editions APDCA, 1997).

Brédier, Sophie, *Corps étranger* (Ex Nihilo, Ina, Doc&Co, 2004, 68 minutes).

Calhoun, Craig, ed., *Habermas and the Public Sphere* (Cambridge: MIT Press, 1992).

Camdessus, Brigitte, ed., *L'adoption: Une aventure familiale* (Paris: ESF Editions, 1995).

Candau, Joël, *Anthropologie de la mémoire* (Paris: PUF, 1996).

Carsten, Janet, *After Kinship* (Cambridge: Cambridge University Press, 2004).

Chalvon-Demersay, Sabine, "Le deuxième souffle des adaptations," *L'Homme* 175–176 (2005): 77–112.

Chang, Kil-su, *Susanne Brink's Arirang* (Se Won Films, 1991, 118 minutes).

Chira, Susan, "Babies for Export. And Now the Painful Question," *New York Times*, 04/22/88, http://www.nytimes.com/1988/04/21/world/seoul-journal-babies-for-export-and-now-the-painful-questions.html.

Ch'oe, Kil-seong, "Belief in Malevolent Spirits," in Mutsuhiko Shima and Roger Janelli, eds., *The Anthropology of Korea: East Asian Perspectives*, papers presented at the Seventeenth Taniguchi International Symposium, Senri Ethnological Studies No. 49 (Osaka: National Museum of Ethnology, 1998), pp. 95–110.

Choy, Catherine, "Institutionalizing International Adoption: The Historical Origins of Korean Adoption in the United States," in Kathleen Ja Sook Bergquist, Elisabeth M. Vonk, Dong Soo Kim, and Marvin D. Feit, eds., *International Korean Adoption: A Fifty-Year History of Policy and Practice* (New York: Haworth Press, 2007), pp. 25–42.

Chu, Tammy, *Resilience* (Koroot/Nameless Films/Waterlights Films, 2009, 75 minutes).

Chun, Doo Hwan, *The 1980s: Meeting a New Challenge III: Selected Speeches of President Chun Doo Hwan* (Seoul: Korea Textbook Company, 1984).

Chung, Y. David, and Matt Dibble, *Koryo Saram: The Unreliable People* (DigiBeta, 2007, 57 minutes).
Clark, Donald, "Protestant Christianity and the State: Religious Organizations as Civil Society," in Charles Armstrong, ed., *Korean Society: Civil Society, Democracy, and the State* (London: Routledge, 2002), pp. 187–206.
Clifford, James, "Diaspora," *Cultural Anthropology* 9, no. 3 (1991): 302–338.
Clifford, James, and George Marcus, eds., *Writing Culture: The Poetics and Politics of Ethnography* (Berkeley: University of California Press, 1986).
Colleyn, Jean-Paul, "Fiction et fictions en anthropologie," *L'Homme* 175–176 (2005): 147–164.
Cox, Susan Soon-Keum, ed., *Voices from Another Place: A Collection of Works from a Generation Born in Korea and Adopted to Other Countries* (St. Paul, MN: Yeong and Yeong, 1999).
Cumings, Bruce, *The Origins of the Korean War: Liberation and the Emergence of Separate Regimes, 1945–1947* (Princeton: Princeton University Press, 1981).
Davis, Fred, *Yearning for Yesterday: A Sociology of Nostalgia* (New York: Free Press, 1979).
Deleuze, Gilles, *Cinéma I: L'image-mouvement* (Paris: Les Editions de Minuit, 1983).
Delumeau, Jean, *Le péché et la peur* (Paris: Fayard, 1983).
Deuchler, Martina, "The Tradition: Women during the Yi Dynasty," in Sandra Mattielli, ed., *Virtues in Conflict: Tradition and the Korean Woman Today* (Seoul: Royal Asiatic Society, 1977), pp. 1–47.
——, *The Confucian Transformation of Korea* (Cambridge: Harvard University Press, 1993).
Dorow, Sara, *I Wish You a Beautiful Life: Letters from the Korean Birth Mothers of Ae Ran Won to Their Children* (Seoul: Yeong and Yeong, 1999).
——, *Transnational Adoption: A Cultural Economy of Race, Gender, and Kinship* (New York: NYU Press, 2006).
Douglas, Mary, *Purity and Danger. An Analysis of Concepts of Pollution and Taboo* (London: Routledge, 2001).
Doumeng, Valérie, "Etude comparative de l'adoption française et de l'adoption ouverte aux Etats-Unis," in Agnès Fine and Claire Neirinck, eds., *Parents de sang Parents adoptifs: Approches juridiques et anthropologiques de l'adoption France, Europe, USA, Canada* (Paris: Maison des Sciences de l'Homme, Droit et Société, 2000), pp. 147–167.
Eckert, Carter, and Ki-Baik Lee, eds., *Korea Old and New, A History* (Seoul: Ilchokak; Cambridge: Harvard University Press, 1996).
Einarsdottir, Johanna, *Tired of Weeping: Child Death and Mourning among Papel Mothers in Guinea-Bissau* (Stockholm: Stockholm Studies in Social Anthropology, 2000).
Em, Henry, "Minchok as a Modern and Democratic Construct: Sin Ch'aeho's Historiography," in Gi-wook Shin and Michael Robinson, eds., *Colonial Modernity in Korea* (Cambridge: Harvard University Press, 1999), pp. 336–361.
Etienne, Mona, "Maternité sociale, rapport d'adoption et pouvoir des femmes chez les Baoulé," *L'Homme* 19 (1979): 66–107.
Fine, Agnès, "Le parrain, son filleul et l'au-delà," *Etudes rurales*, no. 105–106, "Le retour des morts," ed. Daniel Fabre (January–June 1987): 123–146.
——, "Les parentés parallèles," in Gérard Althabe, Daniel Fabre, and Gérard Lenclud, eds., *Vers une Ethnologie du Présent* (Paris: Éditions de la Maison des Sciences de l'Homme, 1992), pp. 195–210.

———, "Pluriparentalités et système de filiation dans les sociétés occidentales," in Didier Le Gall and Yamina Bettahar, eds., *La pluriparentalité* (Paris: Presses Universitaires de France, 2001), pp. 69–93.
Fine, Agnès, and Claire Neirinck, eds., *Parents de sang, Parents adoptifs: Approches juridiques et anthropologiques de l'adoption: France, Europe, USA, Canada* (Paris: Maison des Sciences de l'Homme, Droit et Société, 2000).
Finley, Moses, *Mythe, mémoire, histoire* (Paris: Flammarion–Nouvelle Bibliothèque Scientifique, 1981).
Foley, James, *Korea's Divided Families: Fifty Years of Separation* (New York: Routledge Curzon, 2003).
Fonseca, Claudia, "Patterns of Shared Parenthood among the Brazilian Poor," in Toby Alice Volkman, ed., *Cultures of Transnational Adoption* (Durham, NC: Duke University Press, 2005), pp. 142–161.
———, "Transnational Connections and Dissenting Views," in Diana Marre and Laura Briggs, eds., *International Adoption: Global Inequalities and the Circulation of Children* (New York: NYU Press, 2009), pp. 154–173.
Foucault, Michel, Discipline and Punish: The Birth of the Prison (Vintage Books, 1979).
———, "The Political Technology of Individuals," in Luther H. Martin, Huck Gutman, and Patrick H. Hutton, eds., *Technologies of Self: A Seminar with Michel Foucault* (Amherst: University of Massachusetts Press, 1988), pp. 145–162.
Geertz, Clifford, *Works and Lives: The Anthropologist as Author* (Cambridge: Polity Press, 1988).
Gellner, Ernest, *Nations and Nationalism* (Oxford: Blackwell, 1983).
Gernet, Jacques, *La Chine ancienne* (Paris: Presses Universitaires de France, 1964).
Ginsburg, Faye, "Aboriginal Media and the Australian Imaginary," *Public Culture* 5, no. 3 (1998): 55–78.
Ginsburg, Faye, Lila Abu-Lughod, and Brian Larkin, eds., *Media Worlds: Anthropology on New Terrain* (Berkeley: University of California Press, 2002).
Ginsburg, Faye, and Rayna Rapp, *Conceiving the New World Order: The Global Politics of Reproduction* (Berkeley: University of California Press, 1995).
Glaeser, Andreas, *Divided in Unity. Identity, Germany, and the Berlin Police* (Chicago: University of Chicago Press, 1999).
GOA'L, *The TOAK: GOA'L Newsletter: A New Beginning* (2003).
Godelier, Maurice, *Métamorphoses de la parenté* (Paris: Fayard, 2004).
Goody, Jack, "Adoption in Cross-Cultural Perspective," *Comparative Studies in Society and History* 2 (1969): 55–78.
Grimes, Ronald, *Research in Ritual Studies: A Programmatic Essay and Bibliography* (Metuchen, NJ: American Theological Library Association and the Scarecrow Press, 1985).
———, *Ritual Criticism: Case Studies in Its Practice, Essays on Its Theory* (Columbia: University of South Carolina Press, 1990).
Grinker, Roy Richard, *Korea and Its Futures: Unification and the Unfinished War* (New York: St Martin's Press, 1998).
Gutton, Jean-Pierre, *L'adoption* (Paris: Collection Courants Universels Histoire-Publisud, 1993).
Halbwachs, Maurice, *Les cadres sociaux de la mémoire* (1925; Paris: Albin Michel, 1994).
———, *La mémoire collective* (1950; Paris: Albin Michel, 1997).

Hardacre, Helen, *Marketing the Menacing Fetus in Japan* (Berkeley: University of California Press, 1999).
Harré, Rom, *The Social Construction of Emotions* (Oxford: Basil Blackwell, 1986).
Heinich, Nathalie, "Les limites de la fiction," *L'Homme* 175–176 (2005: 57–76.
Héritier, Françoise, *L'exercice de la parenté* (Paris: Seuil/Gallimard, 1981).
Héritier-Augé, Françoise, and Elisabeth Copet-Rougier, *La parenté spirituelle* (Paris: Editions des Archives Contemporaines, 1996).
Hill, Reuben, *Families under Stress: Adjustment to the Crisis of War Separation and Reunion* (New York: Harper, 1949).
Hobbs, Christopher J., and Jane M. Wynne, "Child Abuse and Sudden Infant Death," *Child Abuse Review* 5 (1996): 155–169.
Hobsbawm, Eric J., and Terence O. Ranger, eds., *The Invention of Tradition* (Cambridge: Cambridge University Press, 1992).
Holt Children's Services, "Discourse of President Kim Keun-Jo," in *Holt International Conference* (Seoul: Holt Children's Services, October 2002), pp. 16–17.
———, *Together with Holt* 1, no. 1 (January 2003).
Homans, Margaret, "Origins, Searches, and Identity: Narratives of Adoption from China," *Contemporary Women's Writing* 1, nos. 1–2 (2007): 59–79.
Hong, Sŏkki, "Les cimetières d'Ile de France et de la région Seoul Kyeonggi" (PhD diss., Sorbonne, Institut de Géographie, 1994).
Howell, Signe, *Kinning of Foreigners: Transnational Adoption in a Global Perspective* (Oxford: Berghahn Books, 2006).
———, "Return Journeys and the Search for Roots: Contradictory Values Concerning Identity," in Diana Marre and Laura Briggs, eds., *International Adoption: Global Inequalities and the Circulation of Children* (New York: NYU Press, 2009), pp. 256–270.
Hübinette, Tobias, "The Adopted Koreans: Diaspora Politics and the Construction of an Ethnic Identity in a Post-colonial and Global Setting" (paper presented at the Third Space Seminar. Malmö, Sweden, 06/21/02).
———, "Comforting an Orphaned Nation: Representations of International Adoption and Adopted Koreans in Korean Popular Culture" (PhD diss., Stockholm University, 2005).
Hughes-Freeland, Felicia, ed., *Ritual, Performance, Media* (London: Routledge, 1988).
Hughes-Freeland, Felicia, and Mary Markwell Crain, eds., *Recasting Ritual* (London: Routledge, 1998).
Hwang, Kyung Moon, *Beyond Birth: Social Status in the Emergence of Modern Korea* (Cambridge: Harvard University Press, 2004).
Im, Kwon-taek, *Kilsottŭm* (Hwa Chun Trading, 1986, 103 minutes).
Jager, Sheila Miyoshi, *Narratives of Nation Building in Korea: A Genealogy of Patriotism* (New York: East Gate Books, 2003).
Janelli, Roger, and Dawnhee Yim, "The Transformation of Filial Piety in Contemporary South Korea," in Charlotte Ikels, ed., *Filial Piety: Practice and Discourse in Contemporary East Asia* (Stanford: Stanford University Press, 2004), pp. 128–152.
———, "The Cyberspace Frontier in Korean Studies" (paper presented at the biennial conference of the Association for Korean Studies in Europe, Sheffield, England, 07/04/05).
Janelli, Roger, and Dawnhee Yim Janelli, *Ancestor Worship and Korean Society* (Palo Alto, CA: Stanford University Press, 1982).

Jo, Sunny, "The Making of KAD Nation," in Jane Jeong Trenka, Julia Chinyere Oparah, and Shin Sun Yung, eds., *Outsider Within: Writing on Transracial Adoption* (Cambridge, MA: South End Press, 2006), pp. 285–290.

Johnson, Kay A., *Wanting a Daughter, Needing a Son: Abandonment, Adoption, and Orphanage Care in China* (St Paul, MN: Yeong and Yeong, 2004).

Johnson, Kay A., Banghan Huang, and Liyao Wang, "Infant Abandonment and Adoption in China," *Population and Development Review* 24, no. 3 (1998): 469–510.

Jordan, David, *Gods, Ghosts and Ancestors: Folk Religion in a Taiwanese Village* (Berkeley: University of California Press, 1972).

Kadar, Marlene, "Wounding Events and the Limits of Autobiography," in Vijay Agnew, ed., *Diaspora, Memory, and Identity: A Search for Home* (Toronto: University of Toronto Press, 2005), pp. 81–104.

Kang, Myoung-kyu, & Helmut Wagner, eds., *Korea and Germany: Lessons in Division* (Seoul: Seoul National University Press, 1990).

Kang, Soo-jin, "The Change in the Family Structure and the Family Law: The Discussion on the Abolition of 'Family Head System' in Korean Family Law" (M.A. thesis, Harvard University, 2005).

Kendall, Laurel, *Shamans, Housewives, and Other Restless Spirits: Women in Korean Ritual Life* (Honolulu: University of Hawaii Press, 1985).

———, *The Life and the Hard Times of a Korean Shaman: Of Tales and the Telling of Tales* (Honolulu: University of Hawaii Press 1988).

———, *Getting Married in Korea: Of Gender, Morality, and Modernity* (Berkeley: University of California Press, 1996).

———, "Caught between Ancestors and Spirits, A Korean Mansin's Healing Kut", in Korean National Commission for UNESCO, *Korean Anthropology: Contemporary Korean Culture in Flux* (Elizabeth, NJ: Hollym, 2003), pp. 395–421.

———, "Birth Mothers and Imaginary Lives," in Toby Alice Volkman, ed., *Cultures of Transnational Adoption* (Durham, NC: Duke University Press, 2005), pp. 162–181.

Khabibullina, Lilia, "International Adoption in Russia: 'Market,' 'Children for Organs,' and 'Precious' or 'Bad' Genes," in Diana Marre and Laura Briggs, eds., *International Adoption: Global Inequalities and the Circulation of Children* (New York: NYU Press, 2009), pp. 174–189.

Kim, Choong Soon, *Faithful Endurance: An Ethnography of Korean Family Dispersal* (Tucson: University of Arizona Press, 1988).

Kim, Dae-jung, *Tashi saerŏun sichakeul wehayŏ* (In order to start a new beginning) (Seoul: Kimyŏngsa, 1998).

Kim, David, *Who Will Answer for These Children?* (Eugene, OR: Holt International, 2001).

Kim, Eleana, "Korean Adoptee Autoethnography: Refashioning Self, Family and Finding Community," *Visual Anthropology Review* 16, no. 1 (2001): 43–70.

———, "Wedding Citizenship and Culture: Korean Adoptees and the Global Family of Korea," in Toby Alice Volkman, ed., *Cultures of Transnational Adoption* (Durham, NC: Duke University Press, 2005), pp. 49–80.

———, "Our Adoptee, Our Alien: Transnational Adoptees as Specters of Foreignness and Family in South Korea," *Anthropological Quarterly* 80, no. 2 (2007): 497–531.

———, *Adopted Territory: Transnational Korean Adoptees and the Politics of Belonging* (Durham, NC: Duke University Press, 2010).

Kim, Elizabeth, *Ten Thousand of Sorrows, The Extraordinary Journey of a Korean War Orphan* (New York: Doubleday, 2000).

Kim, Janice, *To Live to Work: Factory Women in Colonial Korea, 1910–1945* (Palo Alto, CA: Stanford University Press, 2009).
Kim, Jung-woo, and Terry Henderson, "History of the Care of Displaced Children in Korea," *Asian Social Work and Policy Review* 2 (2008): 13–29.
Kim, Ki-duk, *Address Unknown* (Tartan Video, 2001, 117 minutes).
Kim, Seong-nae, "Lamentations of the Dead: The Historical Imagery of Violence on Cheju Island," *Journal of Ritual Studies* 3 (1989): 251–285.
Kim, Shu-su, "La position légale de la femme coréenne," *Revue de Corée* 17, no. 2 (1985): 28–50.
Kim, Sŏn-mi, *Kugyŏng* (Watching) (Seoul: Communication Books, 2003).
Kim, Young-sam, *Korea's Quest for Reform and Globalization: Selected Speeches of President Kim Young-Sam* (Seoul: Presidential Secretariat, 1995).
Kim, Yung-chung, ed., *Women of Korea: A History from Ancient Times to 1945* (Seoul: Ewha Women's University Press, 1977).
Kim Harvey, Young-Sook, "*Minmyŏnuri*: The Daughter in Law Who Comes of Age in Her Mother in Law's Household," in Laurel Kendall and Mark Peterson, eds., *View from the Inner Room*, (New Haven, CT: East Rock Press, 1983), pp. 45–61.
Kitano, Harry, and Roger Daniels, eds., *Asian Americans: Emerging Minorities* (Upper Saddle River, NJ: Prentice Hall, 1988).
Klein, Christina, *Cold War Orientalism: Asia in the Middlebrow Imagination (1945–1961)* (Berkeley: University of California Press, 2003).
Koh, Frances, *Oriental Children in American Homes: How Do They Adjust?* (Minneapolis, MN: East-West Press, 1981).
Koh, Hesung Chun, "Korean Diaspora and Cultural Strategy in the Internet Age," in Korea Foundation, *Korea's Interface with the World: Past, Present and Future* (Seoul: Chimundang, 2002), pp. 371–400.
Kondo, Dorinne K., *Crafting Selves: Power, Gender, and Discourses of Identity in a Japanese Workplace* (Chicago: University of Chicago Press, 1990).
LaFleur, William R., *Liquid Life: Abortion and Buddhism in Japan* (Princeton: Princeton University Press, 1992).
Lallemand, Suzanne, *La circulation des enfants en société traditionnelle: Prêt, don, échange* (Paris: L'Harmattan, 1993).
Lee, Dong-hoo, "A Local Mode of Programme Adaptation: South Korea in the Local Television Format Business," in Albert Moran and Michael Keane, eds., *Television across Asia: Industries, Programme Formats and Globalization* (London: Routledge Curzon, 2004), pp. 36–53.
Lee, Dong-won, *Taejung Maech'ewa Kajok* (Mass media and family) (Seoul: Yang Seo Weon, 2000).
Lee, Hee-kyung, "Psychologie sociale de la 'coréanité' et la notion de han: Une approche ethno-culturelle" (PhD diss., Ecole des Hautes Etudes en Sciences Sociales, Paris, 1995).
Lee, Jae-hoon, *A Study of "Han" of the Korean People: A Depth Psychological Contribution to the Understanding of the Concept of "Han" in the Korean Minjung Theology* (New York: Union Theological Seminary, 1989).
Lee, Joo-lee, "Recent Trends in Child Welfare and Adoption in Korea: Challenges and Future Directions," in Kathleen Ja Sook Bergquist, Elisabeth M. Vonk, Dong Soo Kim, and Marvin D. Feit, eds., *International Korean Adoption: A Fifty-Year History of Policy and Practice* (New York: Haworth Press, 2007), pp. 189–205.

Lee, Jung Young, *Korean Shamanistic Rituals* (Paris: Mouton, 1981).
Lee, Kwang-kyu, *Kinship System in Korea* (Seoul: Chipmundang, 1978).
Lee, Nam-Hee, *The Making of Minjung: Democracy and the Politics of Representation in South Korea* (Stanford: Stanford University Press, 2007).
Le Gall, Didier, and Yamina Bettahar, eds., *La pluriparentalité* (Paris: Presses Universitaires de France, 2001).
Leinaweaver, Jessaca B., *The Circulation of Children: Kinship, Adoption, and Morality in Andean Peru* (Durham, NC: Duke University Press, 2008).
Lenclud, Gérard, "Croyance," in Pierre Bonte and Michel Izard, eds., *Dictionnaire* (Paris: Presses Universitaires de France), pp. 184–186.
Lévi, Jean, *La Chine Romanesque: Fictions d'Orient et d'Occident* (Paris: La Librarie du 20ème Siècle, 1995).
Lévine, Jacques, "Que savons-nous du vécu des enfants adoptés?" in Zerdalia Dahoun, ed., *Adoption et cultures: De la filiation à l'affiliation* (Paris: L'Harmattan, 1996), pp. 49–94.
Lévi-Strauss, Claude, "Le Père-Noël supplicié," *Les Temps Modernes* 77 (1952): 1575–1590.
———, *La Pensée Sauvage* (Paris: Plon, 1962).
———, *The View from Afar*, translated by Joachim Neugroschel and Phoebe Hoss (Chicago: University of Chicago Press, 1985).
Liem, Deann Borshay, *First Person Plural* (Point of View, 2000, 56 minutes).
Lowenthal, David, "Nostalgia Tells It Like It Wasn't," in Malcolm Chase and Christopher Shaw, eds., *The Imagined Past: History and Nostalgia* (Manchester: Manchester University Press, 1989), pp. 18–32.
Lutz, Catherine, "Parental Goals, Ethnopsychology, and the Development of Emotional Meaning," *Ethos* 11, no. 4 (1983): 246–261.
———, Unnatural Emotions: Everyday Sentiments on a Micronesian Atoll and Their Challenge to Western Theory (Chicago: University of Chicago Press, 1988).
Lutz, Catherine, and Lila Abu-Lughod, eds., *Language and the Politics of Emotion* (Cambridge: Cambridge University Press, 1990).
Malarney, Shaun Kingsley, "The Limits of 'State Functionalism' and the Reconstruction of Funerary Ritual in Contemporary Northern Vietnam," *American Ethnologist* 23, no. 3 (1996): 540–560.
Mankekar, Purnima, *Screening Culture, Viewing Politics* (Durham, NC: Duke University Press, 1999).
Marre, Diana, and Laura Briggs, eds., *International Adoption: Global Inequalities and the Circulation of Children* (New York: NYU Press, 2009).
Martial, Agnès "Partages et fraternité dans les familles recomposées," in Agnès Fine, ed., *Adoptions: Ethnologie des parentés choisies* (Paris: Editions de la Maison des Sciences de l'Homme, 1998), pp. 205–244.
Mattielli, Sandra, ed., *Virtues in Conflict: Tradition and the Korean Woman Today* (Seoul: Royal Asiatic Society, 1977).
Mauss, Marcel, *Essais de sociologie* (1921; Paris: Points Seuil, 1968).
———, *The Gift: Forms and Functions of Exchange in Archaic Societies* (London: Routledge, 1990).
McDonald, Donald, and Donald Clark, *The Koreans: Contemporary Politics and Society* (Boulder, CO: Westview Press, 1996).
McLuhan, Marshall, and Bruce Powers, *The Global Village: Transformations in World Life and Media in the 21st Century* (New York: Oxford University Press, 1989).

Medick, Hans, and David Warren Sabean, eds., *Interest and Emotion: Essays on the Study of Family and Kinship* (Paris: Editions de la Maison des Sciences de l'Homme, 1988).

Meillassoux, Claude, *Mythes et limites de l'anthropologie: Le sang et les mots* (Lausanne: Editions Page Deux–Collection Cahiers Libres, 2001).

Metzler, John, *Divided Dynamism: The Diplomacy of Separated Nations: Germany, Korea, China* (Lanham, MD: University Press of America, 1996).

Meulders-Klein, Marie-Thérèse, and Irène Théry, eds., *Les recompositions familiales aujourd'hui* (Paris: Nathan, 1993).

Middleton, Harry, *The Compact History of the Korean War* (New York: Hawthorn Books, 1965).

Modell, Judith S., *Kinship with Strangers: Adoption and Interpretations of Kinship in American Culture* (Berkeley: University of California Press, 1994).

Moon, Chung-in, and David. I. Steinberg, eds., *Kim Daejung Government and Sunshine Policy* (Seoul: Yonsei University Press, 1999).

Moon, Seungsook, "Begetting the Nation: The Androcentric Discourse of National History and Tradition in South Korea," in Elaine Kim and Chungmoo Choi, eds., *Dangerous Women: Gender and Korean Nationalism* (New York: Routledge, 1998).

Moran, Albert, and Michael Keane, eds., *Television across Asia: Television Industries, Programme Formats and Globalization* (London: Routledge Curzon, 2004).

Moskowitz, Marc L., *The Haunting Fetus: Abortion, Sexuality, and the Spirit World in Taiwan* (Honolulu: University of Hawaii Press, 2001).

Munn, Nancy, "An Essay on the Symbolic Construction of Memory in the Kaluli Gisolo," in Daniel de Coppet and Andre Itéanu, eds., *Cosmos and Society in Oceania* (Oxford: Berg, 1995), pp. 83–104.

Nakane, Chie, *Japanese Society* (Berkeley: University of California Press, 1970).

Nelson, Laura C., *Measured Excess: Status, Gender, and Consumer Nationalism in South Korea* (New York: Columbia University Press, 2000).

Nora, Pierre, *Les lieux de mémoire* (Paris: Gallimard, 1986).

Norgren, Tiana, *Abortion before Birth Control: The Politics of Reproduction in Postwar Japan* (Princeton: Princeton University Press, 2001).

O'Connor, Anne, *Child Murderess and Dead Child Traditions*, FF Communications, no. 249 (Helsinki: Suomalainen Tiedeakatemia, 1991).

Ohnuki-Tierney, Emiko, "Critical Commentary: 'Native' Anthropology," *American Ethnologist* 14, no. 3 (1987): 584–585.

Ong, Aihwa, *Flexible Citizenship: The Cultural Logics of Transnationality* (Durham, NC: Duke University Press, 1999).

Ouellette, Françoise-Romaine, "The Social Temporalities of Adoption and the Limits of Plenary Adoption," in Diana Marre and Laura Briggs, eds., *International Adoption: Global Inequalities and the Circulation of Children* (New York: NYU Press, 2009), pp. 69–86.

Overseas Koreans Foundation, *Community 2004: Guide to Korea for Overseas Adopted Koreans* (Seoul: OKF, 2004).

Park, Chung-Shin, *Protestantism and Politics in Korea* (Seattle: University of Washington Press, 2009).

Park, Tae-ho, *Changne-ŭi yŏksa* (History of funerals in Korea) (Seoul: Sŏhaemunjip, 2006).

Pentikäinen, Juha, *The Nordic Dead-Child Tradition: Nordic Dead-Child Beings*, FF Communications, no. 202 (Helsinki: Suomalainen Tiedeakatemia, 1968).

Peterson, Mark, *Korean Adoption and Inheritance: Case Studies in the Creation of a Classic Confucian Society* (Ithaca: Cornell University Press, 1996).

Prébin, Elise, "Adoption internationale: Les revenants de Corée" (PhD diss., Paris Ouest-Nanterre la Défense, 2006).

———, "Korean Orphans, Domestic Adoptees, and International Adoptees: Three Outcomes of Child Circulation and Family Separation Practices," in Kim Park Nelson, Eleana Kim, Lene Myong Petersen, eds., *Proceedings of the First International Korea Adoption Studies Research Symposium* (Seoul: IKAA and Dongguk University Press, 2007), pp. 125–131.

———, "Three-Week Re-education to Koreanness," *European Journal of East Asian Studies* 7, no. 2 (2008): 321–353.

———, "Looking for 'Lost' Children in South Korea," *Adoption and Culture*, no. 2 (2009): 223–261.

———, "Towards a Franco-American Self-Ethnography," *Cahiers d'études coréennes de l'I.E.C.* 8 (2010): 398–410.

———, "Le projet transnational des familles sud-coréennes de la class moyenne," *Autrepart*, no. 57–58 (2011): 281–298.

———, "Cremation's Success in Korea: Old Beliefs and Renewed Social Distinctions," in Natacha Aveline-Dubach, ed., *The Invisible Population: The Place of the Dead in East Asian Megacities* (Lanham, MD: Lexington Books, 2012), pp. 138–164.

Punwani, Jyoti, "Portrayal of Women on Television" in Rehana Ghadially, ed., *Women in Indian Society: A Reader* (New Delhi: Sage, 1989), pp. 224–232.

Reinschmidt, Michael, "An Interview with Professor Lee Kwang-Kyu," *Acta Koreana* 10, no. 1 (2007): 121–137.

Republic of Korea National Red Cross, *The Dispersed Families in Korea* (Seoul: RKNRC, 1977).

Revel, Jacques, *Jeux d'échelles: La micro-analyse à l'expérience* (Paris: EHESS-Hautes Etudes, 1996).

Ricoeur, Paul, *Time and Narrative*, vol. 2 (Chicago: University of Chicago Press, 1986).

———, "Life in Quest of Narrative: Narrative and Interpretation," in David Wood, ed., *On Paul Ricoeur* (London: Routledge, 1992), pp. 20–33.

Robertson, Roland, *Globalization: Social Theory and Global Culture* (London: Sage, 1992).

Robinson, Katy, *A Single Square Picture: A Korean Adoptee's Search for Her Roots* (New York: Berkley Books, 2002).

Roesch-Rohmberg, Inge, "Korean Institutionalised Adoption," in Fiona Bowie, ed., *Cross-Cultural Approaches to Adoption* (London: Routledge, 2004), pp. 81–96.

Rothschild, Matthew, "Babies for Sale: Koreans Make Them, Americans Buy Them," *The Progressive*, January 1988.

Ryu, Je-hun, *Reading the Korean Cultural Landscape* (Elizabeth, NJ: Hollym, 2000).

Sahlins, Marshall, *Stone Age Economics* (London: Routledge, 1988).

Savage, Judith, *Mourning Unlived Lives: A Psychological Study of Childbearing Loss* (Wilmette, IL: Chiron, 1989).

Schechner, Richard, *Essays on Performance Theory 1970–1976* (New York: Drama Book Specialists, 1977).

———, *The Future of Ritual: Writings on Culture and Performance* (London: Routledge, 1993).

Schechner, Richard, and Willa Appel, eds., *By Means of Performance: Intercultural Studies of Theater and Ritual* (Cambridge: Cambridge University Press, 1990).

Schmid, Andre, *Korea between Empires* (New York: Columbia University Press, 2002).

Schneider, David M., *A Critique of the Study of Kinship* (Ann Arbor: University of Michigan Press, 1984).

Schwartz Barry, and Mi Kyoung Kim, "Honor, Dignity, and Collective Memory: Judging the Past in Korea and the United States," in Karen Cerulo, ed., *Culture in Mind: Toward a Sociology of Culture and Cognition* (New York: Routledge, 2002).

Segalen, Martine, *Rites et rituels contemporains* (Paris: Nathan-Université, 1998).

Selman, Peter, "The Movement of Children for International Adoption: Developments and Trends in Receiving States and States of Origin, 1998–2004," in Diana Marre and Laura Briggs, eds., *International Adoption: Global Inequalities and the Circulation of Children* (New York: NYU Press, 2009), pp. 32–51.

Seth, Michael J., *Education Fever, Society, Politics, and the Pursuit of Schooling in South Korea* (Honolulu: University of Hawaii Press, 2002).

Shima, Mutsuhiko, "Retrieving the Past with Genealogies," in Mutsuhiko Shima and Roger Janelli, eds., *The Anthropology of Korea: East Asian Perspectives* (papers presented at the Seventeenth Taniguchi International Symposium, National Museum of Ethnology, Osaka, Senri Ethnological Studies, no. 49, 1998), pp. 37–64.

Shin, Gi-wook, and Michael Robinson, eds., *Colonial Modernity in Korea* (Cambridge: Harvard University Press, 1999).

Son, Chin-t'ae, *Chosŏn minjok-ŭi yŏngu (A Study of Korean People)*, (Seoul: Ŭryu Munhwasa, 1948).

Song, Hyŏn-dong, "Ŭirye-wa sahoe pyŏnhwa. Changnye sikjang chungsim-ŭro" (Changes in South Korea: focus on funerary parlors), *Chongkyo Yŏngu* 35 (2004): 313–338.

Sorlin, Pierre, "Children as War Victims in Postwar European Cinema," in Jay Winter and Emmanuel Sivan, eds., *War and Remembrance in the Twentieth Century* (Cambridge: Cambridge University Press, 1999), pp. 104–124.

Strathern, Marilyn, *Reproducing the Future: Essays on Anthropology, Kinship and the New Reproductive Technologies* (Manchester: Manchester University Press, 1992).

Takeda, Akira, *Ancestor Worship and Posthumous Marriage* (Tokyo: Jinbunshoin, 1990).

Tamanoi, Mariko, "Overseas Japanese and the Challenges of Repatriation in Post-colonial East Asia," in Nobuko Adachi, ed., *Japanese Diasporas: Unsung Pasts, Conflicting Presents, and Uncertain Futures* (London: Routledge Curzon, 2006), pp. 217–235.

Tedesco, Frank, "Rites for the Unborn Dead: Abortion and Buddhism in Contemporary Korea," *Korea Journal* 36, no. 2 (1996): 61–74.

Théry, Irène, *Le démariage, justice et vie privée* (Paris: Odile Jacob, 1993).

———, *Couple, filiation et parenté aujourd'hui: Le droit face aux mutations de la famille et de la vie privée* (Paris: Odile Jacob, 1998).

———, ed., *Recomposer une famille, des rôles et des sentiments* (Paris: Textuel, 2001).

Todorov, Tzvetan, *Les abus de la mémoire* (Paris: Arléa, 1995).

Tonkin, Elizabeth, *Narrating Our Pasts: The Social Construction of Oral History* (New York: Cambridge University Press, 1992).

Trenka, Jane Jeong, *The Language of Blood* (Saint Paul: Minnesota Historical Society Press, 2003).

Tsuya, Noriko, and Larry Bumpass, *Marriage, Work, and Family Life in Comparative Perspective: Japan, South Korea and the United States* (Honolulu: University of Hawaii Press, 2004).

Van Gennep, Arnold, *Les rites de passage* (1909; Paris: Éditions A. et J. Picard, 1981).

Vernier, Bernard, *Le visage et le nom: Contribution à l'étude des systèmes de parenté* (Paris: Presses Universitaires de France, 1999).

Veyne, Paul, *Comment on écrit l'histoire* (Paris: Seuil, 1978).

Volkman, Toby Alice, ed., *Cultures of Transnational Adoption* (Durham, NC: Duke University Press, 2005).

———, "Seeking Sisters: Twinship and Kinship in an Age of Internet Miracles and DNA Technologies," in Diana Marre and Laura Briggs, eds., *International Adoption: Global Inequalities and the Circulation of Children* (New York: NYU Press, 2009), pp. 283–302.

Wade, James, "Korea's Goals, Real and Illusory," in In-Hah Jung, ed., *The Feel of Korea: A Symposium of American Comment* (Seoul: Hollym, 1966), pp. 87–95.

Watson, James, "Virtual Kinship, Real Estate, and Diaspora Formation: The Man Lineage Revisited," *Journal of Asian Studies* 63, no. 4 (2004): 893–910.

Watt, Lori, *When Empire Comes Home, Repatriation and Reintegration in Postwar Japan* (Cambridge: Harvard East Asia Press, 2009).

Wolfe, Charles, "A Time for Pride," in In-Hah Jung, ed., *The Feel of Korea: A Symposium of American Comment* (Seoul: Hollym, 1966), pp. 116–126.

Wolff, Janet, "The Global and the Specific: Reconciling Conflicting Theories of Culture," in Anthony King, ed., *Culture, Globalization and the World-System* (Albany: State University of New York Press, 1991), pp. 161–173.

Wood, David, ed., *On Paul Ricoeur* (London: Routledge, 1992).

Yi, Jeong Duk, "Globalization and Recent Changes to Daily Life in the Republic of Korea," in James Lewis and Amadu Sesay, eds., *Korea and Globalization: Politics, Economics and Culture* (New York: Routledge Curzon, 2002), pp. 10–31.

Yi, So-hoe, Min-ja Chŏng, and Kyŏng-hŭi Kim, eds., "Ihon kajok" (divorced family), in *Hyŏndae kajok pokjiron* (Sŏul: Yangsŏwon, 1998), pp. 163–197.

Yngvesson, Barbara, "Placing the 'Gift Child' in Transnational Adoption," *Law and Society Review* 36, no. 2, Special Issue on Nonbiological Parenting (2002): 227–256.

———, "National Bodies and the Body of the Child: 'Completing' Families through International Adoption," in Fiona Bowie, ed., *Cross-Cultural Approaches to Adoption* (London: Routledge, 2004), pp. 211–226.

———, *Belonging in an Adopted World: Race, Identity, and Transnational Adoption* (Chicago: University of Chicago Press, 2010).

Yngvesson, Barbara, and Susan Bibler Coutin, "Backed by Papers: Undoing Persons, Histories, and Return," *American Ethnologist* 33, no. 2 (2006): 177–190.

Yngvesson, Barbara, and Maureen Mahoney, "'As One Should, Ought and Wants to Be': Belonging and Authenticity in Identity Narratives," *Theory, Culture and Society* 17, no. 6 (2000): 77–110.

Yoon, Hong-key, *Geomantic Relationships between Culture and Nature in Korea* (Taipei: Chinese Association for Folklore, 1976).

Yun, Yŏl-su, *Wonhyangŭl ch'ajasŏ t'osoksinang-ŭi musokhwa* (*Searching for the Origins of Folk Religion: Painting of Shamanism*) (Seoul: Kahoep'ammulgwan, 2004).

Zempléni, Andras, "Initiation," in Pierre Bonte and Michel Izard, eds., *Dictionnaire de l'ethnologie et de l'anthropologie* (Paris: PUF, 2000), pp. 375–377.

Index

Abandonment, 22, 39, 94, 104, 118, 161, 164, 167–168, 170, 171, 184n5, 185n10, 185n11, 186n22, 186n29, 195n3, 203n1; in "Arirang," 56, 188n10; by boyfriend, 24, 43, 45; cases of, 104, 106, 153, 154, 163, 195n4; justification of, 153–154, statistics, 184n9; versus relinquishment, 109–110

Abelmann, Nancy, 81, 194n13

Abortion: in Japan, 165, 203n3 ; in Korea, 164–165, 170, 203n4; in Taiwan, 170

Ach'im madang: aftermaths, 122–132, 151–157, 161–162, 169, 171, 179; description, 1, 3, 5–7, 11–12; hosts, 6, 68, 69–76, 78–81, 82–86, 90, 104, 111–115, 119, 128–130, 151–157, 169, 174, 190n2, 191n15, 191n27; interpreter, 3, 73, 74, 79, 80, 98, 120, 123–124, 126–130, 156, 192n27; and kinship, 103–104, 105–109, 111–117, 119; opening credits, 68, 85; origins of, 75, 88–90, 93, 98, 194n1; paid audience, 1, 6–7, 8, 68, 71, 73, 76–77, 80, 155, 192n34; participants, 68–69, 70, 74, 75, 86, popularity of, 69, 74, 75–77, 81–82, 190n4, 191n25; preparation of, 70–71, 72, 75, 77, 94, 123, 127; professor, 68, 84–86, 90, 97, 111, 119, 152–153; scenario writer, 69–75, 82, 94, 98, 112, 123, 127, 154; viewership, 5–6, 7, 11, 39, 68–69, 71–72, 75–78, 81–83, 88, 112, 115, 119, 169, 174, 175, 192n27, 192n28, 193n71

Adoptees: agency, 9, 14, 16, 66, 177, 183n7, 190n12; associations, 28, 66, 74, 131, 187n42, 187n44, 189n3, 191n6; as depicted by Korean media, 2, 10, 21–22, 27, 28–29, 32, 88, 100, 109, 161–162, 175, 178, 185n11; as diasporic Koreans, 16, 21, 29–34, 37, 47, 50, 52, 54, 57, 63–66, 92–97, 131, 162, 168–170, 178, 189n6, 190n11; gathering, 28–29, 32, 66, 113, 159, 161; honorary citizenship, 58–60; stereotypes, 25, 35, 38–47, 47–51, 54–55, 61–62, 88

Adoption: advertisement of, 23, 184n1; agencies, 9, 22, 25; Holt, 1, 3, 5, 22, 23–28, 38–40, 41–42, 43, 46, 51, 54, 65, 74, 106, 109, 113, 120, 131, 158–159, 161, 168, 183n1, 184n10, 185n15, 186n21, 186n24, 190n10, 197n48; domestic, 23, 25, 27–28, 106, 109–110, 116, 185n11, 186n35, 201n2; as gift, 13, 106; law, 13–15, 177, 185n11, 188n6; practices in Confucian Korea, 13, 42, 196n33, 198n52; practices in contemporary Korea, 22–23, 27–28, 106, 109–110, 116, 185n1

Adoptive: citizenship, 179; country, 33, 66, 161, 177; family, 4, 14, 18, 27, 105, 106, 107, 108, 110, 131, 149, 178, 179, 180, 196n20, 197n48; filiation, 42, 63, 156; parents, 13, 14, 16, 29, 48, 65, 80, 81, 96, 103, 106, 109, 110, 123–124, 126, 130, 147, 155, 181, 183n11, 184n12, 185n15, 188n2; relationship (ties), 181

America (United States of), 22, 23, 42, 121, 145, 147, 196n19; adoption practices in, 14, 23, 24, 25, 27, 109, 184n3, 184n5, 185n15, 186n21, 201n3; anti-Americanism, 26; education, 32, 47, 50, 58, 188n16, 188n18; Korean adoptees in, 1, 7, 29, 32, 39–40, 43, 53, 54, 57, 58, 66, 74, 79, 85, 96, 127–128, 156, 188n2, 199n73; Korean-Americans, 25, 30–31, 32, 36, 43, 46, 48–49, 73, 74, 79, 85, 157, 189n10, 190n5; Korean War, 23; military, 23–24, 24–25, 45, 89, 90, 123, 128, 185n18; newspaper, 22, 24, 184n

Ancestors, 44, 83, 166, 170; rituals for, 49, 125, 139, 147, 162, 172, 174, 175, 183n5, 200n10

Anderson, Benedict, 74

Benedict, Ruth, 171
Birth control, 126, 165; education on, 185n10; in Japan, 203n3
Blood: and ethnicity, 33, 50, 57, 63, 67, 79, 96–97, 148; and feelings, 79–80, 97, 114, 148, 172, 178, 181; kinship based on, 11–13, 14–15, 79, 132, 156, 162, 180–181; patriline, 33, 40, 44–46, 60, 114, 172; and racism, 8, 24–25; test, 118, 127–128; ties, 15, 37–38, 40, 44–46, 49, 162, 178, 179
Boarding house, 77, 135

Carsten, Janet, 132, 201n4, 203n36, 206n1, 206n2
Child: best interest of, 27, 185n11; Buddhist views on, 165–166, 170; circulation of, 13, 17, 103–110; Confucian views on, 166, 204n6, 204n7, 204n8; European history, 169–170, 203n35, 205n19; child-mother relationship, 110, 114–116, 171, 205n17, 205n24; representation of dead, 134, 164, 166–170, 203n2, 204n6, 204n9, 204n12, 204n13
China: Chinese in Korea, 145; domestic adoption, 196n20; influence on pre-modern Korea, 201n3; Korean War, 23, 175; Koreans in China, 31, 46, 188n14; "one-child" policy, 165; representation of the dead, 168
Confucian view: on dead, 125, 166; on nation, 92; on relationships, 81, 110–112; rituals, 201n1, 201n2; on women, 105, 114, 115, 180, 199n70, 199n71, 204n11
Cultural program (summer school), 1, 3, 5, 7, 51, 52–67, 158, 159, 183n1

Death: abnormal or inauspicious, 44, 134–136, 163, 168, 169, 175, 204n9, 204n13, 205n18, 205n23, 205n24; of child, 134–136, 163–172, 199n73, 203n1, 203n2, 204n6, 204n7, 204n11; of Bertha Holt, 25; of Harry Holt, 24, 58; of parents, 41, 104, 105, 107, 112, 115, 116, 124, 151, 198n52
Delinquency: international adoption as a solution for, 189n7; mafia, 39; and orphans, 40, 45, 188n7

Discipline: adoptees' resistance to, 53, 55, 61, 66, 158, 159; in cultural programs, 53, 56, 60, 63, 189n4; infantilizing, 53–58; for orphans, 40, 189n7
Divided families, 17, 87, 88–93, 96–99, 174, 185n16, 206n28; meetings, 89, 90, 93, 94–95, 99, 172–175; Red Cross videos, 172
Divorce, 4, 87, 94, 105, 113–114, 116, 131, 134, 144, 157, 171, 196n15, 198n56, 199n75
Douglas, Mary, 51, 63
Drama, 1, 34, 38, 42, 74, 75, 81–82, 147, 193n58, 193n59, 193n60

Emigrants: compared to international adoptees, 47–49, 50, 62, 90, 92, 99; experience in Korea, 32–33, 35, 37–38, 46
Emotion(s): construction of, 7, 11, 12, 17–18, 67, 75–78, 80–81, 83, 92, 112, 162, 174, 199n68, 205n20; during meetings, 8, 15, 77, 88, 93–95, 119, 201; negative (feelings), 9, 12, 15–16, 18, 65, 70, 88, 92, 99, 132, 151–155, 156–158, 159, 161–162, 165–167, 168–169, 170–171, 172–174, 175, 188n10, 202n10, 205n14, 205n23; tender feelings, 29, 31, 80–81, 93, 96, 97, 112, 114–115, 155–156, 159, 160–161, 183n4, 205n14

Family: building, 132; law, 105, 116, 185n11, 195n7, 196n15, 199n74, 199n75
Father, 1, 3, 4, 25, 25, 28, 87, 118; absence of, 104, 105, 107, 113, 114–117, 120–122, 131, 134, 136, 138, 151, 154, 167, 169, 174, 180, 195n7, 198n53, 199n73, 199n75; adoptive, 80, 106, 123–124, 199n75; in Confucian family, 41, 45, 110, 114, 121, 152, 195n7; foreign, 24–45, 45, 123; meeting, 73, 76, 96, 114–115, 118, 130–131, 154, 157, 174; memory of, 84, 96, 105, 106, 123, 124, 126, 129, 134, 145, 148, 153, 157, 163, 171
Foley, James, 92, 99, 172–174
Food, 54, 57, 60, 80, 107, 125, 125, 128, 139, 143, 145, 156, 167, 193n53, 198n60
Fosterage, 1, 42, 103, 104, 106–108, 110, 195n1, 197n47, 197n48, 197n49, 198n50, 198n61, 203n1; foster mothers in contemporary Korea, 112–113

Gender, 77, 80, 118, 177, 190, 199, 141, 161; in adoption practices, 27–28, 106, 186n39, 201n2; inequality, 25, 36–37, 43–44, 57, 60, 75, 114–115, 116, 138; of nation, 96, 112, 115–116

Ghost (spirit), 43, 44–45, 100, 118, 164, 165–168, 205n17, 204n9, 204n10, 204n12, 205n17, 205n18

Gift, 13, 33, 52, 56, 65, 69, 106, 124, 130, 135, 138, 140, 142, 143–144, 147, 161–162, 170

Globalization, 10, 14, 16, 18, 21, 28, 29–30, 31–32, 52, 74, 177, 191n22, 192n53; and child circulation, 110; and diaspora politics, 28, 30–34, 47, 52, 57, 63–66, 86, 92, 97, 131, 161, 178, 189n4, 189n9, 190n13, 191n22; and education, 50, 188n17; and nostalgia, 81, 193n63; and reproduction, 177

Grinker, Roy, 91, 205n14, 206n29

Guilt, 5, 18, 22, 99, 110, 115, 120, 131, 140, 154, 155, 157, 158, 165, 167, 170; versus shame, 154, 171, 202n10

Happy end: at *Ach'im madang*, 82, 119, 126–127, 154; warning against, 97, 118, 206n29

Head of the family, 116, 139, 195n7, 199n74, 199n75

Holt, Harry, 24–25, 28, 58, 64

Holt, Molly, 24, 28, 41–42, 46, 54, 59, 187n40, 188n8, 196n24

Holt Center (Ilsan), 5

Ilsan, 5, 24, 53, 56–58, 60, 64, 124, 126

Imperialism, 16, 25, 32, 57, 60, 63–64, 66, 90, 97, 159, 187n60, 190n11

Inchon, 4, 5, 47, 64, 87, 130, 133, 135, 137, 144, 145, 146

Japan, 3, 5, 26, 36, 44, 48, 62, 90, 143, 148, 187n60, 190n14, 199n73; and abortion, 165–166, 168, 170, 171, 203n3; annexation and colonization, 30, 201n3, 204n8, 206n31; Koreans in, 31, 46

Kendall, Laurel, 40–41, 46, 185n18, 201n1, 201n2, 202n4

Kim, Choong Soon, 82, 91, 95, 185n16, 198n53, 199n71

Kim, Dae-jung, 28, 37, 90, 93, 95, 96, 194n8, 194n9, 194n15

Kim, Eleana, 183n2, 183n7, 183n11, 184n9, 187n42, 189n3, 195n4

Kim, Young-sam, 31

Kinship, 2, 9, 10, 11, 12–16, 91–92, 100, 103, 105, 120, 122, 149, 156, 164, 177, 189n6, 195n1, 198n62, 200n3, 206n1; compensatory versus legal, 114; ideal versus pragmatic, 9, 12, 15–16, 106, 110, 112, 118, 162; real versus fictive, 11, 12, 13, 17, 18, 162, 179, 197n46; relatedness, 12, 15–16, 132, 150, 201n3, 203n36

Korean War, 23, 88, 91, 93, 98, 99, 153, 175; casualties, 185n16; children, 1, 17, 64, 86, 164, 195n3; partition (division), 11, 12, 17, 23, 86, 87–88, 90–91, 95, 97, 99, 172, 178; poverty, 17, 23, 34, 85, 94, 98, 100, 104, 105, 107, 153, 157, 164, 203n2

Marginality, 12, 35, 42–46, 49, 51, 63, 69, 86, 166, 169, 195n15

Marriage, 4, 7, 28, 36, 38, 40–43, 44, 46, 55, 62, 71–72, 85, 103, 105–107, 113–114, 121, 122, 124, 131, 133, 138, 142, 144–147, 149, 157, 158, 180, 189n8, 197n46, 199n74, 199n75, 201n2; celibacy, 44; ceremony of, 60, 62–63, 66, 152, 162, 201n2; endogamic, 63; posthumous, 168; remarriage, 4, 48, 105–106, 113–114, 122, 123, 131, 171, 198n53, 199n71; unmarried dead, 166

Media, 1, 2, 14, 22, 27–30, 32, 38, 74, 97, 100, 109, 116, 118, 150, 155, 161, 171, 172, 175–176, 178, 179, 183n10, 185n11, 190n12, 203n1, 203n3; anthropology of, 10–11, 17–18; development, 88–89, 194n7; social welfare, 18, 169, 170

Memory (collective), 17, 30, 69, 78, 81–84, 175, 193n61, 194n76; authors of, 84–86; of childhood, 39, 63–65, 82–86, 112, 128; sites of, 89, 128

Modell, Judith, 183n8, 201n3

Mother: adoptive, 43, 81, 156, 183n12;

Mother (cont'd): birth, 48, 104, 109–110, 112, 120, 122, 130–132, 149, 168, 175, 178, 196n32; Confucian mother figure, 96, 115–116; emancipated, 116, 199n71; foster, 110, 112–113, 197n47, 197n48, 197n49, 198n50; single, 22, 43, 44, 52, 64–65, 103, 105, 108, 109, 116, 123, 168, 177, 184n9, 184n10, 205n17

Motherland, 16, 33, 49, 52, 54, 64–66, 190n11; love for, 29–30, 92, 96, 161; tour, 52, 88

Narrative, 10, 11, 40, 92, 119, 180; of family separation, 11–12, 17, 34, 67, 69, 75, 77–78, 82, 104, 152–153; and sublimation, 82, 83, 85–86, 180

North Korea, 17, 91- 92, 174; Cold War, 89, 93; family meetings, 87, 88, 90, 99, 172–174, 194n13; Korean War, 23, 87, 93, 163–164, 175; reunification, 87, 95, 152, 173, 175, 206n29; Sunshine Policy, 89, 90, 92, 93–97, 118, 194n8

Nostalgia, 30, 81, 82, 128, 175, 193n61, 193n63

Olympic Games, 22, 203n3

Orphan, 1, 9–10, 23–24, 32, 35, 38, 50, 64, 168, 178, 184n5, 184n10, 185n11, 185n16 ; at *Ach'im madang*, 70–74, 85, 86, 97, 115, 157, 172; orphanage, 4, 24, 27, 52, 64, 65, 87, 104–108, 114- 115, 127- 128, 151, 163- 164, 171, 188n6, 195n3; stereotypes, 38–47, 72, 86

Park, Chung-hee, 186n26, 194n7, 194n9, 195n3

Patriline, 13, 27, 33, 41, 49, 96, 105, 112, 114, 116, 117, 164

Postadoption services, 54, 64, 74, 120, 158

Prostitute, 25, 43–45

Protestant, 24, 25, 54, 79, 125, 140, 165, 186n19, 189n5, 190n10, 203n4

Race, 8, 14, 24–25, 33, 50, 57, 63, 67, 79–80, 96–97

Resemblance, 17, 50, 69, 78, 79, 114, 115, 146, 199n68

Resentment, 12, 16, 18, 44, 45, 56, 151, 156, 157, 159, 161, 167, 188n10, 202n28, 205n14

Rites: expulsion, 169; initiation, 60, 64, 65, 66, 204n7; of passage, 16, 52, 60, 62, 65–66, 151, 152, 162, 168, 169, 170; phases, 66

Seoul, 2, 22, 24, 28, 35, 36, 38, 43, 46, 47, 48, 53, 54, 56, 57, 59, 61, 62, 64, 65, 69, 77, 90, 95, 96, 106, 107, 113, 120, 123, 124

Shaman, 40, 163, 166–170, 174, 204n10, 204n12, 204n13, 205n17, 205n18, 205n20

Shame, 22, 25, 35, 77, 131, 154, 171, 202n10

Siblings, 6–7, 39–40, 41, 68, 72, 78, 80, 92, 103, 104, 105, 107, 110, 111, 115, 123–130, 153, 154, 155; half-sibling, 114; households, 171; love for, 72, 77, 107, 111–112, 127, 156, 174–175, 178, 197n44

Suwon, 40, 56

Tears (cry, weep), 1, 4, 5, 6, 18, 39, 40, 49, 64, 65, 68, 76–77, 78, 81, 93, 95, 98, 112, 115, 116, 118, 119, 120, 121, 122, 124, 127, 130, 134, 138, 153, 155–157, 159, 163, 173, 169, 174, 204n6, 205n20; absence of, 8, 173, 174; scene of, 75, 77, 78, 93, 94–95, 112, 116, 176

Telethon, 88–90, 92–95, 98, 151, 198n53; aftermaths, 118, 200n1

Television, 1, 5–11, 17, 22, 26, 27, 28, 38, 60, 68, 69, 71, 87, 109, 111, 112, 114, 191n21, 194n1; impact on society, 11, 17, 81, 83, 109, 152, 156–158, 168, 169, 179, 192n28, 206n27; pedagogical tool, 1, 17; political instrument, 11, 93, 96, 112, 173, 194n7

Tomb, 49, 64, 119, 125, 126, 127, 129, 131, 134, 136, 140, 200n8, 200n10

Van Gennep, Arnold, 51
Volkman, Toby Alice, 183n12

About the Author

Elise Prébin was born in South Korea in 1978 and was raised in France. She obtained her PhD at University of Paris Ouest-Nanterre la Défense in social anthropology in 2006, was a postdoctoral fellow and lecturer at Harvard University from 2007 to 2009, and served as an assistant professor at Hanyang University (South Korea) from 2010 to 2011. She is now an independent scholar and lives in New York City with her husband and daughter.